THE ORIGIN OF THE GODS

RICHARD CALDWELL

THE ORIGIN
OF THE GODS

A Psychoanalytic Study of
Greek Theogonic Myth

OXFORD UNIVERSITY PRESS
New York   Oxford

Oxford University Press

Oxford   New York   Toronto
Delhi   Bombay   Calcutta   Madras   Karachi
Kuala Lumpur   Singapore   Hong Kong   Tokyo
Nairobi   Dar es Salaam   Cape Town
Melbourne   Auckland   Madrid

and associated companies in
Berlin   Ibadan

Published by Oxford University Press, Inc.,
198 Madison Avenue, New York, New York 10016-4314

First issued as an Oxford University Press paperback, 1993.

Oxford is a registered trademark of Oxford University Press.

Library of Congress Cataloging-in-Publication Data
Caldwell, Richard S.
The origin of the gods : a psychoanalytic study of Greek
theogonic myth / Richard Caldwell.
p.   cm.
Includes index.
ISBN 0-19-505504-7
ISBN 0-19-507266-9 (pbk)
1. Gods, Greek—Psychological aspects.
2. Mythology, Greek—Psychological apsects.
3. Psychoanalysis and religion.—I. Title.
BL785.C27   1989
292'.13'019—dc19
88-1506   CIP

68975
Printed in the United States of America
on acid-free paper

FOR ARIEL MIRANDA CALDWELL

I have long been haunted by the idea that our studies on the content of the neuroses might be destined to solve the riddle of the formation of myths.

Sigmund Freud, *Dreams and Folklore*

No anthropologist henceforth should suppose that he knows enough to write about primitive religion, unless he has read Freud.

Weston LaBarre, "Freud and Anthropology"

The theories of Freud and his followers as to religion and the origin of myth have not been considered, since, in the writer's opinion, they are scarcely to be taken seriously.

Lewis Spence, *An Introduction to Mythology*

It would admittedly be wrong to regard a myth simply as a product of some kind of unconscious mentality.

G. S. Kirk, *The Nature of Greek Myths*

For the moment we can only deplore the bad taste of the Boeotian farmer-poet, Hesiod, for using rubbish.

Charles Seltman, *The Twelve Olympians*

PREFACE

This book is about the psychological, or emotional, aspect of Greek myth. Its theoretical premises are simple and can be stated briefly in regard to both mythic function and mythic form. The generally accepted view that myths are multifunctional is certainly correct, but the meaning of multiple function and the systematic relationship between functions should be clarified. Multiple function should mean not only that different myths may have different functions, but also that any individual myth typically includes several functions. In the case of psychological functioning, I would argue that myths have three purposes in addition to whatever nonpsychological functions they may fulfill: these are (1) to allow the expression of unconscious, usually repressed, ideas in a conventional and socially sanctioned form; (2) to use the emotional content attached to these ideas to energize the nonemotional function of myth; and (3) to provide a societal response to psychological needs, whether universal or culture-specific, shared by the individuals who make up the society.

Since these psychological functions seems to be present in all (or nearly all) myths, the relationship between psychological and nonpsychological functions is reciprocal: the former provide emotional energy for the latter, and the latter provide an opportunity for the emergence of the former. Since it is unlikely or impossible that either type of function could exist, at least in mythic form, without the other, this reciprocity is virtually symbiotic.

No matter what the nonpsychological function of a myth may be, the pervasive presence of psychological functioning has a determining effect on the form of myths, since nonpsychological concerns must be formulated in a structure that allows the expression of psychological needs. An extreme example of this appears in the subject of this book, the Greek theogonic myth, in which cosmological and theological matters are presented and defined in terms of familial configurations, especially the relationships between father and son and between son and mother. The intellectual question, it seems, must be phrased in such a way as to allow the emotional question to be asked simultaneously.

If we wish to understand the psychology of myth, the only appropriate theoretical model available to us is psychoanalysis. I do not intend to argue this point beyond the implicit argument of its validity in the present book, although I know that the mere mention of psychoanalysis or of Freud's name is sufficient to produce a negative reaction in some people (particularly classicists). When Freud arrived in America on the twenty-seventh of August 1909 and saw a crowd of admirers waiting to greet him, he is supposed to have said to his companion Jung, "If only they knew that I was bringing the plague." Many people even now would agree with this statement, although not in the sense meant by Freud; in their view, psychoanalysis is at worst an unmitigated pestilence and at best something like malaria, a disease that should go away now that modern science has found the cure.

Whether one regards the "plague" as psychoanalysis itself or as that alien internal world to which Freud introduced us, it would be difficult in 1988 to deny that the plague is still with us. Nevertheless, those who hold the former view will find no polemics here. My intended reader is the person who wants to know what myths mean and why hearing or reading a myth, from no matter how far away in time or space, is intensely exciting, and I ask of the reader only the provisional acceptance that myth and psychoanalysis can be allies against the plague.

My principal aims in this book are to describe, in clear and comprehensible language, those aspects of psychoanalytic theory relevant to the understanding of Greek myth, and then to use a psychoanalytic methodology to interpret the Greek myth of origin and succession. Our authority for this myth is the archaic poet Hesiod, who in his poem, the *Theogony,* told of the world's beginning from unbounded Chaos and of the generational conflicts that led finally to the defeat of the Titans and the enthronement of Olympian Zeus as king over gods and men.

The *Theogony,* appearing at the very beginning of Greek literature, crystallized Greek theogonic beliefs in a fixed form, which was to remain, for virtually all later Greeks, as the standard mythic version of the origin of all things. Despite the fact that the *Theogony* has been read and studied for almost 3000 years, there remain a number of problems and questions, both large and small, which have yet to receive satisfactory explanations. Why, for example, does the world begin with the spontaneous emergence of four uncaused entities—Chaos, Gaia, Tartaros, Eros—and why do they appear in this order? Why does Ouranos, the first Sky-Father, prevent his children from being born by confining them in their mother's body? Hesiod may say, and commentators agree, that Ouranos is frightened by their "fearsome" nature, but how can he know this before they are born? Why is Ouranos castrated by his son Kronos, and why is the goddess Aphrodite born from the god's severed genitals? Why are both Ouranos and Kronos overthrown by their *youngest* sons, and what is the logic of the steps taken by Zeus to avoid the same thing happening to him in turn? What do the ambivalent myth and status of the god Hephaistos suggest about his *implicit* role in the succession myth?

These are some of the questions I will try to answer in Chapter 4, "Origin and Succession." Before reaching this point, however, there are certain preliminary matters we will have to consider. Our situation in regard to Greek myth is analogous to that of the psychoanalyst and his patient (the "analysand"). Just as the analyst must know in advance certain things if he is to understand the analysand, there are some things we must know if we want to understand the psychology of myth.

The first requirement for the psychoanalyst is that he know what he is doing, since without an adequate knowledge of psychoanalysis he is merely an amateur making guesses. The same is true for us; we must know psychoanalytic theory if we intend to use it (or criticize it), and the purpose of Chapter 2, "Applied Psychoanalysis," is to provide such knowledge. Too much of what passes for psychoanalytic interpretation, and even more of what claims to be criticism of psychoanalytic interpretation, is based on little or no acquaintance with psychoanalysis itself. Whether or not our conclusions will be accepted, ignorance is a danger that can and should be avoided.

Chapter 2, then, is an exposition of psychoanalytic theory as the basis for an interpretive methodology. Its emphasis is on childhood psychosexual development and the theory of dreams, the two areas of psychoanalytic theory most appropriate to the study of myth. It is intended to serve as an introduction to the psychoanalytic interpretation of myth in general, not merely the myth of origin, and illustrative examples are taken where appropriate from various myths rather than from clinical data. The chapter is not as long as it could be, since so much of psychoanalysis must be left out; it could, in fact, be much shorter, since the Greek origin myth is practically self-evident from a psychoanalytic standpoint. My only rule for determining its length, I must confess, was that it not be longer than Chapter 4; if it is no shorter, it is because there was nothing I could omit without seriously misrepresenting psychoanalysis as a method for interpreting myths other than the origin myth.

The other requirement for our psychoanalyst is that he know as much as possible about the present situation and past history of the analysand. Here the analyst has a great advantage over us, since the analysand is present to provide associations and information (which may or may not be true, but is nevertheless meaningful). Lacking this opportunity, we will have to make up for it by situating the Greek creation myth (our "analysand") in its historical and mythic context; this is the purpose of Chapter 3, "Texts and Contexts." Its first section is a sketch of Greek prehistory before Hesiod, sections 2–4 are a discussion, with summaries, of the principal Near Eastern myths that may have influenced Greek theogonic myth, and sections 5–6 examine the concept of divine food in Hindu and Greek myth as an example of similar concepts in two mythic traditions far removed from a possible common ancestor. Sections 7 and 8, respectively, are translations of the *Theogony* and the theogony that begins Apollodoros' *Library*.

As will be seen, the discussion of psychoanalysis is limited to those parts of the theory particularly germane to the analysis of myth and should not be taken as an outline of all of psychoanalysis. I have chosen those aspects I regard as essential for myth interpretation, and I have tried to make these as clear as possible. As a result, there is no discussion of many of the most important components of the theory as a whole (instinct theory, for example) and in some cases (the nature of primary process thought, for example) the discussion is extended, for the sake of clarity, beyond what might seem required by the importance of these cases.

The same is true of the discussion of theogonic myth in Chapter 4. Although the text on which this chapter is based is Hesiod's *Theogony,* I make no attempt to deal with the *Theogony* as a whole, but confine the discussion to theogonic phenomena strictly and literally defined: that is, to the procreative activities of the first gods and to the related process that leads to the final dominance of Zeus. Little attention is paid therefore to such important parts of the *Theogony* as the initial invocation to the Muses, the praise of Hekate, the story of Pandora, or the various unions and offspring that follow the accession of Zeus.

It may seem strange to omit Pandora from a book about origins, but my subject is the origin and succession of gods, not men. In any case, the Pandora story is not a myth about the origin of the human race, but about the origin of the evils and troubles (including woman) that beset mankind. While the Greeks were sporadically concerned with the original state of humanity, as in Hesiod's account of the "golden race" of men who lived under the reign of Kronos, they seem not to have been much interested in the actual creation of the first humans. Hesiod says that gods and humans "were born from the same source" and names no creator of the first humans, but simply says that the anonymous "gods made a golden race of mortal men" (*Works and Days* 108–10). The "same source" is presumably the earth, the mother from whom the gods are descended.[1] Whenever, in sparse later accounts, a creator of the human race is named (such as Prometheus), he usually makes the first humans from earth mixed with water, and various local legends said that the first men (in their area, at least) were born from the earth. Whether this virtual omission of the creation of humanity from the body of Greek myth is an act of humility or of hybris depends, I would think, on one's general estimate of ancient Greek culture and character.

My discussion of psychoanalytic theory in Chapters 2 and 4 is governed by the firm conviction that this material can and should be presented in ordinary language, free of jargon and technical obscurity. There is a proper place for dense and difficult argumentation, to be sure, but more and more I have become convinced that any interpretive theory (whether of myth or literature or mental functioning) that cannot be translated into ordinary language is probably of little practical use. Theorizing about theory has its attractions (and is certainly the main current of contemporary humanistic studies), but rarely answers, or even pretends to answer, the obvious questions posed by any intelligent student or layman.

It is precisely this group for whom my book is intended. Classicists and psychoanalysts alike may find some of what I say familiar and perhaps simplistic, but I make no apology on this score; on the contrary, I hope that even experts in these fields will find some things new and interesting.

I wish to assure those who may be bothered by the frequent use of the masculine pronouns to refer to young children of either sex, in Chapter 2 and occasionally elsewhere, that this usage is intended only to avoid awkward periphrases and does not reflect the bias of psychoanalysis or myself.

All translations from Greek are my own, with these exceptions: Alexandra Papoutsaki and Jonathan Paris assisted in the translation of Hesiod's *Theogony* in Chapter 3, and for nostalgic reasons I have used Jowett's translation of a few lines from Plato's *Symposium* in Chapter 4. The translation of the *Theogony* and an earlier version of sections of Chapter 3 first appeared in my *Hesiod's Theogony* and are used here with the kind permission of the publisher, Focus Information Group.

I am grateful to Barry Goldfarb, Jeffrey Henderson, and William Levitan for their careful reading of successive drafts of this book and for their many helpful and intelligent suggestions and criticisms.

Finally and far too belatedly, I want to express my gratitude to the American Council of Learned Societies for a fellowship that enabled me many years ago to study and teach psychoanalysis; that year, more than any other factor, is responsible for whatever of value this book contains.

Santa Ana, Calif.   R.S.C.
August 1988

CONTENTS

THE ORIGIN OF THE GODS

CHAPTER ONE

INTRODUCTION
The Nature and Function
of Myth

THE MEANING OF MYTH

Four recent theoretical studies of Greek myth by eminent authorities in this field, Walter Burkert and G. S. Kirk, have given us detailed analyses of the formal aspects and multiple functions of myth.[1] For all our indebtedness to these scholars, however, they have not told us much about the psychological meaning and function of myths. This lack does not diminish the value of these books, all of which reflect the learning and prestige of their authors, and in fact is largely a consequence of the assumptions and methods they employ. Nevertheless, these matters are important and this book is an attempt to deal with them, both generally and in the specific instance of theogonic myth (that is, myths concerned with the beginning of the world and the gods).

For Burkert, myth is practically, if not theoretically, subordinate to ritual. He refers to fables and to certain charter myths, such as the genealogical myth of the descendants of Aiolos, as examples of myths that are independent of ritual (there are, of course, many others), and he notes that many rituals are not connected with any myth, but his chief concern is with ritual, which he regards as historically prior to myth. With few exceptions, therefore, the meaning of myth for Burkert is a function of its relation to ritual, and the meaning of ritual is to be found in its societal purpose. Through the manipulation of emotions, such as anxiety and relief, in a shared and recurrent demonstration, rituals help individuals to deal with biological, emotional, and societal needs and problems, and thereby promote the stability and cohesiveness of a community. Traumatic occurrences like death, marriage, and disease are regularized by being ritualized, and extended by being shared; things happen not to one alone, but to all, and it does not happen only now, but also in the past (and presumably always). The myths that Burkert studies are therefore those that reinforce this ritual function, and their meaning is to be found in some connection with the elements of a given ritual.

Kirk, on the other hand, treats myth independently of ritual for the most part, although his definition of myth as traditional tales which "are on the one hand good stories, on the other hand bearers of important messages about life in general and life-within-society in particular"[2] is not far from Burkert's conception of the function of ritual and ritual-related myth. Nevertheless Kirk emphatically (and correctly) denies any necessary connection between myth and ritual, at the same time as he (wrongly) rejects any theory that implies for both "a common origin in the alleviation of a rather motley collection of psychic needs."[3] In Kirk's view, there are many kinds of myth and many functions of myth; the best one can do is to identify certain general characteristics, types, and functions. Myths may have begun as functional entities, or simply as entertaining stories (which may or may not acquire a different function later on); they tend to embody responses to problems and to have a "fantasy-and-dislocation" aspect, but neither characteristic is inevitable or predictable. Kirk discusses and occasionally applies several theories of mythical meaning (notably the structuralist), but ends by finding all theories inadequate as general explanations; a given theory may work with one myth or a group of myths, but cannot be used to explain, or even describe, myth in general.

Kirk's approach is highly eclectic (a characterization he willingly accepts)[4] and contains many interesting observations and discussions, especially his orientation of Greek myth in the wider context of the eastern Mediterranean and western Asia, but his few attempts to interpret specific myths are unpersuasive. A single example may suffice: unless it is intended to be read as a parody of the structuralist method, Kirk's identification of the "underlying message" of the Greek origin and succession myth—"excesses and irrational acts in the realm of sex and childbirth give rise to counterbalancing and deterrent excesses in the other direction"[5]—misses the point of the myth altogether.

It is unfair to criticize Kirk for not doing what he does not set out to do. If he avoids systematic interpretation of specific myths, it is because his chief concern is with the typology and phenomenology of myth on narrative and functional levels. His interpretations rarely go beyond whatever is necessary to assign a myth to a general functional category like "etiology" or "charter" or even "entertainment."

In the end Kirk is deluged by his data. Because of the great variety of mythical forms, the only formal definition he finds inclusive enough is that myth is a traditional tale with an important message. Mythic functions are also numerous, and Kirk distinguishes three broad functional types: (1) narrative and entertaining; (2) operative, iterative, and validatory (including myths associated with rituals and religion, charter myths, and etiological myths); (3) speculative and explanatory (myths that reflect or explain fundamental paradoxes or institutions).[6] Recognizing that these distinctions concerning form and function say nothing about the most striking characteristic of myth, its use of fantasy and symbol, Kirk suggests the establishment of another typology "of motives and expressive modes, that would subsume all the subjective aspects of myths."[7] After rejecting several theories, however, including the psychoanalytic and psychoanalytically oriented, Kirk abandons the typology project and concludes that the element of fantasy enters myth gradually but erratically, because of three possible factors: (1) an accident in storytelling; (2) a possible connection with dreams "at least in societies that are particularly dream-conscious"; (3) the influence of religion and the supernatural.[8]

Burkert's definition of myth, more elaborate and more fully argued than Kirk's, is summarized in four theses: (1) "Myth belongs to the more general class of traditional tale"; (2) "the identity of a traditional tale, including myth, independent as it is from any particular text and from direct reference to reality, is to be found in a structure of sense within the tale itself"; (3) "tale structures, as sequences of motifemes [recurrent motif units], are founded on basic biological or cultural programs of action"; (4) "myth is a traditional tale with secondary, partial reference to something of collective importance."[9]

These theses essentially add only the concept of fictiveness to Kirk's definition and could be paraphrased as follows: myth is a fictional traditional tale with an important message. For Burkert, the "specific character of myth seems to lie neither in the structure nor in the content of a tale, but in the use to which it is put,"[10] and the functional categories of myth include charter myths, myths connected with ritual, myths that deal with nature, the seasons, and food supply, myths that treat general problems of human society (such as marriage rules and incest) and individuals (such as disease), and myths concerned with the organization of nature and the universe.[11]

Burkert's major contributions to the study of Greek myth are his keen sense of the role of historical development in the successive crystallizations and applications of myth, and the frequently stunning detective work in which he seeks out connections between myths and ancient, often obscure, cults and rituals. Because he uses myths chiefly as data in his investigation of the cultural role of ritual, the question of what a specific myth might mean per se rarely arises. Myths are linked to rituals, and rituals themselves are links in a vast continuum that extends to the Neolithic and even earlier, a mysterious and powerful tradition centered on the confrontation between human groups and the facts of aggression, anxiety, and death.

Both Burkert and Kirk tell us a great deal about myth, particularly its phenomenological aspects, but they tell us little about the psychological meaning and function of myth. In Kirk's case, this omission is more culpable and the reason for it is easily discernible. For Burkert, on the other hand, the omission is both more justifiable and also less obvious.

My position, for which I present this book as partial argument, is that the formal definition of myth must be expanded to include its psychological structure and that among the functions of myth the psychological function must be given priority. I will take up the matter of formal definition again in a few pages, but for now I would simply add a clause to Burkert's definition: myth is a fictional traditional tale, *which regularly represents through symbolic transformation unconscious ideas and conflicts*. And to all the functions, uses, and concerns of myth, none of which I would deny, I would add the three psychological functions mentioned earlier: (1) the expression of unconscious ideas in a specific form;

(2) the transfer of emotional energy to nonpsychological matters and functions; (3) the provision of a societal response to shared psychological needs.

It may seem that the first of these "functions" is formal rather than functional, but I would argue that the expression of repressed ideas in mythic form is functional in the same way that dreams are functional; both maintain psychic health and stability through the allowable (because transformed, or disguised, or sanctioned by society) expression of repressed ideas. What is functionally important is that repressed material appears in mythic or oneiric, not symptomatic, form. There are, of course, important differences between dreams and myths, most obviously the distinction between private and public, or individual and society. Nevertheless, just as individuals must eat and societies therefore take on the task of food procurement and distribution, and just as individuals protect themselves and societies provide for the common defense, so also individuals must dream and societies, which are groups of individuals, produce myths as dreams for the group.

In any case, the distinction between individual and society, like the anthropological distinction between personality and culture, is not so clear-cut as it may seem and may indeed be a "false dichotomy," as Melford Spiro calls it.[12] The observations of the distinguished American anthropologist Weston LaBarre on this matter merit quotation at length.

> Oddly enough, anthropologists are happily content to make large *ethnographic* generalizations about generic group behavior, but are curiously alarmed at *psychological* statements about generic ethos. However, "culture" and "personality" are both abstractions, on different levels, *from the same data,* reverberant inter-individually influenced behavior in a social animal. Culture is the abstraction of the regularities of behavior among members of a group—resulting from the influence of individuals upon individuals. Personality is an abstraction of the regularities of behavior in an individual—resulting from the influence of individuals upon an individual. Those who denigrate culture as an abstraction should remember that Society and Structure are equally abstractions from the same socially reverberant behaviors of the same animal.[13]

As LaBarre notes on another occasion:

Personality *as behavior* is only the culture of an individual. And culture *as behavior* is only the personalities of individuals. The mystery evaporates when we look at the actual phenomena and try to remember what we are talking about.[14]

Burkert establishes in effect a hierarchy of mythic functions, since his preoccupation with ritual requires that one function—the expression and transmission through myths of knowledge about ritual—be given precedence. Still it would not be difficult to recast Burkert's views on ritual and its associated myths in terms of psychological function, especially in light of Burkert's emphasis on the emotional dimension of ritual, its concern with aggressive and erotic feelings, with mourning, fear, and anxiety. For example, in Burkert's view

> anxiety is involved in many human rituals, and one might be tempted to make this the definition of religious ritual . . . many religious rituals seem intentionally, and artificially, to produce the atmosphere of awe, using all the registers of darkness, fire, blood, and death. What happens, then, is a concentration and shift of anxiety from reality to a symbolic sphere, and this makes it possible to handle anxiety to some extent. . . . Religious ritual, by producing anxiety, manages to control it. . . . Even feelings of pollution and guilt become manageable, as highly artificial taboos are set up with expiatory ritual in the background to make up for each transgression. And as anxiety tends to draw a group together, group solidarity is all the more established by the experience and performance of anxiety overcome.[15]

Kirk, on the other hand, is resolutely opposed to psychoanalytic interpretation, although he admits that "wish-fulfillment" motifs that appear in folktale may occasionally slip into a myth. His problem with psychoanalysis is that he does not know what it is. It is ultimately this failure, I believe, that underlies Kirk's extreme eclecticism, as well as his inability to identify any central characteristic of myth and his difficulty in explaining the role of fantasy in myth. Kirk refrains from citing examples of the psychoanalytic approach to myth, but attacks the method with a series of assertions, that range from the mistaken to the uninformed, as in the following selections:

> Not many of Freud's special theories are widely accepted today . . . his emphasis on infantile sexuality, in particular, is seen to be exaggerated.[16]

> There is, indeed, an obvious connection [between dreams and myths], and we do not need mechanistic theories about unconscious dream processes to convince us of that.[17] Dreams [are] not a form of thought.[18]

> It would admittedly be wrong to regard a myth simply as a product of some kind of unconscious mentality.[19]

> His "Oedipus complex" has not, in the end, won many converts and its interest from the point of view of specifically Greek myth is surprisingly slight.[20]

Since no purpose would be served by responding to these assertions with counter-assertions, I will content myself with advising the reader who agrees with Kirk's opinions about psychoanalysis that he or she will probably find an ample source of aggravation in the pages to follow.

There are three primary reasons (and a host of lesser ones) why I chose the Greek origin myth as my example for psychoanalytic interpretation. First, its chief source, the *Theogony,* is early and definitive; what came before Hesiod remains only conjecture, and what comes after him either repeats his version or departs from it for specifically literary reasons (for example, Aristophanes, *Birds* 685–704) or sectarian purposes (for example, the Orphic cosmogony). Second, much has been written on the psychoanalysis of Greek heroic myth, particularly those myths that are contained in famous works of literature, but the origin and succession myth has received little attention beyond a famous (and erroneous) footnote in Freud's *Interpretation of Dreams.* Third, and perhaps most important, it is precisely this mythical pattern that has been identified by Kirk as the type of myth least receptive to psychoanalytic interpretation.

As we saw earlier, Kirk criticizes psychoanalysis by assertion rather than argument. His only real argument against psychoanalytic interpretation of myth is the same argument he uses against all unified theories of myth, that there are many instances of myth that do not fit the theory even if there are some that do. Ironically, as far as the subject of this book is concerned, his argument against psychoanalysis specifically identifies *creation and origin myths* as the exceptions that prove the inadequacy of a psychoanalytic approach:

> Many myths are patently concerned with other things than the reduction of anxiety or the sublimation of our baser instincts: charter-type myths, *myths of creation,* and so on.[21]

> The association of *paradise myths* with unconscious reminiscences of the happiness of childhood is surely arbitrary.[22]

> The irrelevance of both wish-fulfillment fantasy and adjustive or adaptive responses to the whole class of *origin and emergence myths* is just one example of the nongenerality of such [namely psychoanalytic] theories.[23]

A reply to this kind of argument cannot be based on an abstract definition of myth, especially since a rearrangement of definitional terms to fit one's bias is exactly the kind of strategy Kirk rightly condemns. Still less should it be based on a debate over the intrinsic validity of psychoanalysis. The only possible and proper response is an interpretation of the creation myth itself, and the only grounds of judgment are whether or not this method explains the myth better than others. If in fact the interpretation of the creation myth is persuasive, it might then be argued *a fortiori* that the psychoanalytic approach has privileged applicability to other kinds of myth as well.

I have little expectation of persuading Kirk about the efficacy of psychoanalysis—arguments between friends and enemies of psychoanalysis have always the air of a religious debate—but I hope that those who have not yet made up their minds will agree, at least, that psychoanalysis should have something to say about a myth in which the first father marries his mother and is then castrated by his son.

DEFINITION

My intention in the following remarks is not to explain the nature of myth and its functions exhaustively and definitively, a task that has eluded many more learned than I, but rather to make some tentative suggestions concerning this problem. It would be quite presumptuous, in any case, to claim the last word on this subject; scholars have been puzzled and preoccupied with the problem of definition since myth first became an object of study and speculation in antiquity. There are virtually as many definitions of myth as there are definers of myth, and the tendency in recent years seems to be toward more and more complex definitions (and, thus, more variables and more inclination to define in accordance with one's set of presuppositions). And yet, if we confine ourselves to Greek myth, everyone knows what a myth is, even if each attempt to define myth exactly seems to differ in at least some detail from all other attempts.

The problem, of course, is that no one has yet been able to come up with a simple explanation of myth that includes everything the definer regards as myth and excludes everything else. The desire for definitional exactitude thus leads often to a proliferation of conditions and provisos, or to reliance on abstract and ambiguous language, or to a combination of the two.

A parallel exists in the scholarly discussion, since Aristotle, of the nature and definition of Greek tragedy. Even more has been written on this subject than on myth, but no one definition has yet been offered that satisfies even a minority of those who debate the matter. Still we all know that *Agamemnon* and *Alkestis* are Greek tragedies, even though if we were asked to give a concise definition of tragedy that corresponded to only these two examples (and which would be capable of general acceptance), we would have to answer in terms of simple description: A Greek tragedy is a text composed for dramatic performance on certain ritual occasions by a chorus and a limited number of actors, usually on a mythological subject, generally serious in tone, with certain linguistic, metrical, and staging conventions.

The question of tragedy is complicated because it concerns the same issues of language, religion, and social and political context as does myth. So suppose we turn to a far less complicated object to define, and ask the question philosophers are fond of asking, "What is a table?" A definition acceptable to most people who speak English and claim to know what a table is, would probably be something like this: An object, usually furniture and most often with one or more legs, with a flat horizontal surface on which things can be placed. This seems simple enough, but again problems arise, which may be classified as pertaining either to form or to function. In the case of form, is a house built on pillars and with a flat roof, on which objects are placed such as a television antenna or the trees and plants of a roof garden, therefore to be considered a table? Of course not, most people would answer, since a house is not a piece of furniture. Then what about a bed? No, the answer runs, a bed is not a table since the objects to be placed on a bed are supposed to be people, while the objects put on the table are food or writing materials or something else, but not people. Then why is an operating table not an operating bed? Because, even though people lie on the table as on a bed, their purpose in lying there is to be just like objects on a table, to be cut up by the tools of someone standing or sitting next to the table.

The definition of a table, it seems, must include purpose or function if it is to exclude the house and bed. Conversely, if we spread our lunch on the surface of a large ball or write a letter on the hood of a car, this does not make the ball and car into tables, since the formal requirements of shape and appearance are not met. We may, however, say that the ball or car functions as a table, just as a table may function as a ladder (if we climb on it) or as a chair (if we sit on it).

To summarize, a table is something that both looks like a table and is used like a table. Exactly the same can be said of a myth: it is something that both looks (or sounds) like a myth and is used like a myth. The first part of the definition is fairly easy, although many definitional battles have been fought in this arena. A Greek myth, we all know, is a traditional story (that is, handed down over generations) about gods or heroes (and their families) of either the remote or more recent past (a remote past in creation myths, for example, and a more recent past in such quasi-historical myths as the Trojan War); in addition, as we saw earlier, we should add that a Greek myth regularly represents in various transformations unconscious ideas and conflicts. And just as we might say that a table usually is a piece of furniture and most often has legs, we might add that myths are often, but not necessarily, connected with rituals, and that they are usually expressed poetically (although this is no more than a likely inference when applied to the preliterate stages of Greek culture).

FUNCTION

The formal definition of myth is not difficult; anyone familiar with Greek myth can recognize a myth as easily as he can recognize a table. But the matter of mythic functions is far more complex, as can be seen in this list taken from a recent attempt to define these functions: (1) myth as source of cognitive categories; (2) myth as form of symbolic expression; (3) myth as projection of the subconscious; (4) myth as world view; (5) myth as charter of behavior; (6) myth as legitimation of social institutions; (7) myth as marker of social relevance; (8) myth as mirror of culture, social structure, and so forth; (9) myth as result of historical situation; (10) myth as religious communication; (11) myth as religious genre; (12) myth as medium for structure.[24]

What all these functions of myth seem to have in common is the use of myth as some kind of model for thought or behavior. There is, however, an additional function of myth that should be mentioned and that does not, at least ostensibly, point to something external to myth itself: this is its aesthetic function, its capability of producing some sort of pleasure or satisfaction. Similarly, to return to our definitional analogy, a table may be something we eat off or write on, but it may also be a satisfying aesthetic creation in itself, both when first created and also now when we view it in a museum. Clearly it is this function of Greek myth that has accounted for its attractiveness during the many centuries (including later antiquity) during which other functions were no longer operative.

Most analysts of Greek myth ignore this function, or dismiss it by a brief reference to the entertaining quality of myth, or view the emotional effect of myth as due not to myth itself but rather to the literary or visual art form in which the myth is contained. Such views, of course, fail to answer adequately the questions of why mythical subjects have been so dominant in Western art (in Renaissance and Mannerist painting as well as in ancient art) and literature (from medieval times through Romantic poetry), or why even a prosaic retelling of a Greek myth holds interest and affective power for a modern audience. There is something special and yet elusive about myth which compels our attention and which cannot be much different from what compelled Greek artists, poets, and especially dramatists to use myth as their primary subject.

Aesthetic issues are exceedingly complex, but it seems clear that one reason for the bypassing of this function by most scholars of Greek myth is that taking it seriously would eventually require raising the third function in the previous list (myth as projection of the unconscious) to a position of priority. Since real consideration of myth as an aesthetic object (beyond references to "good stories" and "entertaining tales") would necessarily bring up the question of psychological functions in myth, the whole subject is left untreated.

Kirk, for example, refers mysteriously to the "special imaginative power" of myth which "elicits a special kind of imaginative response . . . akin to the impact of great music or poetry,"[25] and notes "an obvious connection" between the symbols of myth and dreams, but rejects psychoanalytic explanations for reasons that clearly derive from his rejection of psychoanalysis itself.[26] This view is not uncommon among students of myth, although many anthropologists demonstrate both more knowledge of psychoanalytic theory and more appreciation of its applicability to the interpretation of myth.[27] While this is not the proper occasion to speculate on the reasons for classicists' aversion to psychoanalytic explanations, it might be pointed out in passing that this attitude coincides with their general reluctance to employ explanatory models outside the limits and jurisdiction of a discipline inherited from the librarians and textual critics of Hellenistic times (and largely unchanged since).

The usefulness of any model, however, does not depend on its disciplinary location, nor can usefulness be denied by impugning the theories from which the model is constructed. If we no longer hold the "solar" or "nature" or "vegetation" explanations of myth, which dominated the field in the late nineteenth and early twentieth centuries, it is not because the theories were themselves fallacious but rather because as models they did not seem to fit the facts of the myths.

The use of a psychoanalytic model to interpret myth neither assumes nor requires a prior conviction or belief in the validity of the theory, therapy, or explanatory models of psychoanalysis. I ask only an open mind on these matters, since an already held belief *or* disbelief simply makes much of the argument to follow superfluous. In any case, the "proof" of a heuristic model has not much, if any, value beforehand; what matters is the coherence, economy, and persuasiveness of a substantial number of applications of the model. The proof of a pudding is in its eating, and the validity of an explanatory model lies in the results of its explanations.

Similarly, the *therapeutic* usefulness of psychoanalytic theory is almost totally irrelevant to its use in studying myth. The theory itself is a model of how the human mind works and is still a very tentative model, given the current state of neurological research. Some day, as Freud pointed out almost a hundred years ago, we will have exact knowledge of the chemical and electrical operations of the mind and we will no longer need theoretical concepts such as repression or the unconscious. That day is still a long way off, however, and until it arrives we will need to use a model based on the current state of our knowledge (just as we must use a model to comprehend the functions of electricity while its exact nature remains a mystery). And just as the usefulness of any one application of the electrical model—to provide light, for example—does not depend on the success of other applications, so also the validity of the psychoanalytic explanation of myth is a separate issue from the efficacy of psychoanalysis in treating mental illness.

The general function of myth is the fulfillment of a variety of human needs, but among all the needs that receive representation and response in myth it is emotional needs that are primary. There is no doubt that myths have multiple functions; Kirk is certainly right when he says that myths have purposes other than anxiety reduction or instinctual sublimation, but he is wrong in his implied notion that the matter of function is an either/or proposition (a notion he elsewhere rejects). It is possible that a given myth (or, more frequently, a part of a myth) may have a purpose or motive completely apart from emotional needs; some genealogical myths, for example, might seem to have as their sole purpose an answer to the question, "Why do these people with these names live in these places?" (although even this question may well have a psychological motive). Functions that appear to be nonpsychological appear often throughout Greek myth; on a few occasions no other function is readily apparent, but in most cases the nonpsychological is joined to a psychological function or is a minor element in a larger myth with an overall psychological function. Whatever other functions may appear in parts of myths or in scattered whole myths, it seems clear to me that a model based on psychological or emotional function best explains myths in general, large mythical patterns and sequences, and the majority of puzzling and anomalous details in individual myths.

It is the same with dreams. The correspondence between dreams and myths will be discussed later, but two preliminary observations might be helpful in our analysis of myth's function. First, dreams incorporate elements from a variety of sources (people, objects, events, wishes, fears): some are from the recent past, some are from the remote past, some might occur during the actual time of the dream, some are from preconscious memories, and some are from the unconscious. There are a number of possible reasons why any one element might appear in a dream: it may be something the dreamer was thinking of during the waking period preceding sleep; it may be something from long ago that the dreamer likes to remember (or doesn't like to remember!); it may be some chance stimulus, like the unwanted ring of a telephone or alarm clock or a physical pressure like hunger or thirst; it may be an object of curiosity or intellectual concern; or it may be present simply to provide a connection between other elements in the dream. But for dreams in general, and for almost any individual dream, there are only two principal functions, both of them conducive to the health of the dreamer: to guard against the interruption of sleep and to allow some kind of expression, usually disguised or distorted, for repressed ideas. Even the simplest dreams may contain unexpected complexity. For example, the sick child who goes to bed hungry and dreams of eating cake and ice cream may be responding on one level to the stimulus of hunger that threatens to wake him up (a threat defended against by the dream), on a second level to happy (or unhappy) memories of holidays and birthday parties whether recent or long past, and on a third level to unconscious fantasies of gratification and prohibition.

Second, research experiments in which people who are systematically prevented from dreaming become very nervous and anxious and within a week or so acquire a kind of artificial psychosis (depression, hallucination, etc.)[28] would seem to indicate that an important function of dreams is the preservation of mental health through the allowable expression of repressed ideas. There is, at any rate, no apparent reason why the prevention of any other presumed function of dreams would so radically alter a subject's mental state. Although it has been shown that changes in chemical metabolism accompany dream deprivation, it should not be assumed, with Kirk, that chemical and psychological processes are mutually exclusive.[29]

These characteristics of dreams are easily transposed to the psychological model of mythical functions. Particular elements in myths may come from different sources and have different purposes, but the most important function of myth in general and of most individual myths is to answer an emotional need through the representation in some way of unconscious ideas.

These ideas are unconscious (that is, repressed) in the first place because of their connection with wishes or fears that provoke anxiety. And just as individuals seem to need their own idiosyncratic dreams and private rituals in order to prevent anxiety and preserve sanity, it would seem that societies need shared myths and public rituals to maintain the emotional integrity and collective health of the group. For any society to function properly, every individual must appropriate to himself the needs of the whole, and the whole must embody the needs of the individual. Whatever need it is that makes it necessary for people to dream (and we are assuming here that it is the psychological need to allow repressed ideas some measure of expression), this need appears on a social level as myth.

CHAPTER TWO

APPLIED PSYCHOANALYSIS

REPRESSION AND SEXUALITY

It is not necessary to know all or even most of psychoanalytic theory in order to use the theory to interpret myth since the aspects of psychoanalysis most relevant for this undertaking are, for the most part, the basic and early discoveries Freud referred to as the cornerstones of psychoanalysis: the existence of the unconscious, the role of repression, and the importance of childhood events and fantasies.

The unconscious mind was neither discovered nor created by Freud. His great achievement was not the realization *that* we all think unconsciously but rather the study of *how* we think unconsciously, and how this affects our conscious life and behavior. The term *unconscious* refers in psychoanalysis to a dimension of thinking that is separate from consciousness or awareness, a dimension whose existence can be easily demonstrated in cases of amnesia or through hypnotic suggestion. Freud's notion of the unconscious, which struck some of his contemporaries as unscientific or preposterous when first proposed, is now generally accepted. Nevertheless we should be careful about the exact meaning of the word unconscious in psychoanalytic theory. It does not denote simply any mental process of which we happen to be unaware at any given time, but rather refers to those processes which cannot be admitted into consciousness under normal circumstances. Freud therefore distinguished between three areas of thinking: *conscious* ideas are those of which we are aware at any given moment; *preconscious* ideas are those of which we are not aware but can bring into awareness with little or no effort; *unconscious* ideas are those of which we usually cannot become conscious except in a disguised form such as dreams or neurotic symptoms. A person's memory is comprised of preconscious and unconscious ideas; the former have relatively free access to consciousness while the latter are kept from consciousness by an internal mental barrier.

This barrier is *repression,* a hidden censor that keeps certain ideas and the fantasies in which they occur away from consciousness. Repression is one of the mind's defense mechanisms, a mental strategy that flees from danger and seeks to protect conscious thinking from the threat posed by repressed ideas. This "danger" or "threat" is anxiety, which typically arises from a conflict between a wish and an opposed prohibition or fear, originally the fear of loss of love.

Two important characteristics of repression are commonly misunderstood. First, repression is itself an unconscious activity, carried on below the threshold of awareness. It does not depend on conscious willing or on a conscious resolution not to think of something because it is wrong or dangerous (which might be called suppression or inhibition), but operates completely outside the domain of consciousness. Second, despite the fact that it is unconscious, repression is not some instinctual process totally isolated from external reality, but is in fact largely the result of socially determined factors.

CHILDHOOD

The ideas that are most subject to repression (and, therefore, the ideas that figure most importantly and frequently in the content of the unconscious) are typically ideas from early childhood and especially ideas connected with prohibited, dangerous, and anxiety-provoking thought and behavior of childhood. During childhood the individual learns what he can and cannot do, should and should not do, in order to take his place as an accepted member of the family and the larger society. To cite an obvious if crude example, the observation of young children tells us that an infant would probably prefer to play with his own feces than with the inanimate rubber objects in his crib, but soon learns as a result of the withdrawal and bestowal of affection by his parents that this preference cannot be maintained. His coprophilic wish comes into conflict with a fear of anticipated punishment or the loss of affection, and the resulting anxiety causes the repression of the wish.

Ideas enter the unconscious through repression (or through association with already repressed material), and since repression is simply one of the conditions of growing up in a given family and a given culture, the unconscious ideas of adults are chiefly a remnant of this maturational process. Not every stimulus received by the mind leaves a memory; when memories do occur, some remain preconsciously, some are repressed, and many disappear forever. Those memories that are subject to repression tend to be those concerned with sexuality, as the developing individual learns that the ideas connected with his strongest feelings and desires are also the ideas that attract the prohibitions and strictures of his society. This does not mean that children below the age of six think only or mostly of sexual matters or that these are the most important concerns of children; it means only that sexuality is the area of childhood experience most likely to be affected by repression. Clearly children do many things, want many things, and are curious about many things that have nothing to do with sexuality; but these are not usually the areas of experience where repression is likely to occur.

The concept of childhood sexuality, one of the best-known and most controversial doctrines of psychoanalysis, has acquired much wider acceptance now than when Freud first began to speak of it. At a medical meeting in Hamburg in 1910, the noted neurologist Weygandt said of Freud's theories, "This is not an issue to be discussed at a scientific meeting. This is a matter for the police!" but Freud himself observed that childhood sexuality had always been recognized by nannies and observant parents.

A combination of factors made it difficult for many people then (and, to a lesser extent, now) to accept the idea of childhood sexuality: a lack of knowledge based on accurate observation of children, the fact that one's own childhood is almost entirely subject to a general repression (usually called "infantile amnesia"), and especially a misperception of the meaning of sexuality in psychoanalysis. For most people sexuality means adult genital sexuality, and admittedly psychoanalysis finds the roots of adult sexuality, and even of adult perversions, in childhood; nevertheless, even a slight acquaintance with the earliest psychoanalytic writings on this subject shows that psychoanalysis has always meant by sexuality something much broader than the usual notion, both for adults and especially for early childhood before the dominance of genital organization. Freud stressed this extended meaning of sexuality many times, as when he compared it to the range of meanings encompassed by the German verb *lieben* (to love) or by Plato's use of the Greek noun *eros* (desire).

While it includes the activities and pleasures oriented toward a genital function, sexuality also refers in psychoanalysis to all activities, wishes, and fantasies that aim at producing a specific organic pleasure and that cannot be adequately explained in terms of a basic physiological need such as breathing, hunger, or excretion. Thus sexuality originally appears in the early life of the individual when a pleasurable activity carried on in the service of a biological function first continues to be engaged in after the biological need has been satisfied and is no longer present; the most obvious example is the infant who sucks his thumb or some other object not because he is hungry but for the pleasure of sucking. Even in this earliest manifestation, important characteristics of infantile sexuality are already apparent: the child can take his own body (or a part of his body such as the thumb) as a sexual object, the pleasure can occur in a non-genital location (the mouth in this instance), and the plasticity of the sexual impulse is evident from the start. That is, the same pleasure can be achieved by sucking at the breast, the bottle, the pacifier, the blanket, or the thumb; furthermore, since the last four items in this series seem to be substitutes for the first, it would seem that already a rudimentary kind of fantasy or symbolic thinking is taking place.

It has become customary to divide childhood psychosexual development into three phases named for the parts of the body (*erogenous zones*) that predominate in behavior and fantasies aimed at organic pleasure: the *oral* phase from birth to two years, the *anal* phase from two to four, and the *phallic* phase from four to six. These time periods, of course, are statistical generalizations and cannot be applied meaningfully to the experiences of individuals, except to say that most children go through these three phases and in this order. The oral phase does not end when the anal phase begins, nor do these two end with the onset of the phallic phase. Oral, anal, and phallic phenomena coexist throughout childhood and continue to play a part in adult life, depending on individual circumstances; the only purpose in giving a name to childhood phases is to designate a situation in which the stimulation of a certain part of the body is emphasized, especially in fantasies related to this period. All three phases have two significant attributes in common: beginning from infancy, the erogenous zones are the principal paths of exchange between the interior of the body and its surroundings, and they are also the parts of the body that receive the most attention, care, and stimulation from the mother.

SYMBIOSIS AND THE ORAL PHASE

Before discussing in detail these phases of psychosexual development, however, we should turn our attention first to a remarkable event, occurring during the first year of life, which will be of great importance in our analysis of the Greek creation myths: the child's initial awareness of himself as a separate being, and the ambivalent emotional situation that results from this awareness. One of the most important trends in psychoanalytic theory during the past thirty years has been an increasingly greater emphasis on, and knowledge of, the infant's acquisition of identity and his first attempts to deal with an environment that is perceived as separate from himself. For all of his emphasis on childhood, Freud can be said to have neglected infancy as a state, a neglect due no doubt to his conviction that the oedipus complex, occurring at the end of the phallic phase, was the culmination of childhood development and the crucial psychological event of the individual's entire life. However, thanks largely to research done on the causes and treatment of childhood psychoses, especially autism, psychoanalysts have discovered that the earliest events of childhood have great importance in themselves and a far-reaching effect on later life, and that the oedipus complex itself is best seen not as an entirely original situation but as a final childhood repetition of mental and emotional structures that go back to the first year of life.

Freud's case studies show clearly his tendency always to search for an original event from which later developments were derived by an unconscious line of descent, and some early analysts, notably Otto Rank, believed that the so-called birth trauma was the origin and prototype of all later anxiety. Recent studies, however, including physiological research that stresses the minimal disturbance of the passage from prenatal to postnatal existence, have indicated that the real trauma of infancy is not the physical birth of the child but rather what has been called the "psychological birth of the individual."[1] For the first six months or so after birth, the infant lacks a stable perception of himself as a separate being surrounded by other separate beings. The technical term for this situation prior to the discovery of the difference between self and other is *symbiosis,* a biological metaphor referring to the infant's attachment and dependence upon the mother and her complementary involvement with her child, and also to a state of undifferentiation and fusion in which the "I" is not yet distinguished from the "not-I." For the symbiotic infant, the self is the whole world (admittedly a tiny world, especially during the first weeks when undeveloped eyesight can barely see beyond the confines of the crib), and the whole world consists essentially of the illusory fusion of two separate (but not perceived as such) individuals, the child and the mother. Although consciousness is quite rudimentary, memory-traces of pleasure and unpleasure are acquired, which will be important later on and which have been demonstrated empirically by the beginning of the third month. Long before the infant becomes aware of the mother as a person and of his own self, these memories (sometimes called *engrams*) reflect his responses to maternal care and his environment.

The symbiotic state is followed by the state of *individuation,* or *separation-individuation:* these terms refer to an emerging awareness of self, or individual identity, as a result of differentiation between self and other, subject and object. The symbiotic state ends, one could say, when the infant is first able to look in a mirror and recognize himself. In reality, however, the mirror in which the infant first sees himself is not an actual mirror but rather the image of another human being, usually the mother, and it is a result of his perception that the mother is a separate being that the infant begins to think of himself as separate. The beginning of individuation is due to innate maturational processes and a sufficiently helpful environment, but the infant knows nothing of these causes. What strikes the outside observer as a sign of the child's growing independence, alongside his new ability to sit up and move around, must be rather the opposite from the child's viewpoint.

For the child individuation is the occasion for feelings of dependence, aloneness, and loss, as he realizes for the first time that the
person on whom he depends for the satisfaction of his basic needs
and wishes is not part of himself but is a separate person who may
leave the room and never return.

It is because of individuation, not physical birth, that the infant
first experiences separation anxiety (the newborn infant does not
cry when left alone or even know that he is alone). One half of
what had been the symbiotic unity now becomes known as a separate person; this perception, on which subsequent awareness of the
self as separate is based, is precipitated by the intermittent loss or
absence of the other person, and thus we might say that the subject comes into existence through perception of the other as lost
object.

The symbiotic infant is conscious, but his consciousness is
like that of a dream, from which he is awakened by individuation. As mental faculties are separated into conscious and unconscious systems at the time of, and as a result of, individuation,
memory-traces of the symbiotic state become the first contents of
a "primal" unconscious and the state of individuation itself serves
to repress these memories, to bar them from consciousness. Symbiotic memories persist in the unconscious, however, and the first
unconscious desires, based on these memories, will aim at regain-
ing the lost part of the once all-inclusive self. The images that signify this lost and desired state, memories of a lost world, will be
the standard against which later pleasurable experiences will be
measured.

The loss of symbiosis produces a set of mutually contradictory wishes and fears that will last through life and are similar to
what many sociologists and psychologists regard as the specific ills
of modern mass industrial civilization. On one hand is the desire
to escape separateness and loss and to return to the symbiotic
state, while on the other hand is the desire, virtually inseparable
from the instinct of self-preservation, to maintain separate identity and to keep clearly defined the distinction between the "I" and
the "not-I." The first desire is countered by the fear of loss of identity, of being swallowed up or engulfed by a larger entity, of being
a faceless, nameless part of an enormous whole, while the second
desire is countered by the fear of alienation and estrangement, of

losing the ability or opportunity to have emotional bonds or meaningful relationships with other people.

Desire, appearing for the first time as a result of the perception of loss, will have as its object that which maintains the existence of the individual: nourishment, security, and love, represented in objects momentarily lost and thus generating both anxiety and desire. But desire itself will be essentially modeled on the memories of the lost symbiotic state; even the adult manifestations of the sexual drive will base their aims and objects on the experiences of the symbiotic state and will find their culmination in the act that comes closest, in the experience of the post-symbiotic individual, to a recapturing of symbiotic fusion.

The infant's mother, traditionally regarded by analysts as the irreducible object from which other, substitute objects of desire will be derived, may herself now be seen as the first symbol, the first separate entity whose loss signifies for the infant the lost symbiotic state. Strictly speaking, the desire to return to symbiosis is not the same as desire for the mother, since what has been lost is not a separate being but rather a part of the self, which becomes known as the mother. The goal of symbiotic desire is not an object but a state, an undifferentiated state without subject or object; since nothing can be lacking in this all-inclusive state, there can be no desire (which depends on the perception of lack) and thus the desire to return to symbiosis is the paradoxical desire not to desire.

Although the desire for symbiosis is desire for a state, not an object, it is important to recognize that this desire first appears already focused on a symbolic object, the mother, and that symbiotic memories and desires become attached to, and influence, later relationships throughout childhood and throughout life. Symbiotic desire may appear connected with desire for the mother as lost object during the second year of life, with desire for the parent as incestuous object during the oedipus complex, or with desire for the sexual object of adulthood. The unconscious memory of symbiosis persists as the prototype of total gratification, and the unconscious desire for symbiosis remains as the prototype of desire as impossible, unsatisfiable, and total.

The difficulties involved in the observation and analysis of early childhood are obviously great, but it is not difficult to see the role that this desire plays in certain cultural projections. The goal of much Eastern mystical religion, for example, is virtually identical to a recovery of the symbiotic state: the overcoming of individuality through merger or dissolution into a cosmic whole, the attainment of a state of zero desire and perfect equilibrium, the absolute loss of the self.

The best-known and most widespread cultural representation of the symbiotic state occurs in mythical and religious fantasies, found throughout the world, of an original paradise in which the first humans lived for a time before exile to a life of loss, desire, time, suffering, alienation, and death. The Garden of Eden in Genesis 1–3 and Hesiod's "Golden Age," for example, portray the first humans as living in a timeless and effortless nirvana in which nothing is desired since nothing is lacking. The emergence of desire is equivalent to the loss of this state, and this loss appears as a primal prohibition. The inevitable fact of individuation, like the angel with the fiery sword at the gates of Eden, prohibits return to paradise and condemns mankind to a life of separation and lack. A similar situation appears in the Near Eastern epic of Gilgamesh, as Enkidu (the "natural man") is seduced from his solipsistic wilderness by a harlot who leads him "like a mother" to culture, strife, and death, while Gilgamesh in his search for immortality travels through a great expanse of impenetrable darkness (like the abyss of Genesis or the Chaos of Hesiod's *Theogony*) before reaching the magical garden of the gods and the woman who tells him of life's inevitable limitation.

Symbiotic wishes also appear prominently in literature from antiquity to the present: the temptations of infinite bliss and loss of identity offered to Homer's Odysseus by Kalypso's island, Nausikaa's kingdom, and the land of the lotus-eaters; the paradisal gardens of medieval and Renaissance poetry; the magical island of Avalon in Arthurian legend; the idyllic Arcadia of pastoral poetry; the frenzied search for an impossible happiness that leads the heroes of Shelley's longer poems to their death.

Death would seem to be the only means (other than autism or some other psychosis) of liberation from the limitations imposed on individuated life, and this may be one of the reasons why religion has such a difficult time deciding whether paradise comes at the beginning or at the end of life, whether it is located in Eden or in Heaven. Freud wrote about this meaning of death, without realizing the significance of what he was saying, when in *Beyond the Pleasure Principle* he attributed the "death instinct" to a universal tendency in organic life "to restore an earlier state of things which the living entity has been obliged to abandon under the pressure of external disturbing forces."[2]

Symbiosis and individuation, like all phases of infantile development, are important chiefly because they inscribe permanent unconscious records of paradigms—important feelings, ideas, and situations that happen for the first time. The presence of such a paradigm in the oral phase was noted by Freud in his observation that anyone who has seen an infant fall into a sleep of utter contentment after nursing at his mother's breast should realize that he has seen a state of absolute satisfaction to which all later gratifications will be unfavorably compared. In general, all concerns with the loss or protection of identity, or with separation from or union with a loved object, may be traced back ultimately to oral models. When adults speak to or of the person they love and from whom they anticipate receiving the most intense pleasure possible, they inescapably regress to the language of childhood and to the oral imagery that embodies the unconscious model of the most intense sensual satisfaction. We speak of loved ones as something good to eat ("sweetie," "honey") and in so doing express both the strength and the infantile basis of our feelings.

THE ANAL PHASE

The importance of the anal phase is also chiefly paradigmatic, since it is during this time that the child begins to learn how to relate to his environment. Eager proponents of psychoanalytically oriented upbringing once claimed that proper toilet training of the child insured the mental health of the adult, but now it is generally recognized that styles and methods of toilet training, within very broad parameters, have in themselves little effect on adult life. Nevertheless anal effects do appear in adult life, as for example in excessive rebelliousness or passivity, in the tendency to expel or retain words or possessions, or in the personality traits of compulsive orderliness, cleanliness, and miserliness, which together make up what is called the "anal personality." More importantly, the child experiences for the first time constraint and manipulation and learns how to manipulate in turn. From his lonely perch in the bathroom, the child learns the processes of reciprocity and exchange, the basic structures of all social organization and the basis of religious sacrifice.

Sacrifice in primitive religion is based on the principle of *do ut des* ("I give so that you will give"); by giving up something of value, the sacrificer tries to insure that he will receive something of value from the gods. Sacrifice is the means by which the weaker party (the human being) is able to protect himself, to get what he wants, and to appease the stronger party (the gods). The more valuable the thing desired, or the greater the need for protection, the more valuable must be that which is sacrificed: the best crops, the finest animal, perhaps even other human beings. Thus, in order to win from the gods the favorable sailing conditions that will bring him what he desires most, victory over the Trojans, Agamemnon consents to sacrifice his own daughter Iphigeneia.

The relationship between child and parents during the anal phase is almost exactly analogous to that between the sacrificer and the gods. To the young child, his parents are like omnipotent and omniscient gods; they have absolute power over him and they have in their possession everything he wants. In order to satisfy his wishes, the child learns that he must do and be what his parents expect of him. And, as in the primitive sacrificer's relationship with his gods, the child comes to believe that despite the absolute power differential between him and his parents there are ways in which he can manipulate and influence them.

Since the affection and approval that the child wants from his parents are by far the most important things in his young life, he comes to believe that the price he pays, the possession he must give up in order to win what he wants, is equally valuable (a belief supported by the parent's attitude and attention). This price, of course, is his feces, a part of his body which must be surrendered to the demands of the parents. The disgust felt by adults toward these bodily products is not at first shared by children and is learned with some difficulty; how can something so vile and worthless be also the eagerly awaited and applauded object of parental attention, and the "cash" with which the child is able to buy parental affection?

Like the oral phase, the anal phase is important for later life because it provides a set of models based on events and ideas oc-

curring *for the first time.* During this period the child first experiences demands made of him, both positive and negative; he learns
the difference between good and bad, yes and no, dirty and clean.
He learns that he must please in order to be pleased, give something in order to get something, and with his feces (the only possession of convertible value he has) he takes his place in the
system of symbolic exchange that will govern so many of life's
activities. Since feces are his first money, the currency of his first
transactions, both the overestimation and underestimation of money
in later life may be derived from the ambivalent position of feces
in childhood: on one hand they are disgusting and abhorrent, but
on the other they are as supremely valuable as the all-important
love to which they are equivalent in a reciprocal process.[3]

The appearance of reciprocity during the anal stage would
seem to be one instance in which Haeckel's law that ontogeny re-
capitulates phylogeny (i.e., individual development repeats the development of the race) may be valid; just as every child enters society via his role in a system of exchange, so the most elementary
structures of kinship and social organization that first create human society also constitute a system of exchange, the exchange of
women by men according to the rules that define society and one's
place in it.[4] Just as in an exogamic situation a man from one clan
or social group must give up a woman from his group in order to
receive a woman from another group, the child gives up his feces
in order to receive love. For the purposes of the relationships thus
established, all women are the same, all feces are the same, and
feces are the same as love; all that matters is the act of giving and
the maintenance of the relational structure.

SEXUAL QUESTIONS

The unbounded curiosity of a child is the innate mechanism by
which he grows mentally, and it is natural that some of this curiosity be concerned with sexual subjects. It may be only a small
percentage of all his attention and concern, but it is a very important percentage for the contents of unconscious fantasy, since
the child's sexual questions concern his status in the world of his
family, tend to arouse emotional reactions in parents and others,
and are liable to be subject to repression.

The two great sexual questions of childhood are the origin of babies and the difference between the sexes. They usually occur in this order, most often around the end of the anal phase and beginning of the phallic phase (that is, around three to five years of age), and the child's attempt to answer them is based in part on experiences during the anal phase.

The question of where babies come from, sometimes stimulated by the arrival of a new baby brother or sister, is ultimately a generalized expression of the child's concern as to his own origin. While it may seem to be a precocious philosophical investigation— the child is asking about the circumstances of his own nonexistence—in fact the child's curiosity does not go back further than the situation of his own coming-to-be (or, if it does, it does so because of the child's emotional connection with prior events and relationships, as we shall see).

A variety of answers are suggested to the child by his parents and other respondents and by his own imagination, but it is ultimately his own experience that validates the answer the child comes to believe. He knows that babies are present inside the mother's body—and their mysterious growth within, clearly observable from outside in the changing shape of the mother's body, is the physiological prototype of *magic* in human experience—and he knows that somehow they become separate from the mother. The questions of the child, thus, are "How does the baby get out?" and "How did he get in?"

In seeking an answer to the first question, the child, no matter what he is told by truthful or evasive parents, must turn finally to his own experience for an answer. He knows that something grows within him and is subsequently detached, and that this object is of immense value: the feces he exchanges for love. Since the baby seems to go through a similar process—first inside the mother's body and then separate from her—and since the baby's value seems even greater than that of the child's feces—for the newborn baby immediately wins away the attention and affection of the parents (and everyone else) from the older child—it must be that the baby becomes separate in the same way as feces, and the process of birth must be parallel to defecation. The production of feces wins love, and so does the new baby's presence; this is why the younger child is favored in folklore or takes away the elder child's birthright in myth, and why Zeus and Kronos, who each inherits his father's position as ruler of the world, are their parents' youngest son.

The "anal birth fantasy," as it is called, may be represented in dreams by scenes of laboriously seeking an exit from narrow twisting passages, and appears in myths and art around the world as the attempt to escape from (or enter) a labyrinthine maze. Labyrinths occur as early as the stone age rock art of Europe and Africa and appear in one form or another in the ancient or primitive cultures of every inhabited continent. Labyrinthine rituals and myths indicate that emergence from the labyrinth signifies birth or rebirth, and the form itself of the labyrinth symbolizes human anatomy, more specifically the internal organs of the mother.[5] The opposite significance, that the passage *into* the center of the labyrinth symbolizes death, is equally widespread (e.g., in Egyptian labyrinth tombs of the fourth and third millennia B.C.) Both meanings are supported by the symbiotic fantasy that death is the means of re-establishing union with the mother, a return to the earliest state. As Earth says in Shelley's "Prometheus Unbound,"

> And death shall be the last embrace of her
> Who takes the life she gave, even as a mother,
> Folding her child, says, "Leave me not again."
> 3.3.105–107

The best-known labyrinth of Western mythology is that which Minos, king of Crete, built to house the Minotaur, the half-human, half-bull child of his wife Pasiphae. When the Athenian prince Theseus kills the Minotaur (the "Minos-Bull") in the center of this labyrinth, then emerges with the help of an umbilical thread to escape with the Cretan princess Ariadne, the fantasy of anal birth is combined with oedipal rivalry and triumph. In the center of the mother's body, the hero meets and overcomes the representation of paternal sexuality (the Minotaur) and thus takes for himself, immediately after birth, the desired and forbidden female.

There is, of course, one other way the child knows in which a solid object can be ejected from within the body: it can be vomited through the mouth. This fantasy appears in the myth of Kronos, father of Zeus, who swallowed his children (except for Zeus) as soon as they were born and later was compelled to vomit them up.

THE PHALLIC PHASE
AND THE OEDIPUS COMPLEX

Once the problem of the baby's manner of birth is solved, the child's curiosity turns to the question of how the baby got inside the mother in the first place and consequently to the second great problem of infantile sexual curiosity, the difference between the sexes. The urgency of this question, the natural outgrowth of the child's preceding concerns, is intensified by the fact that it typically arises at the beginning of the phallic phase, the period during which the child's fantasies of obtaining pleasure are centered on genital stimulation. It is difficult to say (in fact impossible outside of individual examples) whether sexual curiosity promotes interest in the genitals or vice versa, but in any case the combination of the two leads the child into the fantasy world of the oedipus complex.

The four- or five-year-old's interest in the genitals is not difficult to observe. The child develops habits of touching and stimulating his own genitals, he wants to inspect the sexual anatomy of his pets and toy figures, he may amuse himself (and expect others to be amused) by crude childish references to the sexual organs, and, as every parent knows, the child who was apparently asleep and content will suddenly appear in the parents' bedroom, complaining of thirst, as soon as strange noises are heard from inside their closed door.

Far more important than the actual genitals, however, are the child's fantasies concerning parental sexuality, just as the fantasized wishes and behavior of the parents are more important than the actual wishes and behavior around which fantasies are constructed. The child (especially but not only a male child) at first may believe or want to believe that the mother has a penis, that she does not lack this valuable possession. The discovery of the difference between the sexes leads naturally to this kind of evaluation, for a number of reasons. The child's thinking about the fact that some people have a penis while others do not will tend, as we have seen, to incorporate his own experiences; in particular, the anal equation of feces and baby will now be extended to include the penis, which also is regarded as both valuable and detachable. A general principle of childhood, known well by parents, is that almost always a child will want to have something rather than not have it, whatever the something may be. In addition, even the very young child quickly learns that it is better to be male than female, an unfortunate but virtually inescapable lesson imprinted on children by society and the family. Thus the penis, the male possession, succeeds to the position of value held by feces and baby, with which it also shares the characteristic of being detachable (since half of the people in the world have one and the other half do not). How could the mother, the figure most awesome (in both a positive and a negative sense) in the child's world not have this valuable possession?

When later the child comes to accept the idea that the mother does not have a penis, the old fantasy that denies this may recur in situations that stress the terrible power of the mother or the female in general. This fantasy of the "phallic mother" appears in primitive myths around the world, in fairy tales and medieval beliefs about witches and broomsticks, and in the frequency in Greek myth of hybrid female monsters (e.g., the Sphinx, the Echidna, the Harpies). Half-woman, half-animal monsters like these always have the face, and often the breast, of a woman, but their lower parts, the parts to which the sexual curiosity of the child is directed, are a lion or serpent or bird of prey, all common animal symbols of powerful male sexuality.[6]

Along with the new importance attached to the difference between the sexes or more specifically to that which constitutes this difference, the phallus (a term that refers to the symbolic representation of the penis and to its function in fantasy), the child begins to wonder about the sexual behavior of his parents, especially that secret activity, from which he is excluded, which produces both pleasure and babies. Several factors—the emergence of the genitals as leading erogenous zone, fantasies about the origin of babies, curiosity about parental sexual organs and behavior (a curiosity whose intensity is only slightly modified by variations in parental openness or reticence)—combine to produce in the child the famous *oedipus complex:* that is, the childhood phase during which the child wants the exclusive attention and affection of the parent of the opposite sex, and views the parent of the same sex as a rival or enemy to be replaced.

Since by the time of the oedipus complex repression has come to play a major and appropriate role in the child's mental life, oedipal phenomena rarely appear undisguised in the conscious memories of post-oedipal individuals, and parents or other observers usually notice nothing more than occasionally excessive jealousy or possessiveness. But the unconscious fantasies of the oedipal phase, appearing later in more or less disguised fashion in symptoms, dreams, character, and imaginative creations, are exceedingly complicated and significant—so important, in fact, that Freud called the oedipus complex the "nucleus of the neuroses" and taught that the key to mental health or mental illness lay largely in the successful or unsuccessful resolution of this complex. Although psychoanalytic theory has undergone a considerable shift of emphasis, in the years since Freud, from the oedipus complex to pre-oedipal developments, the general tendency has been not so much to devalue the oedipus complex as to realize that earlier phenomena are also, and perhaps equally, important. Even though some aspects of the oedipus complex once thought to be original now may be seen as repetitions of earlier structures and psychic conflicts, nevertheless the oedipus complex is the definitive point of entry for the individual into human society; it is this complex that puts a final, lasting, and in a sense, culturally approved seal on patterns of desire and prohibition, which may, however, go back far before the beginning of the oedipus complex.

For example, if we define the essential basis of the oedipus complex as the expression of a wish for union with a parental object and the ultimate failure of this wish because of an overwhelming prohibition, it is clear that the same definition describes exactly the earlier wish to return to symbiotic union with the mother and the impossibility of fulfilling this wish because of the prohibition of individuation, a prohibition given personal form in the figure of the father or stranger who interrupts the dyadic relation between child and mother. In the symbiotic situation, things happen for the first time and patterns are established that may affect much of what happens later, including the oedipus complex. In the oedipal situation, however, things happen for the last time; the emotional dialectic of childhood is crystallized in a form that will define the individual's desires henceforth while accomplishing his passage from the closed world of the family into the society outside. Furthermore, the oedipus complex, which introduces the individual into society, has as its societal correlate the universal incest taboo, the basis of primitive social organization. The principle of ex-

change, then, which every individual learns in bargaining for parental affection, appears first at the beginning of human society in
the agreement of men to exchange women, and subsequently in
the resolution of the individual oedipus complex; the child is forced
to give up the object of his desire within the family in order to receive later a substitute object from outside the family.

In any discussion of the oedipus complex and its relationship
with both later and earlier developments, it must be remembered
that mental and emotional phenomena do not necessarily proceed
in a unidirectional sequence. The effect of early phases on later development is unmistakable, but there are also ways in which later
development may influence the memories of earlier experiences.
The oedipus complex may be seen as a repetition of a symbiotic
configuration, but it is also possible that each step in the developmental process may produce alterations in the memories of former
steps; that is, it may be equally likely that the events of symbiosis
and individuation, registered as memories at the time of their occurrence, receive real psychic force only later, when new but similar events supply earlier experiences with retroactive significance.
Freud called this mechanism "deferred action," and a striking example in myth of this reciprocity between separate stages of psychic activity appears in the Greek creation story. In an obvious
scenario of transition from symbiosis to individuation, just where
we would expect to find some representation of the new individuals's first experience of loss and frustration, we encounter instead
a symbolic representation of oedipal loss, the eternal frustration
inflicted in Tartaros on those (e.g., Tityos and Ixion) who are
punished for having attempted to fulfill forbidden oedipal desires.[7]

Freud gave the name "oedipus complex" to this combination
of love for one parent and hate for the other because of its famous
and relatively undisguised representation in the Greek myth of
Oidipous, who killed his father Laios and married his mother
Iocasta. Writing to his friend Fliess in 1897, Freud said, "the
Greek legend seizes on a compulsion which everyone recognizes
because he feels its existence within himself." In fact, this identification of the myth of Oidipous with the oedipus complex needs
clarification in at least two areas.

First, the central meaning of the myth (which must not be
viewed as exactly equivalent to Sophocles' dramatic version of it)
is concerned not so much with the undiluted representation of an

individual's hidden wish to kill his father and marry his mother, as with the emotional ambivalence that complicates a person's effort to come to terms with sexuality both inside and outside the family. Oidipous and his father Laios represent the opposite poles of this ambivalence, and their relationship is duplicated in the conflict between Oidipous' sons, Polyneikes and Eteokles.

Second, the depiction of oedipal themes is not confined to the Oidipous myth as an isolated instance, but is a general and important characteristic in all heroic myth. We meet an oedipal situation wherever we find a triangular relationship between a hero, the forbidden object of his desire, and a prohibiting figure who denies the hero access to his own possession. Usually these mythical figures are not literally son, mother, and father, as they are in the Oidipous myth, and even when they are, one aspect of the triangle is generally missing or altered—Ouranos marries his mother Gaia, but doesn't overthrow his father (he doesn't have one); and both Kronos and Zeus overcome their fathers but then marry their sisters, not their mothers—however, this brings the myths closer to, not further from, the oedipus complex and real life. The real significance of the oedipus complex lies not in the child's family, but in its effect on his life beyond the family, and the significant characters in the complex are not so much the real mother and father as the parents of fantasy and other figures who inherit the function of the fantasized parents. In myth and in life, what matters is not the specific identity of involved parties, but rather the persistence of a specific structure and functions.

Seen in this light, the oracle warning Laios not to have a son, because that son will kill him, is merely a simpler version of the many oracles warning fathers of daughters not to allow their daughters to marry, since the father is fated to be killed by his son-in-law or grandson or some other bearer of the son's function. And every suitor who must perform an apparently impossible task to win the hand of a daughter from her forbidding father or guardian is as much as Oidipous as Oidipous himself, just as we in actuality fight our oedipal battles and pursue our oedipal desires not with our real fathers and mothers but with those figures who function as oedipal parents in fact and in fantasy.

THE BLINDNESS OF TEIRESIAS

Oedipal desires and sexual curiosity combine during the phallic stage (although here again "deferred action" may play a major role) to produce the "primal scene" fantasy, the child's fantasy of observing the sexual intercourse of parents. This fantasy, which expresses both the child's curiosity as to what his parents do and also his wish to know what *he* should do, occurs often in myth, perhaps most interestingly in the three versions of how the Theban prophet Teiresias was blinded. Teiresias plays a major role in the myth of Oidipous and in Sophocles' *Oidipous the King,* and it could be argued that *his* myth reveals more about the oedipus complex than that of Oidipous.

According to the mythographer Apollodoros, Teiresias was blinded by the gods because: (1) he revealed the secrets of the gods; (2) he saw the goddess Athena naked; (3) when asked by Zeus and Hera whether men or women had more pleasure in sex, he answered that women did and was blinded by Hera.

1. The gods of myth represent, in general, the parents, and the "secrets of the gods," which mortals are forbidden to know, are the secrets of parental sexuality. The nature of the secrets revealed by Teiresias is not specified, but in the parallel instance of Sisyphos, also punished for revealing the gods' secrets, we learn that Sisyphos saw Zeus rape Aigina and informed her father Aisopos, and on another occasion Teiresias himself is said to have told Amphitryon that his wife had spent the previous night with Zeus.

2. In the second variant Teiresias is blinded by Athena after he accidentally sees her bathing in a stream. As in the first variant, the object of "accidental" curiosity is parental sexuality, but this time the father is eliminated and the primal scene consists only of the mother's sexuality revealed. It may seem strange that Athena, the most resolutely virginal and anti-maternal of goddesses, would represent the mother, but this conforms with the common mythical situation (and possessive childhood fantasy) in which the mother of a divine or favored child is a virgin; the child's possessive jealousy is duplicated in the exclusion of a father from the scene. In any case, the identification between the naked goddess and the forbidden body of the mother is further substantiated in the account

of this episode by the Hellenistic poet Callimachus; Teiresias sees not only Athena but also his mother Chariklo, the favorite nymph of Athena, naked together in the stream.

3. The third variant is divided into two related events, in each of which Teiresias is punished. In the first, he saw two snakes copulating, attempted to interfere with them, and was changed into a woman; some years later she saw the same snakes doing the same thing, again tried to interfere, and was changed back to a man. Later chosen by Zeus and Hera to arbitrate their sexual argument on the basis of his ambisexual experience, he angered Hera with his answer and she blinded him. The copulating snakes are another primal scene—snakes are often associated with the older generation in Greek funerary and hero cults—and the knowledge gained by Teiresias both experientially and visually, as well as the question asked of him by the divine couple, represent the chief motivating question of the primal scene fantasy: What are the sexual roles of male and female?

The primal scene fantasy underlying this myth appears in three forms: as the sexual secret (or forbidden knowledge) revealed by Teiresias, as the naked goddess, and as the copulating snakes. Something is lacking in each representation (the exact content of the secret, a male companion for Athena, a human counterpart to the snakes), but they repeat and complement one another to form a picture of the knowledge that is the object of sexual curiosity and oedipal wishes, the knowledge that equips Teiresias to answer the question of Zeus and Hera.

The *function* of the primal scene is both to gratify curiosity and also to inform the child of what he would have to do if he were able to replace the rival parent and then have the loved parent all to himself. This knowledge, at the same time desirable and threatening, is the prototype of all later forbidden knowledge and this origin helps to explain why that which is unknown so often combines allurement and danger.

Freud believed that the male oedipus complex came to an end because of the child's fear that persistence in his wishes would bring him into direct conflict with his father. In this contest the child could only lose and the price of defeat would be castration (a conclusion reached by the child on the basis of the importance of the phallus in this sexual conflict, especially in light of his discovery that not all people possess this organ). The anxiety caused by the child's fantasies of paternal revenge, whether general or specific, is called *castration anxiety,* and it is this anxiety that compels the child to give up his oedipal desires and to make his peace with the father (by a process that substitutes identification for rivalry and leads to the origin of the superego, or conscience).

In the myths of Teiresias' blindness, the gratification of incestuous curiosity is punished four times by a symbolic castration. Blinding, which ends each of the three mythic variants, is a frequent punishment in myth for a sexual crime (and an appropriate one, since the primary sexual organ of the curious child or voyeuristic adult is his eyesight); the best-known example, of course, is the self-blinding of Oidipous after his discovery that he has killed his father and married his mother. Similarly, the change of sex undergone by Teiresias in the third variant is a symbolic castration, particularly in a society as male oriented and phallocentric as ancient Greece.

Furthermore, the overthrow of the primal father Ouranos by his son Kronos at the beginning of Greek mythology is accomplished by a real rather than symbolic castration; while still within his mother Gaia, Kronos castrated Ouranos during the act of parental intercourse.[8] This myth represents the fulfillment of an oedipal wish, particularly since Kronos is aided by his mother who gives him the sickle with which he accomplishes his victory. In real life, however, this wish is countered by the fear that sexual conflict, with castration as its ultimate outcome, will result in the defeat of the son by his much more powerful father; it is this fear, Freud believed, that causes the boy to renounce his oedipal desires.

Freud thought that progress through the oedipus complex is quite different for the girl, for two main reasons: castration cannot be a threat to her as to the boy, and she must change her primary love object from mother to father while the boy keeps always the same object, the mother. In fact, Freud said, castration (threatened) ends the male oedipus complex but castration (perceived) begins the female oedipus complex; the discovery that she and her mother are "castrated" leads the girl to transfer her principal love to the father, and her concomitant wish to have a penis is transformed into a wish to have a child by her father. *Penis envy,* a notorious term in contemporary psychoanalysis, means nothing more or less than the observable fact that little girls in a male-dominant culture may feel deprived of something boys have. What matters, of course, is the effect this childhood perception has on later life, an effect which may be significant or negligible, depending on societal circumstances. Like the color of one's skin, the shape of one's genitals is a neutral biological fact that acquires meaning from a society that prizes or devalues certain biological differences.

We would expect the incidence of penis envy to be high in a strongly patriarchal culture like ancient Greece, but the overvaluation of male activity and attributes results in the virtual absence from historical records of any direct information about the psychological behavior of women. If we turn to Greek myth, we find that two of the five Olympian goddesses, Artemis and Athena, reject the sexual and maternal roles of women and tend to adopt the activities and attitudes of men. The only occasion on which this facade is penetrated is when Athena the warrior and Artemis the huntress put aside their weapons and clothing to bathe. We already saw how Teiresias was punished when he discovered Athena in this situation, and a similar incident involves Artemis and the Theban hunter Aktaion; having come upon Artemis bathing in a stream, he was changed into a deer and killed by his own dogs. Before seeing these two goddesses, or the related myth of the Amazons, as examples of a feminine wish to be a man, however, we must remember that these myths, like virtually all of Greek myth, are presumably male fantasies. It is much more likely that Athena's masculine behavior is related to her general helpfulness to mythical heroes than that it reflects a woman's desire to escape from femininity. In other words, if penis envy was a significant factor in Greek society and myth, we should look for it not in the form of actual representations, but rather in male responses to a hypothetical phenomenon.

The male castration complex, on the other hand, does seem to appear frequently in Greek myth. In addition to the earlier examples, we might note the presence of monsters who threaten some kind of real or figurative castration, like the Harpies, Gorgons, or Erinyes.[9] Here, however, we are presented with an obvious problem: if castration anxiety, as usually described by psychoanalysis, concerns the son's fear of his hostile father, why are these castrating monsters usually female? And why, in the stories of Teiresias's punishment for oedipal offenses, is blindness inflicted not by a god but by the goddesses Athena and Hera? Or, to put the question in another form, can the male child's oedipal anxieties and fears center as much or more around the figure of the mother as that of the father?

THE ANXIETY OF BELLEROPHON

A possible answer to this question is suggested by the Argive myth of Bellerophon, grandson of the oedipal criminal Sisyphos (Apollodoros 2.3.1–2; *Iliad* 6.155–93). Having accidentally killed his brother, Bellerophon was forced to find a foreign figure of authority who would purify him for this deed. Proitos, king of Tiryns, agreed to perform the purification, but while Bellerophon was staying with him, Proitos' wife Stheneboia fell in love with their guest. When Bellerophon rejected her advances, she went to her husband and falsely told him that Bellerophon had tried to seduce her. Proitos believed his wife and was obliged to punish Bellerophon, but because of the special relationship now existing between purifier and purified he had to find an indirect means of vengeance. He therefore sent Bellerophon to his father-in-law Iobates, king of Lykia, with a sealed letter requesting Iobates to kill the bearer of the message. Iobates commanded Bellerophon to fight the terrible Chimaira, a flying female monster who combined the forms of a lion, a serpent, and a goat and breathed fire on her enemies. At first helpless, Bellerophon was aided by Athena, who gave him a magic bridle with which he was able to tame and ride the winged horse Pegasos. In the midair conflict between Bellerophon and Chimaira, the hero was ultimately victorious (in one version, by putting a lump of lead on the end of his spear and poking it into Chimaira's fiery mouth, causing the monster to swallow the molten metal and die of lead poisoning). Iobates then sent Bellerophon on a number of missions which, he was sure, would cause his death; Bellerophon was forced to fight, with the help only of Pegasos, against the Amazons, the Lykian army, and the king's own bodyguard. When Bellerophon, like Samson, singlehandedly defeated this multitude of foes, Iobates realized the futility of his intention and made Bellerophon his successor by giving him a share of his kingdom and marriage with his daughter Philonoe.

This myth is only one of many examples in Greek and other

myth of what is called the Potifar's Wife Motif (named for the Old Testament story of the slander by the Egyptian Potifar's lecherous wife against the innocent Joseph). Whether the story concerns a husband, wife, and unrelated third party (as in the myths of Bellerophon and Joseph) or a father, son, and stepmother (as in the well-known Greek myth of Theseus, Hippolytos, and Phaidra), the triangular relationship clearly represents the oedipal situation of father, mother, and son. But why then would the son, whose primary oedipal wish is presumably to have his mother to himself, reject the mother's offer to gratify this wish and, furthermore, deny the existence of the wish itself? The obvious, and psychoanalytically orthodox, answer would be that he fears being punished by his father, even if the father were merely to learn of the existence of the wish. In every case the father does attempt to punish the supposedly innocent son, and in most instances he is successful.

Without denying the plausibility of this explanation, however, we might entertain the possibility of a different motive for Bellerophon's behavior and a different answer to the question of why he denies his oedipal desire. At the time of his stay with Proitos and Stheneboia, Bellerophon is hardly as yet a hero, although his causing the death of a brother does hint at oedipal aspirations. It is only after he receives Pegasos and triumphs in the exploits on which he is sent by Iobates that he becomes a great hero and receives in marriage the sister of Stheneboia. Now it might be argued that this outcome supports the view that oedipal renunciation results from fear of the father; through becoming a hero and defeating Iobates' armies, Bellerophon overcomes both his fear and his paternal enemies. At first so inadequate and powerless that he had to deny his wishes, he now is invincible and receives from the father himself the double of the woman he had earlier rejected. The secret of his success, the difference between Tiryns and Lykia, is Pegasos, a doubly determined symbol of phallic superiority.[10] In this grandiose wish fulfillment, the weak and helpless child becomes sexually powerful, conquers the world, and replaces the father.

Still this argument leaves certain aspects of the myth unexplained, in particular the role of the woman who represents the mother. While her sexual advances might be explained as a projection of the child's wishes, why is it that in all versions of the Potifar's Wife story it is the mother who is principally responsible for the punishment of the son? If the myth is about father–son enmity, why are Proitos and Iobates essentially instruments of Stheneboia's desire for revenge? Why is it that the enemies Bellerophon and Pegasos must initially face are female, Chimaira and the Amazons?

A different interpretation (and perhaps a more persuasive one, since it takes all elements into account) would begin from the fact that everything happens in this myth because of the hostility of a maternal figure whose sexual demands are unfulfilled. We should then ask what sort of fantasy on the part of the male child would produce such a situation. Both before and during the oedipus complex, the child's primary desire is to please his mother, and in order to do this he must first learn what his mother wants him to do. The child's desire is always a function of his mother's desire, or, more specifically, of the child's fantasy of what his mother's desires are. During the oedipus complex, when the child wants to replace the father as his mother's sexual companion, he creates on the basis of his knowledge of that relationship (the primal scene fantasy) a fantasy of maternal sexual expectations: what will he have to do if he takes his father's place? What is the nature of his mother's relationship with his father, and what will she therefore expect of him? How will he satisfy her sexual wishes and demands?

It seems entirely likely that this fantasy will generate anxiety and fear concerning the child's inability to satisfy the mother, particularly as a result of comparison between his own size and abilities and those of his mother and father. How will he possibly be able to do whatever it is that his father does, and how will he be able to gratify the *imagined* needs of his mother? Antecedent to fear of punishment by the father (castration anxiety), then, may be prior fear of inadequacy and inferiority (a kind of "performance anxiety") which, in my view, is of earlier and perhaps greater significance.

There is a good deal of clinical support for this infantile performance anxiety, including Freud's famous case history of "Little Hans"[11] and other studies by early psychoanalysts. Further evidence appears in the frequent complaint by adult male neurotics that their penis is too small; in a situation of stress and conflict, the neurotic regresses to a paradigmatic occasion of failure in childhood, when both he and his penis were literally too small to achieve success. Even in so-called normal behavior, the common emphasis on penile size in "male" humor and jokes (as well as allusions to female insatiability) suggests that this anxiety is pervasive. And the typical anxieties of adolescents of both sexes in anticipation of first sexual activity display a striking repetition of their oedipal anxieties: girls tend to worry about bleeding, being wounded, and pain, while boys tend to worry about ability and performance.

The prevalence of performance anxiety can be demonstrated in many areas, in anthropological and sociological studies as well as in myth and imaginative literature. The custom in medieval and primitive societies of the *ius primae noctis* (right of the first night)—the assignment of the defloration of a virgin to a king, lord, or chief instead of her new husband—is probably due not so much to the lecherous tyranny of the lord, as is commonly thought, as to the anxiety of the new husband, who is thereby freed from the ordeal of the first night.

The clearest and best-known example in literature of this phenomenon occurs in the first two sections of Swift's *Gulliver's Travels,* "A Voyage to Lilliput" and "A Voyage to Brobdingnag." While he is staying among the giant Brobdingnagians, Lemuel Gulliver is a child among greatly exaggerated adults. He spends most of his time with the women of the court, who keep him and treat him like a pet, and the chief characteristic of his stay is his acute shame at his smallness, which is intensified when he is stripped naked and dandled on the breast of one of the women, or when he is obliged to urinate in their presence or they in his. At the sight and smell of these immense naked female bodies, Gulliver is overwhelmed by horror and aversion, a reaction which he attributes specifically to the difference between his size and theirs. The land of the Lilliputians, on the other hand, is a place where childhood dreams of phallic enormity come true. The Lilliputians are filled with wonder at Gulliver's capacity for wine (he drinks many tiny barrels at a time) and his consequent urinary potency. When they are planning a parade, they ask Gulliver if he will be a colossus, standing astride the boulevard while the population marches between his legs; he agrees, on condition that they not look upward (his breeches having been torn in the shipwreck), but they are unable to restrain themselves from looking up in "awe and amazement." This wish-fulfilling fantasy is finally ended by a thinly disguised oedipal adventure, the fire in the Queen's chambers. The tiny Lilliputians with their tiny hoses could not put out the fire, but Gulliver, who had drunk his usual amount of wine that day, succeeded in extinguishing the blaze by urinating on it. A psychoanalyst would have no difficulty interpreting a similar dream of one of his patients. The Queen is the mother, and the fire is her erotic desire, which no one who is too small can possibly gratify. Gulliver's saving act, by means of his giant "hose," expresses a wish for phallic enormity and potency, and overcomes the anxieties of Brobdingnag. When Gulliver is now put on trial and condemned to death by the Lilliputians, since urination in the royal precinct is a capital offense, we can see that the elimination of performance anxiety does not prevent the appearance of castration anxiety. Then, as though to stress the infantile nature of the fantasy, Gulliver's sentence is changed from death to blinding, reminiscent of the fates of Oidipous and Teiresias.

When mythical and legendary heroes must overcome a terrible male adversary to win a princess, the psychology of the confrontation concerns castration anxiety and the rivalry between son and father (or brother, who often represents the father). But when the obstacle to be overcome is female, whether a female monster, as so often in Greek myth, or the inaccessibility or power of the desired woman herself, as in the Arthurian legends, we are dealing with performance anxiety and the child's feeling of impotence and inadequacy.

In Greek myth fathers of marriageable daughters invariably demand that their daughter's suitors perform what seems to be an impossible task if they want to win a bride. Often this involves defeating or imitating the father in something the father does better than anyone else, and the meaning of the imposed ordeal is clearly male oedipal rivalry. At times, however, the task is to overcome a fearsome female, as Perseus must defeat the Gorgon Medousa in order to win the princess Andromeda or Bellerophon must defeat Chimaira to win Philonoe. An interesting variant is the story of Admetos' courtship of Alkestis, whose father Pelias demanded that his daughter's suitors succeed in yoking a boar and lion to a chariot. The god Apollo, who at this time happened to be obligated to Admetos, accomplished the yoking for him and thus Admetos received Alkestis. On the wedding night, however, he opened the door to the marriage chamber and found the room full of coiled snakes. Like the snakes on Medousa's head, they represent female (that is, maternal) sexuality as something dangerous and frightening, and Admetos' failure is appropriate; a surrogate, not Admetos himself, performed the test of manhood, and so now Admetos cannot even enter the bedroom.

Stheneboia, the unsatisfied woman in the myth of Bellerophon, and other versions of Potifar's Wife would then represent the unsatisfiable woman, the mother whose sexual needs and wishes, as imagined by the oedipal son, are so overwhelming and frightening that he must deny his own wishes and project them onto the mother: it is not *I* who want her, it is *she* who wants me. But the father always believes his wife's lying accusation, and the reason is that it is not in fact a lie. The son really does desire the mother (although he cannot admit it), he really is guilty, and so he must be punished. In those instances where the punishment is successfully carried out, we would suppose that a prime determinant of the myth is castration anxiety and fear of the father. In those cases where punishment fails, it would seem that performance anxiety is uppermost; this is especially evident in the myth of Bellerophon, who marries Iobates' other daughter and replaces the father after demonstrating his phallic heroism.

In the myth of Teiresias, his blinding by Athena in the absence of any paternal agent of punishment would then represent the same motive: the sexual knowledge gained through incestuous curiosity may be desirable but it is also frightening and castrating, revealing to the child that his most important desire is impossible and unfulfillable. This knowledge, which Teiresias possesses as a result of having seen both the primal scene and the maternal genitals, is what enables him to answer the sexual question of Zeus and Hera; and his answer, which causes Hera to blind him, is that there is a great disproportion between male and female in the matter of sexual capability and potential for pleasure. It may seem at first that Teiresias is comparing an adult male with an adult female (and his answer is not invalid on this level, since it would reflect adult male performance anxiety and fear of female insatiability), but the viewpoint of the other versions of his punishment, which clearly portray a childhood oedipal situation, suggests that the answer he now gives to the gods is a sexual comparison between mother and son. His answer, his viewing of the maternal genitals, and the maternal sources of his punishment all indicate that the major source of anxiety for the son is the mother, the discrepancy between his and her physical size and sexual capability, and the impossibility of his attaining her. The two occasions on which Teiresias sees parental copulation reveal the sexual nature of his desire to see the mother naked, since similarity of punishment indicates similarity of crime, and at the same time the primal scene demonstrates to the son not only that his mother is an impossible object, but also that he would have to measure up to an impossible model, his father. Sexual curiosity in all its manifestations leads inevitably to the perception that the castration threat is real and also to the enforced realization that an inescapable limitation is imposed on the son's greatest wish.

The model of an impossible love, of a desire that cannot be realized, is the sexual love of a son for his mother. Teiresias' knowledge of maternal sexuality, the paradigm of that forbidden and inaccessible knowledge for which he, like other wise men and seers, is blinded, is thus also the knowledge of human limitation. On a specific and infantile level, the knowledge of the prophet is that what the mother wants the child cannot give. On a generalized experiential level it is knowledge of the eternal disproportion between our desire and our capabilities, a discrepancy that turns the child away from his first love and is reformulated in every act of sex afterward, which psychoanalysis expresses as the conflict between the pleasure principle and the reality principle. The paradox of human life is that the continual restless search for immediate instinctual gratification is continually resisted by the inhibiting factors of reality; happiness is always, at best, a fragile compromise between these essentially irreconcilable principles.

Seen in this light, the oedipus complex, which ends the phallic stage and infantile psychosexual development, is childhood's final adaptation to reality. During the oral stage the child was forced by the fact of individuation to repress fantasies of symbiotic union. During the anal stage he learned to deal with the world of others and lost his illusions of omnipotence in the necessity of having to give something in order to acquire something. And now in the phallic stage he learns that there are some things he cannot give, and consequently, that there are some things he can never acquire.

THE NATURE OF DREAMS

As Freud and the other early analysts quickly learned, the study of dreams opened a window both on the meaning of myths and on the ways in which we think unconsciously; in Freud's famous phrase, dreams are "the royal road to the unconscious." Most importantly, since dreaming is something that every person regularly does, what we can learn from dreams is applicable to a general psychology, not just to a psychology of neurotics or children or primitives.

Every dream exists, for the purposes of analysis, on two levels, manifest content and latent content. The manifest content is the dream as it is remembered, typically a brief visual narrative that may be quite sensible, or quite nonsensical, or anything in between. The latent content is the collection of ideas combined together and transformed into the manifest content. The process of transformation from latent content to manifest content is called by Freud the *dreamwork,* and it is perhaps helpful to compare this process to translation from one language to another (although this is not quite accurate, since the manifest content is often a severely compressed abridgement of the latent thoughts). The reason that any dream may be viewed as existing on two levels, as well as the necessity of transformation in the relationship between the two levels, is that a kind of censorship operates in dreams, a particular instance of the general function of repression in mental activity. Because of the special conditions of the state of sleep, especially its lack of motility—its requirement that all action take place in hallucination rather than in reality—dreams allow certain repressed ideas to enter consciousness momentarily. Nevertheless, repression is lifted only partway; since expression of these unconscious ideas in their actual form would still threaten too much anxiety, a partial repression or censorship disguises them, a function facilitated by condensation and displacement, the principal modes of unconscious thinking. This transformational characteristic of the dreamwork can be seen most clearly in the case of symbolism, as in the episode from *Gulliver's Travels* discussed earlier: the queen is the mother, the bedroom fire is her sexual desire, Gulliver is the male child, urine is semen, and so forth.

The various ideas, or *dream-thoughts,* that make up the latent content of the dream fall into three categories: chance stimuli, day residue, and unconscious wishes.

1. A chance stimulus is any disturbance, whether external or internal, which affects a person while asleep, especially if this stimulus threatens the continuation of sleep. A ringing telephone or alarm clock, for example, may be incorporated into a dream, sometimes as itself but more frequently as some other noise, and thereby the dreamer is able to go on sleeping. Similarly, an internal stimulus such as hunger, thirst, urinary pressure, or pain may appear in a dream as an alternative to waking the sleeper.

2. Day residue, or *residue of the previous day,* refers in general to all of a subject's unrepressed memories and more specifically to those memories incurred during the waking period immediately prior to the sleep during which the dream occurs. Although all preconscious memories are available for the dream-thoughts, the majority of those that actually appear are typically from the previous day.

3. The most important element in the latent content of the dream is an unconscious wish, repressed material that usually has some connection with childhood and with sexuality. It is the presence of a wish that gives the dream its motive and energy, and the virtual necessity of this presence led Freud to define the dream itself as the hallucinatory fulfillment of an unconscious wish. Even anxiety-provoking dreams such as nightmares or punishment dreams, which seem far from expressing a wish, are only apparent exceptions; the wish would not be repressed were it not for a corresponding fear or opposing wish, and it is this conflict that is represented in such dreams (and in neurotic symptoms as well). The sexual content of dreams has received an unexpected confirmation from empirical research on the physiology of dreaming, which has shown that dream states are invariably accompanied, in both sexes, by some degree of physically evident sexual arousal.[12]

The third category is (almost) always present in dreams, the second is usually present, and the first occasionally. All three categories have distinct functions: the first and third categories promote health, whether physical or mental, and the second provides the material for the dream's development and embellishment. The whole process is quite similar to the technique of a novelist who begins with a basic idea or structure (the unconscious wish), elaborates it and fleshes it out with material from diverse sources, principally his own experiences (day residue), and incorporates into the work chance occurrences that occur during writing or may even provoke the writing process (chance stimuli).

The inclusion of a chance stimulus in the dream clearly promotes physical health, in that it protects sleep; Freud described the dream as "the guardian of sleep" and even spoke of the "fulfillment of the wish to sleep," but he seems here to be speaking not so much of an unconscious wish as of a physical need or preconscious wish (e.g., I don't hear the alarm clock, because I prefer to keep on sleeping and not go to work). The presence of repressed material in a dream would seem to have the same therapeutic function, but on a mental level; the regular expression of unconscious wishes, even (or only) in changed and disguised form, seems to be an indispensable requirement of mental health.

The necessity of dreaming for mental stability has been clearly demonstrated by empirical studies in which subjects are prevented from dreaming (but not from sleeping) for a prolonged period. After a week or so, the non-dreamers begin to display quasi-psychotic behavior—hallucination, anxiety, depression, and so forth—and the resumption of dreaming "cures" these "symptoms."[13] This phenomenon is not so surprising or anomalous as it may seem, but is merely the correlate on a "normal" level of the function of neurotic and psychotic symptoms on an "abnormal" level; symptoms, like dreams, are the disguised representation of psychic conflict and express through this representation a person's attempt to attain health and protect against a greater danger.

This discovery has little practical value for therapy, since we all dream on a regular basis, but it has large and important implications for the study of the function of myth. If dreams are in fact of the same nature as myths—which Freud defined as "the *secular dreams* of youthful humanity"—it would then follow that myths perform the same function for a society that dreams fulfill for the individual. Myths may, of course, have other functions, just as a table may be an objet d'art or a pie may be a projectile, but in each case there is a primary use that suffices for the definition of function: tables are to put things on, pies are good to eat, and myths express unconscious wishes and fears. And just as every individual must dream, every society must have its myths, whether religious, political, or cultural, to maintain its collective mental health.

DREAMS AND MYTHS

The unconscious fantasies represented in myth are also found in dreams, but only a small percentage of dream fantasies appear in myth. There are several reasons for this disproportion, the most obvious and necessary being the requirement that the myth be communicable and that the wishes and fears embodied in it be shared by the majority of its audience. While myths may have had their inception in dreams (a plausible conjecture, particularly in light of the equivalence of myth and dream in certain primitive cultures, but still only a conjecture in the absence of written evidence), nevertheless only those dreams that responded to the emotional needs of a large segment of the community could acquire the status of myth. Dreams, on the other hand, tend to be so personal and idiosyncratic that they appear nonsensical to others, and so heavily disguised that they are usually undecipherable even by the dreamer.

The mythical equivalent of a dream's day residue, the material the dream uses to express an unconscious wish, is the collective past of a society, both the history of the group and also the sum of the individual histories of those who have belonged to the group. The day residue of myths, like that of dreams, is made up of memories, but these are mostly shared memories, the group memory of a mythical and historical past handed down over the centuries by bards and storytellers, and the individual memories of emotional events common to the experience of most members of the group. These memories contain real events and things (wars, migrations, encounters with new peoples; births, deaths, marriages; social institutions and social change; trees, mountains, ships, etc.), but they also contain the dreams and fantasies of the past, the dreams from which myths sprang, and the fantasies whose communicability and universality made them into myths.

Hesiod's *Theogony,* for example, probably consists partly of his own invention and partly of an inherited tradition of creation and succession myths. If this version, both the original elements and also the specific structure he gave to traditional elements, be-

came the canonical cosmogonic myth, it must be because this particular collocation of individual and group memories best satisfied
the society's emotion-laden curiosity about the origins of the world,
the gods, and themselves.

The mythical equivalents of chance stimuli, which are incorporated into a dream to ward off the threat they pose to sleep, are
the great events and sudden changes that threaten the coherence
and stability of a group: a Trojan War, a Flood, a radical political
or technological transition. Thus the widespread destruction of
Mycenean sites at the end of the Bronze Age was mythologized
as the vengeful return of the descendants of Herakles, and the two
great technological advances of early man, the beginning of agriculture and the invention of metallurgy, were incorporated as sexual fantasies into the myths of Demeter and Hephaistos.[14]

The assimilation of external or internal disturbances, however, is only one aspect of myth's stabilizing function. The existence
of a common set of beliefs and of a common structure directing
emotional responses also provides coherence and unity to a society, especially when these beliefs and responses are connected with
communal rituals. But when change becomes too rapid or severe,
as in our own time or in fifth century Greece, this function of myth
is weakened and other means of preventing societal fragmentation
must be found.

Dreams and myths are similar in that they protect individuals,
in the case of dreams, and societies, in the case of myth, from danger through the expression of repressed material. Myths differ from
dreams chiefly in two ways: the latent content of the myth must be
sufficiently general that an emotional response is elicited from the
group, not just from one or a few individuals, whereas a dream requires no psychic relevance beyond the individual dreamer; and
the "day residue," the setting and details with which the myth is
constructed and elaborated, is typically set in the remote past,
while the day residue of dreams usually comes from the immediate past. The best explanation for the second difference—why
are myths set in a distant, or virtually timeless, past?—is probably
to be found in the first difference. The separation of myths from
the recent past removes them at the same time from the experiences of present and recent members of the society, thus making it
possible for the reality of myths to be believed, and this shared
trust in the truth of myths would seem to be necessary for their

full psychological effect to be realized. A dreamer also will usually believe in the reality of his dream while dreaming, but there is no requirement, nor virtually any likelihood, that the dreamer when awake or any other person will believe that the events of the dream actually took place. Myths, however, require a waking consent to their reality, and so must be far enough removed from any past or current reality against which they could be tested and falsified.

THE PRIMARY PROCESS: CONDENSATION AND DISPLACEMENT

Thinking may be defined most simply as the connecting of one idea with another idea. In our conscious thinking, these connections must observe certain linguistic and logical rules if our thinking is to be comprehensible to ourselves and to others; if we do not follow these rules, we will be accused of not making sense. Unconscious thinking, on the other hand, seems to break these rules (especially in regard to logical conventions of time, causality, and negation or contradiction); this is why dreams, to take the most obvious example, usually seem *not* to make sense.

Psychoanalytic theory is largely based on the contention that dreams, as well as all other instances of unconscious thinking, do in fact make sense, but that this sense cannot be discovered without the recognition that the mechanisms of unconscious thinking are different from those of conscious thinking. Not only are the rules of conscious logic usually disobeyed, but also meaning itself is highly allusive and unstable, with the result that the characteristics of unconscious thought seem much closer to the kind of thinking we find in poetry than to ordinary conscious thought processes. Because the principles of unconscious thinking are genetically prior to those of conscious thinking, which develop only gradually as thought-connections are tested against reality, psychoanalysis refers to unconscious thinking as *primary process* thinking, while the system of conscious thought, which develops out of the primary process and represents a modification of it, is called *secondary process* thinking.

The two major principles, or mechanisms, of the primary process are *condensation* and *displacement,* which may be defined most easily in the context of the relationship between a dream's latent and manifest content. *Condensation* means that one idea in the manifest content of a dream may stand for several similar ideas in the latent content; consequently, the latent content will usually be much greater in extent than the manifest content, which, says Freud, is its "abbreviated translation."[15] *Displacement* means that the emotional energy attached to one idea may be transferred to another, seemingly dissimilar, idea; a practical result of displacement in dreams is that an apparently insignificant or indifferent detail in the manifest content may represent the most important element of the latent content—or, conversely, that what seems most important in the manifest content may have little or no importance in the latent content.

We know the unconscious only as it appears in consciousness—in symptoms, parapraxes (slips of the tongue or pen), the clinical practice of psychoanalysis, and especially dreams—and since all these phenomena employ condensation and displacement to disguise, even while expressing, unconscious ideas, it is possible to regard these mechanisms both as characteristics of unconscious thinking and also as aspects of the defensive strategies of censorship and repression. In other words, the much greater freedom with which ideas can be associated with, or substituted for, other ideas in primary process thinking lends itself to the transformation of latent content into manifest content or of repressed idea into conscious symptom.

By unconscious "ideas" or "thoughts," psychoanalysis does not mean the complex and abstract judgments of the secondary process, but rather the concrete contents of acts of thought. Unconscious thinking has access to all ideas that have entered a person's mind and are retained as memories, but typically prefers to employ visual and specific ideas rather than abstract and general ones. Since the contents of the unconscious are formed by repression, the ideas found in the unconscious will be those associated with repressed wishes and fears and organized into fantasies, imaginary scenes or dramatizations portraying the repressed wish and employing various defensive mechanisms.

The "rules" or characteristic associations—the means by which unconscious ideas are organized into fantasies and fantasies are connected with one another—are condensation and displacement, which replace the logical and linguistic rules of the secondary process and are especially appropriate to a mode of mental functioning that tends to think in images rather than words and is indifferent to reality and therefore to negation, doubt, and varying degrees of certitude.

METAPHOR AND METONYMY

Ideas can be connected with one another in two ways, either (1) because they are alike in some way, or (2) because they have some other association that is not principally likeness. For example, "water" may be connected with "wine" because they are similar, both being potable liquids; or "water" may be connected with "bottle," the association being that water is often contained in a bottle. We can call the first kind of connection, which is based on similarity, *metaphoric,* and we can call the second kind, based on some other relationship than similarity, *metonymic.* Suppose someone is asked to say the first thing that comes into his mind in response to a verbal or visual stimulus, and to "automobile" he responds "truck"; auto and truck are related by similarity, and his answer is metaphoric. But if he should respond to "automobile" with "driver" or "wheel" or "highway," he is using another kind of relationship, and his answer is metonymic.

Condensation tends to utilize metaphor, that is, associations based on similarity. This means (1) that one idea may be associated with another idea, or with several ideas, because they are similar; (2) that similar ideas located in separate fantasies may bring the fantasies into connection, so that one idea may represent several fantasies (as though an intersection can represent the several roads that meet at it); and (3) that one idea in the manifest content of a dream, or myth, may represent an indefinite number of ideas in the latent content.

Displacement, on the other hand, uses metonymic associations and is thus better suited than condensation as a disguising and defensive mechanism; in Freud's view, displacement in dreams is entirely caused by the dream's censoring activity, while condensation, which serves censorship, is nevertheless a separate function.

It would seem, however, that metonymic associations can be subjected in turn to condensation. Suppose that A-B-C is one set of metonymic associations, and E-F-G-H is another; if, say, B and

G are similar (or identical), all the associations in both sets can be represented by B or G or by some composite figure BG. Furthermore, although Freud tended to stress the role of similarity in condensation, there seems to be no reason why the same condensation could not occur if B and G were related to one another metonymically rather than metaphorically.

Condensation, then, is probably best understood as meaning that one idea can represent several ideas or several sets of ideas, but the relationship between these ideas may be either metaphoric or metonymic. Displacement would refer to detaching emotional energy and attention from one idea and attaching it to another; again the relationship between ideas could be either metaphoric or metonymic. Still, it is possible to define condensation strictly as a metaphoric operation; if several ideas or fantasies can be represented by a single idea, it is because the several ideas are similar in that they each can be represented by the same idea. We can likewise regard displacement, in strict terms, as metonymic; even if emotional energy is transferred from one idea to a similar idea, the similarity itself must be sufficiently suppressed that it will not be perceived. For example, if a man's fondness for apples is based on a metaphoric association between apples and breasts,[16] the association (and the fondness) are maintained precisely on condition that the similarity between the two objects not become evident.

In summary, condensation and displacement can be differentiated in terms of the typical kinds of association in each (condensation uses metaphor, while displacement uses metonymy), in terms of their relation to emotional energy (condensation accumulates and intensifies energy by gathering several ideas together into one, and displacement transfers energy from one idea to another), and in terms of their defensive function (we might say that condensation disguises an idea by losing it in a crowd of ideas, while displacement disguises the idea by changing its clothes).

Brief examples of the operation of condensation and displacement may help to clarify these distinctions. Condensation might appear in the case of a single figure in the manifest content of a dream who, whatever his role in the dream narrative, has something in common with a succession of authorities in the dreamer's past (father, teachers, employers, etc.). The possession of power over the dreamer is what enables all these figures to be represented metaphorically by a single person; the emotional energy attached to this one person is the sum of the energies connected with the represented figures; and the crucial figure in the condensation, perhaps a parent from childhood or perhaps someone with present power over the dreamer, is disguised by being grouped with others, all of whom are represented by still another.

Although displacement, with its emphasis on the mobility of meaning in unconscious thought, is the most important mechanism in the production of dreams, myths, and other fantasies whose latent meaning is disguised, it occurs most obviously in the case of neurotic phobia, an irrational and excessive anxiety about something that normally would not cause such a reaction. We discussed previously the example of a man whose fixation concerning breasts led to a great love of apples (which we might call melophilia). Now consider another person, who suffers from melophobia: once, while climbing in an apple tree as a child, he had observed a traumatic scene below and had then been caught and punished; the memory of that event has been repressed, but a derivative of the anxiety attached to it survives in consciousness and is directed toward apples. The nature of the phobia is produced by a metonymic series (forbidden viewing and punishment—apple tree—any apple), the emotion (anxiety) connected with the repressed memory is transferred to apples, and the memory is kept safely repressed by the discrepancy between scene/punishment and apple.

Again, however, we must note that the relationship between ideas in displacement, even in a phobia, may be metaphoric as well as metonymic. An apple-phobia, for instance, might use the metaphoric association apple–breast to transfer to apples an anxiety orginally connected with the maternal breast and incestuous wishes.

It may be useful to look at another example, this time taken from language. Whenever we say something—"rain dampens my hair," for example—we simultaneously employ two basic linguistic operations, *selection* and *combination*. That is, in order to arrive at this sentence of four words, we select at each of four points a word from a pool of possible words, depending on the meaning we want to express and the possibilities allowed by the language, and we *combine* the four chosen words consecutively in the temporal sequence of the sentence.[17] This sentence therefore has two dimensions: a vertical (metaphoric) dimension of four pools of words from which four representatives are chosen, and a horizontal (metonymic) dimension consisting of the actual arrangement of the chosen words. All words in a vertical pool exist simultaneously and potentially, and are related to one another by varying degrees of *similarity*. The size of the pool depends on the extent of similarity, both syntactic and semantic; the largest pool for the first selection—"rain"—would contain all nouns, and the smallest would contain synonyms for "rain." The words in the horizontal dimension, on the other hand, exist actually (not potentially) and consecutively (not simultaneously), and are related to one another not by similarity but by position or syntax.

It is not difficult to see why these two fundamental linguistic operations, metaphoric selection and metonymic combination, are regarded by some scholars[18] as equivalent to the primary process mechanisms of condensation and displacement. Condensation and selection both choose one unit to represent a group of similar units, while displacement and combination both connect units in a relationship not necessarily defined by similarity. Nevertheless it is possible to find metonymy in selection and metaphor in combination. If we said "rain dampens my head" instead of "rain dampens my hair," we would be understood as saying practically the same thing, even though "head" is related to "hair" metonymically rather than metaphorically. And in the sentence "warm weather makes me hot," "warm" and "hot" are virtually identical, both semantically and syntactically, yet their relationship in the sentence is based entirely on their position, not on their similarity to one another.

These linguistic examples may seem to complicate an already laborious discussion of condensation and displacement, but it is useful and perhaps important to recognize that there are fundamental affinities between the elementary aspects of any language and the mysterious workings of unconscious thought. A major premise of structuralism, one of the most influential of contemporary critical methodologies, is that primary linguistic processes underlie a wide spectrum of human mental and behavioral activities, ranging from the formation and meaning of myths and social institutions to the ways we eat and clothe ourselves. And yet it is surely possible, and arguable, that language is *not* the basic source and determinant of these other structures, but that language should be included with them as reflecting the ontogenetically prior mechanisms of the primary process. Perhaps Lacan's famous statement that "the unconscious is structured like a language" should be reversed to read "language is structured like the unconcious," and perhaps the difference between humans and other animals is not that humans possess language but that humans are capable of repression.

To conclude this discussion of the primary process on a less complicated note, everything we have been saying about the mechanisms of condensation and displacement may be reduced to two key psychoanalytic notions: overdetermination and defense. Overdetermination means that any product of the unconscious—for example, a symptom, a dream, an element in a dream—is derived from a multiplicity of unconscious elements and is therefore susceptible to a corresponding over-interpretation. Condensation is merely the technical term for a kind of unconscious data processing, which reduces groups to a single representative; our practical concern, as far as condensation is concerned, should be to remember this group presence and to avoid regarding any one interpretation, no matter how satisfactory, as the only possible explanation. Condensation, in other words, is the psychological equivalent of the literary term *ambiguity;* where condensation occurs, there are always several meanings, or layers of meaning, to be discovered.

As for displacement, it is simply one instance of the continual defensive activity required of a mind that is separated into conscious and unconscious systems as the result of repression. It is displacement that makes it possible for unconscious ideas to appear in dreams, myths, and symptoms without being recognized, and it is by retracing the steps of displacement that we arrive at an explanation of these phenomena. All symbolism is a kind of displacement, of meaning if not always of emotion, and even our conscious thinking regularly makes use of symbolic formations. The chief differences between unconscious and conscious symbolism relate to frequency and comprehensibility: symbolism occurs much less often in our conscious thought, and then only on condition of it being understood. We tend to use obvious metaphors and only those metonymic constructions that are conventional and therefore communicable. We may use metaphors like "I'm hungry as a bear" but not "I'm hungry as a hummingbird" (though the second expression connotes greater hunger), and we may resort to metonyms like "The White House announced its policy" but we would not say "A microphone announced its policy." The language of poetry, however, uses both metaphor and metonymy much more frequently and less transparently, and we would not be wrong in regarding unconscious thinking as an extreme instance of poetic styles of thought.

SYMBOLISM

Displacement, the most common mode of expressing unconscious ideas while at the same time disguising them, occurs in three defense mechanisms, which are especially important in the formation and interpretation of myths. It is these three—symbolism, decomposition, and projection—that play the chief role in transforming a simple unconscious fantasy embodying a repressed wish or fear into an enlarged and elaborated narrative, particularly by weaving elements from the day residue (of dream or myth) into the original fantasy structure.

Symbolism, the best known and most frequently used of these mechanisms, is sometimes regarded by Freud as separate from displacement, perhaps because the aspect of metaphor or similarity is so obvious in symbolic formations such as earth for mother or snake for phallus, or perhaps because he thought that dream symbols often existed apart from the dreamer's own experience and therefore could be interpreted only by reference to a cultural dictionary of symbols. Neither reason, however, is sufficient to separate symbolism from the work of displacement: nearly all of the many dream symbols Freud lists in the tenth chapter of the *Introductory Lectures on Psycho-Analysis* are metaphors, but what matters is that the personal connection between the symbol and the idea symbolized not be recognized by the dreamer, despite their metaphoric relationship. The equation earth = mother may be obvious to us and even more obvious to the ancient Greeks, who regularly referred to Earth as "Mother Earth," but displacement and subsequently disguise occur in the hidden equation earth-as-mother = *my* mother.

Freud's other point, that some dream symbols elicit no response from the associations of the dreamer and therefore require for interpretation a kind of universal (or at least culture-specific) codebook, is one of several instances where Freud seems close to agreeing with Jung's fallacious notion of a "collective unconscious." Nevertheless, it would seem that it is precisely the metaphoric nature of most symbols (that is, the analogy or similarity that binds the symbol to the symbolized) that both accounts for the occurrence of the same symbol in the dreams, symptoms, and myths of different individuals and in different cultures, and also explains why the dreamer or patient can furnish no associations: the relationship between symbol and symbolized is so close, the risk of unmasking the disguise and disclosing the repressed idea is so great, that all intermediary links must be rigidly and systematically suppressed.

Despite the existence of symbols that retain the same meaning across individual or even cultural barriers, Freud always insisted on the dangers of "automatic" interpretation and sought wherever possible an explanation of the symbol in the context of the dreamer's associations. These associations are lacking in the study of ancient myth, of course, although the very presence of a symbol in myth is usually sufficient warrant that the symbol has meaning, albeit unconscious, for the members of the society in which the myth occurs; a completely idiosyncratic symbol would probably not become, and certainly not remain, part of a myth. Nevertheless, even if we cannot produce associations to the elements in a myth, we can and should use as a substitute for these associations anything we can learn about the mythical, cultural, and historical context of any given mythic element. We should be especially careful to explain the reciprocity that exists between the symbol and its immediate context in a specific myth; any symbol affects, and is affected by, the other elements of the myth.

An example of the need for contextual interpretation of a symbol appears in the myth of Melampous, a mythical shaman or healer who is called on to cure the impotence of Iphiklos, prince of Phylake (Apollodoros 1.9.1). Melampous learns that the ailment is related to a childhood incident in which Phylakos, Iphiklos' father, frightened the boy with a bloody knife (he had been gelding rams) and then stuck the knife in a tree. Since "knife" and "tree" appear in Freud's list of symbols as representing, respectively, the male and female sexual organs, one might assume that the episode is a primal scene fantasy, that sexual intercourse was seen by the child as a bloody and violent act, and that impotence was the result of this traumatic view. This is a valid explanation, but another interpretation is suggested by what happens to the knife after it is stuck in the tree; the tree's bark grows over the knife and conceals it, and Iphiklos cannot be cured until the knife is found and uncovered. A second interpretation would see the knife as representing not the phallus but the idea of castration at the hands of the powerful father, a fate transferred from the rams to the child. The insertion of the knife into the tree that hides it would represent the repression of this idea, which in turn will have to be brought back into the open if the patient is to be cured. This interpretation is reinforced by the fact that the tree is identified as a "sacred oak"; another sacred oak in Greek history and myth is the oak at the center of the oracle of Dodona, whose rustling leaves brought a message from Zeus. Mythical oracles regularly tell those who consult them of their unconscious wishes and fears (for example, the oracle that tells Oidipous that he will kill his father and marry his mother), and the oak of Phylake contains the hidden castration fear of Iphiklos. The two interpretations are not mutually exclusive but complementary, just as castration anxiety and a primal scene fantasy may be interrelated. In addition, the concealment of the knife within the tree suggests a third interpretation, which returns to Freud's list of symbols: the disappearance of the knife corresponds to the disappearance of the father's penis in the mother's body in the primal scene fantasy, and castration can be seen as something inflicted by the mother as well as by the father.

Even in this brief fragment of a myth we can see how the work of condensation and overdetermination requires an approach that observes both internal and external context of a symbol; the result is a dialectical interpretation that reflects the complex determinants of symbol production.

DECOMPOSITION

Another form of displacement which is very important in myth is decomposition or splitting, the representation of one idea in the latent content of a dream or myth by several ideas in the manifest content. Since the manifest ideas typically represent partial aspects of the latent idea, decomposition is metonymic in the traditional sense of the term as a representation of a whole by one of its parts.

Decomposition occurs frequently and familiarly in fairy tales, where it clearly serves the tale's function of helping children deal with the problems of growing up. One of the major problems of childhood is emotional ambivalence; children tend to oscillate between emotional extremes in regard to the significant persons in their lives, and a great maturational achievement is the ability to maintain a consistent affective stance in one's relationships. A three-year-old child with his mother in a supermarket grows livid with rage when his mother refuses to buy him candy; if she relents, his anger immediately subsides, only to reappear when she will not buy him something else. In psychoanalytic terminology, the childhood problem is the instability of object-relations; in the child's view, how can his mother, the most important person in his life, the one on whom he depends for love, security, and the gratification of his wishes also be this hated woman who denies and frustrates him? The fairy tale helps resolve this conflict by attaching the good (loved) aspects of the mother to one imaginary figure and the bad (hated) aspects to another. The good mother often appears as a fairy godmother, the bad mother as a wicked witch or evil stepmother, and the final victory of the former over the latter allows the child to exorcise his feelings with the assurance that the good mother is the real mother.

The closest counterpart in Greek myth to the fairy-tale plot is the story of Athamas and Nephele (Apollodoros 1.9.1): they had two children, Phrixos and Helle, and then Athamas married Ino and had two children by her; Nephele's children were hated by their stepmother Ino, who used a complicated scheme to compel Athamas to sacrifice Phrixos; at the last second Phrixos and Helle were snatched from the altar by Nephele, who gave them a flying ram with a golden fleece on which to escape. The fact that Nephele's name means "Cloud" perhaps explains her ability to disappear and appear at will throughout the myth. Her sudden arrival out of a clear sky to save her children, like the magical appearance of the fairy godmother in the nick of time, answers every child's anxious question, "When will my mother return?"

Maternal decomposition becomes even more complicated in this myth. A lost tragedy, the *Ino* of Euripides, told how Ino disappeared, leaving her two children with Athamas; he then married for a third time and had twin sons by Themisto; later he found Ino, brought her home, and disguised her as a nurse; Themisto, who knew Ino was alive but did not know where she was, decided to kill Ino's children and instructed the new nurse (Ino, of course) to cover Themisto's sleeping children with white cloth and Ino's with black cloth; Ino did the opposite and Themisto mistakenly killed her own children.[19]

Decomposition, like symbolization, occurs everywhere in myth, as a few examples typical of many myths will show. Future heroes frequently are separated from their parents at birth and raised by foster parents (usually, but not always, of low or even subhuman status), and upon attaining manhood set out to find their true parents. Often it is the struggles of this search for identity and family that confer upon the searcher his heroic reputation (Theseus, for example). This mythical pattern of true and foster parents appears in the fantasies and play of children, who create imaginary parents of great wealth and kindness; someday, they fantasize, they will be discovered to be the long-lost children of Rockefellers or DuPonts.

This fantasy, which constitutes a virtual genre in Hellinistic, Roman, and Shakespearian comedies or the foundling novels of Fielding and Dickens, is not just another example of the child's colossal ingratitude toward the parents who raised and love him, as Freud pointed out, but instead results from the child's over-valuation of his parents. To the young child his parents are perfect and omnipotent (ask any four-year-old who the smartest man in the world is, or the most beautiful woman), but inevitably the child learns that his parents will not or cannot give him whatever he wants whenever he wants. Unwilling to relinquish his former belief, the child subverts a reality he does not want to face by inventing new parents who are simply a continuation of the old idealized parents. Thus, if we compare reality to myth, the true parents of reality correspond to the foster parents of myth and the fantasized parents of reality correspond to the true parents of myth.

In our previous discussion of the Bellerophon myth, we saw how the hero, after denying any desire for the amorous Stheneboia, then killed the monster Chimaira and subsequently married Stheneboia's sister. Both women, as we saw, represented the mother as object of desire, but in the case of Stheneboia desire was opposed by fear, both of the mother's sexual demands and of the father's vindictive anger. By overcoming representations of the feared father (Proitos, Iobates and his armies) and the feared aspect of the mother (Chimaira, the Amazons), Bellerophon was enabled to overcome fear, admit desire, and win the double of the woman he had earlier rejected.

A more complicated version of this pattern is found in the myth of Perseus (Apollodoros 2.4.1–4), who kills the female monster Medousa and then marries the Ethiopian princess Andromeda, whom he finds and rescues in exactly the same situation his mother Danae had been in at the beginning of the myth; each woman was loved by her paternal uncle and had been placed by her father in a situation inaccessible to all suitors. In addition to the decomposition of the mother into Danae, Medousa, and Andromeda, paternal figures appear in this myth as a triple repetition of twin brothers (Akrisios and Proitos, Polydektes and Diktys, Phineus and Kepheus).[20]

The same decompositional motive occurs in the myth of Oidipous, who overcomes the female monster Sphinx by solving her riddle and then is rewarded by receiving his mother Iocasta as his wife. This episode contains many levels of meaning, but it is not difficult to see that one of them is the split identity of the Sphinx and Iocasta. Other confrontations between a hero and a monster usually end with the hero killing the monster, but in this anomalous story the Sphinx commits suicide by jumping from a mountain (a puzzling choice of self-destruction for a winged creature). Similarly, Iocasta commits suicide after Oidipous has solved another problem, the question of her (and his) identity.

Examples of mythical decomposition could be multiplied indefinitely, but we may conclude by noting that this mechanism, essentially the differential representation of the ambivalent relationship between child and parents, is one of the major structural principles in Greek myth and in all (but especially polytheistic) religious systems.[21]

PROJECTION

A third mode of displacement important in myth is projection, the attribution of unpleasant or dangerous internal motives and emotions to some external agency. Primitive societies in general tend to assign much of what we would regard as internal causality, whether psychological or physical, to some outside force—gods, demons, or enemies who cause illness, death, aberrational behavior, or bad fortune—and it might be objected that when Homer, for example, describes someone's irrational act as the result of a deity's physical intervention, it is because Homer, like primitive people, lacked the knowledge and language to identify internal causality and motivation. This may be true concerning disease and death, but it is certainly not true about mental functioning; Homer is no different from us, when we say "the whim seized me" or "the devil made me do it." Projection is a defense mechanism for those who believe it, and an alibi for those who do not.

Of the many forms of projection in myth, the most obvious is the function of oracles, which regularly tell men of their unconscious wishes and fears. The most common reason for consulting an oracle in myth is the failure of a man to have a son, or the birth of a daughter instead of a son. In the first instance, the man is told of his *counter-oedipal* fear: if he has a son, that son will kill him. In the second instance, he is told of his possessive incestuous wish and also of his fear; he should not let his daughter be married, for if she marries he will be killed by his son-in-law or grandson. Therefore, mythical fathers of marriageable daughters typically place some insurmountable barrier between their daughters and any suitor. The ostensible reason for this is the oracle's warning, but the internal motive is the father's desire to keep the daughter to himself; sometimes this is explicitly stated, as in the myth of Oinomaos and Hippodameia (Apollodoros, *Epitome* 2.4), and often it is implied in the fact that the impossible task facing the suitor is competing with the father in something the father does better than anyone else. For example, to win Iole, Herakles must win an archery contest against her father, Eurytos, his own archery teacher (Apollodoros 2.6.1); to win the Golden Fleece and Medeia, Iason must perform the labors of the fire-breathing bulls and the dragon's teeth, tasks that Medeia's father, Aietes, himself can accomplish in a single day (Apollonius Rhodius, *Argonautika* 3.398–430); to win Hippodameia, Pelops must win a chariot race against her father, Oinomaos, whose magical horses were a gift from the god Ares (Apollodoros, *Epitome* 2.5).

Oracles, of course, were a historical as well as a mythological institution, but even historical oracles often embodied the characteristics of dream formation, as in the learned interpretations they required and in the unconscious mechanisms they utilized. There is a great deal of symbolism, sometimes metaphoric (for example, earth as mother) and sometimes elusively metonymic (as in the "wooden walls" of the oracle about the defense of Athens, interpreted by Themistokles to mean the Athenian fleet). The effect of displacement and reversal can be seen in the characteristic response to oracles: men often adopted the popular and obvious interpretation of an oracle, only to learn that its real meaning was obscure and in many cases the opposite of what they had thought. And in a certain sense even historical oracles were subject to projection in that those who consulted the oracle generally did so with a definite purpose in mind and then interpreted the received oracle in accordance with their own predisposed desires.

Projection takes many other forms in myth, as when someone does something because of "fate" or "destiny" or "the will of the gods" or even "by chance" or "unintentionally." The action taken for any of these reasons invariably turns out to be the object or result of predictable unconscious wishes or fears. Bellerophon kills his brother "accidentally" and Oidipous kills his father "unwittingly"; no one ever kills a stranger by chance or ignorance, since the stranger is always revealed as the object of childhood aggression.

REVERSAL

Projection may take the form of a complete reversal of the situation: "It is not I who desire her, it is she who desires me"; "I don't hate him, he hates me." This disguised expression of one idea by its opposite is natural for unconscious thought, which is free from secondary process observance of the law of contraries (that a quality and its contrary cannot both be predicated of the same object at the same time). Primary process tolerance of contradiction and opposition has an analogy in the presence in some languages and scripts, especially ancient ones, of words and signs which can express either of two opposites. Citing examples in Old Egyptian (*ken* meant either "strong" or "weak") and Latin (*altus* is either "high" or "deep," *sacer* is "sacred" or "accursed"), Freud described reversal as an archaic characteristic of the dream-work, one of several similarities between unconscious thinking and primitive forms of expression and writing.[22]

The dream mechanism of reversal is defined by Freud as follows: "An element in the manifest dream which admits of an opposite may stand simply for itself, or for its opposite, or for both together; only the sense can decide which translation is to be chosen."[23] Reversal occurs frequently in symptom formation, most obviously in overcompensation: the compulsive assertion of innocence derives from hidden guilt, the obsessional display of masculinity betrays a hidden anxiety. Although a symbolic mode that allows "black" to represent "white" and "up" to stand for "down" may seem strange and puzzling, it is in fact this strangeness that makes it so appropriate for unconscious thought, since opposites are at the same time farthest apart from one another and most closely related to one another. As simultaneous affirmation and denial, representation by opposition lends itself to condensation, particularly in the portrayal of opposed emotions. A mythological example is the punishment of being turned to stone that Medousa inflicts on those she catches looking at her. The monster herself, like so many female monsters in Greek myth, represents the forbidden aspect of maternal sexuality, the simultaneously feared and desired object of the child's curiosity (which is why the myth portrays the hideous Medousa as having been once the most beautiful of women). Just as a prohibition could not exist without the desire to do what is prohibited, the punishment imposed on those Medousa sees looking at her requires a prior desire to see what is forbidden. The combination of fear and desire, ugliness and beauty, repulsion and attraction, reappears in the punishment of being turned to stone: the victim is dead, immobilized, impotent, but at the same time he is fixed forever in the act of looking, frozen in fascination and fixation before a scene from which he literally can never turn away.

Representation by opposition is considered by some to be the basic structure of thought itself; in the view of Henri Wallon, "Every term identifiable by thought, every thinkable term, requires a complementary term in relation to which it will be differentiated and to which it can be opposed."[24] If this is true and if our earlier hypothesis about the beginning of conscious thought at the time of the passage from symbiosis to individuation is valid, it is possible to identify the content of this first thought, appearing in the original derivation of secondary process thinking from the primary process. The first and most important distinction made by the

child is between the "I" and the "not-I." This would be the first
thought, the initial observance of the law of contraries, which constitutes the self. But in the unconscious memories of the symbiotic
stage, oppositions coexist and the law of contraries has no effect;
"I" and "not-I" are not mutually exclusive, but are instead a unity
(of opposites) which will exert its illogical and invisible attraction
throughout life.

A defense mechanism based on reversal and appearing in
both symptoms and myths is sometimes called "identification with
the aggressor," a variant of what is more popularly called "role
reversal." Its defensive function can be seen, for example, in the
behavior of a child who deals with fear of a parent by becoming
the parent himself, by acting toward a doll, a play-figure, or another child in the way he regards the parent as acting toward him
(or, conversely, in the way he would like the parent to act toward
him). Mythological examples of this kind of identification are
found in two famous confrontations between a hero and a female
monster, in which the hero, after defeating the monster, then assumes the monster's power as his own. After killing the Lernaian
Hydra as his second labor, Herakles dips his arrows in the deadly
poison of the Hydra's gall (the same arrows with which he will
later wound his persecuting stepmother Hera), and Perseus, after
killing the Gorgon Medousa, uses Medousa's head as the weapon
with which he will vanquish all his enemies, save his mother from
an unwanted marriage, and win a bride for himself.

More important than such individual examples, however, is
the function of reversal as a kind of ironic principle throughout
myth. Although usually classified as a type of displacement, reversal clearly depends on a prior condensation, a union of opposites in unconscious thought, and Freud's definition would seem to
allow for both possibilities, since an element may stand "for itself,
or for its opposite, or for both together." As a condensation, reversal is a particularly striking form of the *ambiguity* that, as we
have seen, is a general characteristic of condensation (that is, the
several meanings implied in a condensed idea may include the
opposite of the idea). As displacement, on the other hand, reversal
is closely related to the concept, more familiar in literary criticism,
of *irony*. When Oidipous, according to Sophocles, vows to avenge
the dead king Laios as if he were his own father, or when the
Player Queen in *Hamlet* speaks of her love for her husband (to

which the real queen replies, "the lady doth protest too much, me-thinks"),[25] this is dramatic irony; the truth is the opposite of what a character says or does.

Mythological reversal, however, constitutes irony as a pervasive presence rather than as an occasional occurrence, and thus accounts, at least in part, for the mysterious and uncanny mood of myth. As in the meetings of Oidipous with Laios or Bellerophon with Stheneboia, the stranger killed at the crossroads is really the father and the anxious lover is really oneself.

CHAPTER THREE

TEXTS
AND CONTEXTS

BEFORE HESIOD

Shortly before the end of the eighth century B.C., a Boiotian Greek named Hesiod wrote or dictated a poem of some one thousand lines on the beginning of the world, the emergence of the first gods, and the conflicts between generations, which resulted finally in the permanent seizure of power by Zeus, ruler of the world and king over gods and men.[1] We do not know what name, if any, Hesiod gave to his poem, but it has always been known as the *Theogony,* the "Origin of the Gods" (the Greek word is *theogonia,* from *theos,* "god," and *gone,* "birth" or "offspring" or "generation"). The *Theogony* is also literally a cosmogony, an account of the beginning of the world (from *kosmos,* "world"), but since in Greek myth as in many creation myths the component parts of the universe as it gradually came into existence were also gods and goddesses, the two terms are here synonymous.

Hesiod and his contemporary Homer stand at one of the great dividing points in Greek history, as authors of the earliest surviving works of Greek literature. Although most modern scholars regard Homer as somewhat earlier than Hesiod, this is not certain; the earliest ancient authorities seemed to think that Hesiod was earlier than Homer, and they may be correct. The very fact that priority is disputable shows that there is no incontrovertible evidence that either Homer or Hesiod knew the works of the other. What similarities exist between the two poets should not be taken as borrowings or references, but rather as signs they both were composing within a long-established tradition of oral poetry, which now, for the first time, could be preserved in writing.

Hesiod and Homer invented neither writing nor literature, but their works were the first committed to writing in the alphabetic script the Greeks borrowed from Phoenicia, probably during the eighth century.[2] Once before the Greeks had possessed a method of writing, the syllabic script known as Linear B, which the Myceneans adopted from Minoan Crete. The use of Linear B, however, seems to have ended with the destruction of Mycenean civilization 500 years before Hesiod, and in any case the surviving Linear B material contains nothing literary or mythological except for the names of a few gods, some of them familiar.

It is not only literature that began to receive definite form at the time of Hesiod; Greek history itself can be said to have begun during the eighth century. Everything before this time, despite the brief presence of Mycenean writing, is prehistoric in the sense that virtually all we know about the way people lived, including their religious beliefs and myths, is based on the physical remains studied by archaeologists and not on written records. For this reason almost everything said in the following survey of Greek prehistory is probable at best; the present state of our knowledge does not allow certainty in most matters, and in some of the most important does not even guarantee probability. This is not true, at least to the same extent, of the ancient Near East, where written records and literature existed long before the arrival of the first Greek-speaking people in Greece, starting at the end of the third millennium. Nevertheless the question of influence and exchange between Greece and the East during the prehistoric period is still largely a mystery.

The Greek language is Indo-European; that is, it belongs to the large family of languages derived from a single language spoken by a hypothetical people who lived in northeast Europe or northwest Asia during the Neolithic period. In irregular waves of migration from the beginning of the third millennium to the middle of the second, descendants of this people spread throughout Europe and into central Asia as far east as India. One branch of these Indo-European nomads, who spoke an early form of the language we now know as Greek, entered the mainland of Greece around the beginning of the second millennium. They presumably brought with them both poetry and a polytheistic religion in which the chief god was associated with fatherhood and the sky, since these are elements of the general Indo-European tradition. In Greece they met, probably conquered, and merged with a native people, the early Helladic culture of the beginning of the Greek Bronze Age; before the coming of the Greeks, metallurgy had been introduced into Helladic Greece from the east, just as argiculture, the domestication of animals, and the painting of pottery had come earlier to Greece from Mesopotamia through Asia Minor. We know hardly anything about Helladic religion, of which only a few figurines have survived; whether it may have resembled the religion of nearby Minoan Crete remains a guess.

When the first Greeks entered Greece, one of the great civilizations of the ancient world was already flourishing on the island of Crete to the south. This culture, known as Minoan after Minos, the mythical king of Crete, had been in contact with the Near East and Egypt during the third millennium; thanks to these contacts (which were to increase greatly during the second millennium), a favorable climate, and a protected location, the Minoans had developed a prosperous civilization with large unfortified cities, great royal palaces, and spectacular refinements in art and architecture. The Minoans also possessed writing in the form of a pictographic or hieroglyphic script, which developed later into Linear A, the syllabary that the Myceanean Greeks adopted to write Greek. Since neither Minoan scripts have been deciphered, all our evidence for Minoan religion is pictorial and conjectural. A goddess (or probably goddesses, who may yet represent different aspects of one goddess), presumably associated with the earth and fertility, seems to be the dominant figure; male figures who may be gods appear, and later myths such as Hesiod's story of the infancy of Zeus on Crete (*Theogony* 468–84) may point to a Minoan myth of a son or consort (or both) of a goddess.

Within a few centuries of their arrival, the Greek rulers of the mainland came squarely under the influence of the Minoans. The power and cultural sophistication of the mainland increased rapidly through the Middle Helladic period and reached its height during the late Helladic period, the sixteenth through the thirteenth centuries. Meanwhile the Minoan civilization, at its greatest during the seventeenth and sixteenth centuries, went into decline after the destruction of the palaces, caused perhaps by the eruption of the volcanic island Thera around 1450.

The Late Helladic period, the final phase of the Bronze Age on the Greek mainland, is most commonly named the Mycenean period, since the city of Mycenae in the Peloponnese seems to have been the most important Myceanean center (an assumption strengthened by the pre-eminence of Mycenae and its king Agamemnon in the myths of the Trojan War). The chief Mycenean cities—Mycenae, Tiryns, and Argos in the Argolis, Pylos in Messenia, Thebes and Orchomenos in Boiotia, Iolkos (modern Volos) in Thessaly, Eleusis and Athens in Attika, as well as Knossos on Crete, which was taken over by the Myceneans during this period—all play a significant role in later myth, and it is this period that provides the setting for much of Greek myth as it was later known to Hesiod and Homer.

Minoan influence on Mycenean civilization is so extensive that the few exceptions stand out clearly. There is nothing in Crete like the battle scenes in Mycenean art, or the enormous Cyclopean fortifications that protect the Mycenean citadels (the archaeological term is derived from myths crediting the one-eyed giants called Kyklopes with building these walls; post-Mycenean Greeks did not believe that ordinary mortals could have lifted the great stone blocks). Mycenean frescoes, jewelry, pottery painting and shapes, and architecture (with such exceptions as the distinctive Helladic room-style called the *megaron*) imitated Minoan models so closely that it is often difficult to tell them apart. Whether the same assimilation applied to religion and myth is impossible to say; the iconographic evidence shows great similarity, but the absence of literary records makes these pictorial data difficult to interpret. The figure of a bull, for example, appears everywhere in the Minoan remains—on buildings, frescoes, pottery, and jewelry and in sacrificial, ritual, and athletic contexts—and the bull is very prominent in later Greek myths concerning Crete, but the exact connection between artifacts and myth is impossible to establish. In the case of Mycenean culture we have the advantage of written records in a known language, but since the Linear B tablets are almost entirely inventories and accounting records of the religious and political bureaucracy, all they can tell us are the names of some deities and the facts that sacrificial cults existed and that the religious system was highly organized.

Names on the Linear B tablets that correspond with gods and goddesses in later Greek religion include Zeus, Hera, Poseidon,

Hermes, Enyalios (a double of Ares), Paiaon (an epithet of Apollo), Erinys (an epithet of Demeter, as well as the singular form of the three Erinyes or Furies), Eleuthia, and perhaps Athena, Artemis, Ares, Dione, and Dionysos. In addition, there is a goddess, or many goddesses, called Potnia ("lady" or "mistress"), a name occurring usually but not always with some qualification: Potnia of horses, Potnia of grain, Potnia of the labyrinth, and so forth. Finally there are several deities whose names do not appear later, such as Manasa, Drimios the son of Zeus, and Posidaija (a feminine form of Poseidon). The tablets, on a few of which these names appear, were found in great number at Knossos and Pylos and in smaller quantities at Mycenae and Thebes; they were preserved by the fires that accompanied the destruction of these sites during the fourteenth through twelfth centuries.

The end of Mycenean civilization coincided with general disruption in the eastern Mediterranean area and may be due, at least partially, to the raids of the mysterious Sea Peoples, who appear most prominently in Egyptian records. A major role may also have been played by the movement into central Greece and the Peloponnese of new groups of Greek-speaking peoples from the northwest, the Dorian invasion. Only Athens and its surrounding area, and a few isolated places in the Peloponnese, escaped destruction. Most survivors of this turbulent period probably remained in Greece under the new Dorian regime, but the level of culture changed radically; writing, building in stone, and representational art disappeared, and cultural depression and poverty were widespread, especially in the century or two immediately following the Mycenean collapse. A Mycenean group fled to the island of Cyprus soon after the Dorian invasion; they were followed, toward the end of the second millennium, by large-scale migrations from the Greek mainland to the eastern Aegean islands and the coast of Asia Minor. Aiolians from Boiotia and Thessaly moved into the northern part of this area, Ionians (a mixed group chiefly from Attika and Euboia, but perhaps including temporary refugees in Athens from other parts of Greece) occupied the central section, and Dorians settled in the south, including Crete. A cultural revival began in Athens around 1050, marked by a distinctive pottery style called Proto-Geometric, and gradually spread throughout the Greek world. Other than changes in the Geometric pottery series and a great increase in the use of iron during the eleventh

century, however, there is little we can say about Greek higher
culture during the period 1200 to 800, appropriately called the
"Dark Age" of Greece.

THE QUESTION OF INFLUENCE

The poetic tradition in which Hesiod wrote has obvious connections not only with the Minoan-Mycenean world but also with the
Near East and western Asia. The end of the Dark Age and the
beginning of the Archaic period is marked by an increase in population and prosperity after an extended period of relative calm and
stability. Prosperity both brought and benefited from rapidly ex-
panding trade relations with the Near East, especially Syria and
Phoenicia. A wealth of new ideas poured into Greece, including
the Orientalizing style in pottery and, of course, the alphabet. But
this is not the first time that Greece came into contact with the
great civilizations to the east. The Minoan and Mycenean civilizations both traded actively in the eastern Mediterranean, the Minoans especially with Egypt and the Myceneans especially with the
Ugaritic cities of Syria and the Hittite empire in north Syria and
the interior of Asia Minor. The island of Cyprus, located much
nearer to Syria than to Greece, must have been a favorable place
for the exchange of goods and ideas; after early contacts with Asia
Minor and Syria, it was colonized by Myceneans from the fifteenth
century through the massive migrations of the thirteenth and twelfth
centuries, and seems to have received Syrian and Phoenician colo-
nists during the ninth century.

   These are merely the most obvious times and places for Greek
acquaintance with the Near East. In fact, there is no time throughout and even before the entire Bronze Age and early Iron Age at
which such contact can be absolutely ruled out. Furthermore, a
still more complex network of diffusion and transmission existed
within the Near East itself. The situation is summarized by Kirk:

> The Near East and western Asia in the third and second
> millennia . . . were a cauldron of customs and ideas that
> passed from Mesopotamia to Egypt and occasionally back
> again, to Syria and Asia Minor and into the Aegean, to
> Cyprus and Crete and the Greek mainland. Semitic tribes
> absorbed concepts from Indo-Iranian ones and vice versa.

Indo-European-speaking Hittites derived their theology from the non-Indo-European Hurrians, the Semitic Akkadians from the non-Semitic Sumerians. The Aegean peoples were in contact during the second millennium with Trojans and Hittites in Asia Minor, with Egypt through casual trade and mercenaries, with the Levant through Cyprus and trading posts in Syria and Palestine.[3]

West notes that "Ugarit [or Ras Shamra, the most important city of Canaanite Syria from 1450 to 1350] was an extremely important center of trade—no less than seven languages are represented on the tablets found there."[4] Nor was Ugarit unique in its cosmopolitan connections; a similar situation and the same number of languages existed at the contemporary Hittite capital of Hattusas, where tablets have been recovered written in Hittite, Akkadian, Sumerian, Hurrian, Hattite, Luwian, and Palaic.

No other subject has attracted the attention of scholars working on the *Theogony* as much as the question of how, and how much, his subject was influenced by the myths of the Near East. There are several instances in which it is clear that the Hesiodic theogony is derived from Near Eastern sources, and many for which such derivation is claimed by some and denied by others. In order to demonstrate derivation, it is not enough to point out separate characters, functions, and ideas in Hesiod that have identical or rather similar parallels in Asiatic literature, and then to select the most probable means by which these concepts traveled from East to West. If this approach were valid, little in Hesiod could be regarded as a Greek original, since an Asiatic parallel could be cited for most single and separate elements. Kirk attributes "the apearance in different places of vaguely similar or very general ideas (like those of a mother goddess, a storm god or the moulding of mankind out of clay)" to the continual and widespread diffusion of customs and ideas throughout the eastern Mediterranean and western Asia; the direct influence, however, of one culture upon another cannot be demonstrated by parallels such as these, but "only when a rather complex and specific motif occurs in two distinct places and not elsewhere."[5] Kirk's argument that derivation can be shown only by the similarity of complicated patterns instead of isolated elements is quite true (despite the facts that single elements can be and certainly were transmitted from one people to another, and that, as Kirk admits, the determination of how much complexity is sufficient to prove derivation is always a subjective judgment). A similar argument could be made by comparing Greek myths with those of cultures the Greeks could not have known directly or indirectly. Parallels can be found outside of Europe, Asia, and north Africa for many of the elements in Hesiod; to take Kirk's three examples, the notions of a mother-goddess, a storm-god, and creation from clay appear regularly in the myths of Africa, Australia, and the Americas (as well as the ideas of an original void, the theft of fire, and many others), and there simply were not enough intercontinental land bridges around in the prehistoric era to explain all these parallels as the result of diffusion and influence.

THE *ENUMA ELISH*

Two Eastern myths are most frequently cited as examples of Hesiod's dependence on non-Greek sources. First is the Akkadian-Babylonian creation epic, called the *Enuma Elish* (the first two words of the poem), a ritual text that was recited annually to the god Marduk on the fourth day of the New Year's festival. Although no texts written earlier than the end of the second millennium are known, the epic was once generally regarded as having been composed during the Amorite or Old Babylonian dynasty (nineteenth–seventeenth centuries), the age of the famous lawgiver Hammurabi. More recent opinion, however, has tended to reject this early dating and to place the composition of the epic during the Kassite period (the four centuries following the Old Babylonian period) or even later.[6] Precise dating is not as important in regard to possible influence on Greece as some have thought; even if a late date is correct, the epic is based on earlier Akkadian and Sumerian material, and presumably the theogonic material at the beginning of the poem would be oldest and least resistant to change, as opposed to the detailed accounts of Marduk's new dispensation. The epic is written in the Akkadian dialect and, like most Babylonian mythological texts, is greatly dependent on Sumerian myths.

The Sumerians, whose language was neither Indo-European nor Semitic, were the first great civilization of Mesopotamia. They dominated the area throughout the third millennium, except for two centuries (about 2340–2150) during which Mesopotamia was ruled by the Semitic kingdom founded by the legendary Sargon, king of Akkad. The Sumerians regained dominance during the Third Dynasty of Ur (2125–2000), but disappeared as a separate people after another defeat by Semitic armies. The Sumerian language was no longer spoken, but continued to be written as an official language of some religious, political, and literary documents. Sumerian achievements in religion, literature, architecture, law, astronomy, and economic organization were adopted by succeeding Semitic peoples, and Sumerian culture remained the leading influence on the civilizations of Mesopotamia. When the Old Babylonian empire, perhaps Hammurabi himself, set out to validate their rule and that of their god Marduk, the Summerian creation myth was rewritten to make Marduk the ultimate ruler of all the gods and the *Enuma Elish,* or an earlier version, was composed.

The *Enuma Elish*[7] begins with the union of primal waters, Apsu and Mummu-Tiamat; Apsu is male fresh waters and Tiamat is female sea waters (the epithet Mummu probably means "mother"). Within their waters were born the first gods: Lahmu and Lahamu, then Anshar and Kishar, then their son Anu (Sky) and Anu's son Ea, chief of the gods. The new gods disturbed Apsu and Tiamat by their "loathsome" and "unsavory" behavior within the body of Tiamat, and Apsu decided to destroy the gods. Tiamat protested, but Apsu persisted with his plan. Then Ea, the "all-wise," learned of Apsu's intention, cast a spell upon him, and killed him. Ea now married Damkina and their son was Marduk, a giant with four eyes and four ears.

Some of the gods complained to Tiamat about Marduk and persuaded her to avenge Apsu. With the help of "Mother Hubur" (perhaps the earth goddess), who produced eleven monstrous children, Tiamat appointed Kingu, one of the "older gods," as commander, gave him the "Tablet of Destinies," and prepared for battle. Ea went to Anshar for help and Anshar sent Anu to confront Tiamat, but Anu (like Ea before him) turned back in fear. Anshar then sent for Marduk, who agreed to fight Tiamat if the assembled gods proclaimed him as supreme ruler. They granted Marduk his wish and, armed with a bow, mace, lightning, a net, eleven winds, and a storm-chariot, he went to face Tiamat. At first sight of the "inside of Tiamat" and "Kingu, her consort," Marduk and his followers were temporarily confused and alarmed, but he quickly recovered and engaged Tiamat in single combat; first, however, he accused her of having caused a situation in which "sons reject their own fathers," of having given to Kingu the rightful position of Anu, of plotting evil against Anshar, and of not loving those whom she should.

In the combat Marduk snared Tiamat in his net; when she opened her mouth to swallow him, he sent in winds to hold her mouth open and her stomach distended, then shot in an arrow and killed her. All her helpers, including Kingu and the monsters, were captured and imprisoned, and Marduk cut Tiamat's body in half to create the sky and the earth. He then gave to the great gods (Anu, Ea, and Enlil) their proper places, arranged the weather and the heavenly bodies, and created the features of the earth from parts of Tiamat's body. Finally Ea created mankind from the blood of the rebel Kingu, for the express purpose of serving the gods. The epic ends with the building of a great temple in Babylon for Marduk, where a banquet is held at which the grateful gods recite the fifty honorific names of Marduk.

There are clear similarities between the Babylonian and Greek theogonies, and there are also many differences. Both begin with a primal couple (Apsu and Tiamat/Ouranos and Gaia) from whom the other gods are descended; children remain within the body of the first mother and are hated by their father; a solution is found by a clever god (Ea/Kronos) who defeats the father; the son (Marduk, who replaced Sumerian Enlil/Zeus) of the clever god then becomes king, but first must defeat monstrous enemies (the older gods and the monsters produced by Hubur, who seems functionally equivalent to Gaia and Rhea/the Titans, the Giants, and Typhoeus, all of whom are children of Gaia); mankind is created either by the clever god or during his reign.

Differences between the two epics, however, are more obvious than similarities, as a few examples will show. The first Babylonian couple are both water-gods, while the first Greek couple are Gaia (Earth) and Ouranos (Sky); the clever god Ea overthrows Apsu (Fresh Waters), not his father Anu (Sky), while Kronos overthrows his father Ouranos—in fact, the Babylonian Sky and his son (Anu and Ea) are allies against their common enemy Apsu; likewise Zeus overthrows his father Kronos and Kronos' brothers, while Marduk succeeds his great-grandfather Anshar, who is called "king of the gods," and defeats neither his father Ea nor Anshar, but is their champion against Tiamat.

It is unnecessary to extend the comparison, since it is clear that both myths share the same very general pattern, and that there is not much correspondence in details, especially the family relationships of characters to one another. Another recently discovered Babylonian theogony also displays a pattern similar to the Greek succession myth, but with characters different from either Hesiod or the *Enuma Elish*.[8] In it the first couple are Hain and Earth; Earth commands her son Amakandu to marry her, which he does and kills his father Hain; Amakandu then marries his sister Sea and their son Lahar kills his father and marries his mother; the unnamed son of Lahar and Sea kills both his parents and marries his sister River; their son kills his parents and marries his sister Ga'um; their son kills his parents and marries his sister Ningeshtinna; at this point the tablet becomes unreadable, although the same cyclic pattern of violence and incest seems to continue. While this theogony can hardly be a model for the Hesiodic version, it is nonetheless closer to it than the *Enuma Elish* in its insistence on father–son conflict and incest (both mother–son and brother–sister) as primary motives. On the other hand, incest is found (and is often logically necessary) in creation myths from around the world; this is especially true of the earliest cosmogonic myths of India, although it should be remembered that Hindu myth is Indo-European and therefore shares a common background with Greek myth.

Walcott has made an elaborate and impressive attempt to derive Hesiod's *Theogony* primarily from the *Enuma Elish* and other Babylonian material with which the Greeks became familiar at the beginning of the Archaic period, but his views have not met general acceptance.[9] It is probably best to say that the *Enuma Elish,* whatever its date (Walcott would put it around 1100), represents a common theogonic pattern in the Near East during the second millennium, which regularly was subject to local adaptation (as Marduk could replace Enlil, his Sumerian equivalent, or the Assyrian god Ashur could replace Marduk), and that the Greeks could have learned of this pattern at any time, the most probable guess being during the Minoan-Mycenean era.

"KINGSHIP IN HEAVEN"

Our second example, regarded by most as the closest Near Eastern
parallel to Hesiod, is the Hurrian-Hittite myth called "Kingship in
Heaven" with its sequel, the "Song of Ullikummi." The Hurrians
were a non-Indo-European, non-Semitic people (as were also the
Sumerians) who moved south into Assyria at the beginning of the
second millennium and eventually migrated across northern Mesopotamia into Syria. They adopted many aspects of Mesopotamian
culture, and it may be through Hurrian versions for the most part
that the Greeks came to know Sumerian and Babylonian myths.
The Hittites were an Indo-European tribe who appeared in Asia
Minor about 1800; by the fourteenth century they had won con-
trol of Syria, and during the New Kingdom (about 1450–1200)
they were one of the great powers of the Near East. The Hittites
were approximate contemporaries of the Myceneans, and their two
languages are our earliest examples of a written Indo-European
language (in both cases in a borrowed script—the Myceneans used
the Minoan syllabary and the Hittites used the Babylonian cunei-
form). Some of the more than 10,000 texts found at the Hittite
capital Hattusas are mythological and religious, and most of these
are Hittite versions of Hurrian myths, which had themselves been
influenced by Mesopotamian precedents.

"Kingship in Heaven"[10] begins with the reign of Alalu in
heaven; after nine years, he was overthrown by Anu (Sky) and
went down to the "dark earth"; Anu ruled for nine years and then
was attacked by Kumarbi and fled to the sky; Kumarbi pursued,
seized Anu by the feet, and then bit off and swallowed Anu's genitals; when Kumarbi began to laugh, Anu told him that because of
what he had swallowed he was now pregnant with three gods: the
Storm-God Heshub (the chief god of the Hurrians and Hittites),
the river Aranzaha (the Tigris), and Tasmisu (an attendant of the
Storm-God); Anu now hid in the sky and Kumarbi spat out what
he could (later Aranzaha and Tasmisu will be born from the
earth), but the Storm-God remained inside him; Anu now spoke
to the Storm-God and the two had a long debate about how the
Storm-God should escape from Kumarbi's body; Kumarbi became
dizzy and asked Aya (Ea) for something to eat; he ate something
(variously read as "stone" or "son"), but it hurt his mouth; finally

ABC

the Storm-God, after being warned not to exit through other orifices, especially the anus, came out through Kumarbi's "good place," evidently his penis;[11] at this point the text becomes unreadable, but the Storm-God must defeat Kumarbi and become king.

In the "Song of Ullikummi" Kumarbi plots revenge; he had intercourse repeatedly with a huge female rock, who gave birth to a stone child, Ullikummi; the child was hidden from the Storm-God and placed on the right shoulder of Ubelluri (the Hurrian Atlas), where he grew at the rate of an acre per month; the first battle between the Storm-God and Ullikummi, who was now 9000 leagues high, ended with the Storm-God's defeat; the gods were upset and threatened by Ullikummi, and Ea ordered the "old gods" to bring out the ancient copper "cutter" with which heaven and earth had been separated, and to use this to cut through the feet of Ullikummi; the Storm-God again came to fight Ullikummi (and must defeat him, although the final lines cannot be read).

The parallels between the Hurrian and Hesiodic myths are clear once we eliminate the reign of Alalu: Anu is equivalent to Ouranos, Kumarbi to Kronos, and the Storm-God to Zeus; Anu and Ouranos are both castrated and various gods are born from their severed genitals; Kumarbi and Kronos castrate their fathers and have children inside themselves; the Storm-God and Zeus win the kingship of the gods, then must win a second victory over an enormous monster (Ullikummi/Typhoeus).

The parallels cannot be pressed too far. For example, is the Storm-God the son of Kumarbi, from whom he is born, or of Anu, whose genitals make Kumarbi pregnant, or of both, with Anu as father and Kumarbi as mother? Also, Zeus, unlike the Storm-God, never shares his siblings' fate of being inside Kronos but is rescued by the trickery of Rhea and Gaia. As for the similarity between the monsters Ullikummi and Typhoeus, the Hurrian myth seems closer to the much later version of Apollodoros (1.6.3) than to Hesiod's (but according to Apollodoros it is Zeus, not the monster, whose feet are cut through).[12]

Kirk's use of a structuralist model to show that the Hurrian and Hesiodic versions are independent of one another is no more plausible than his discovery on the basis of this model that the underlying message of Hesiod's succession myth is a combination of "an eye for an eye" and "crime doesn't pay."[13] Nevertheless Kirk's conclusion that "the Greek version may be ultimately derived from a pre-Hurrian *koine* account"[14] is as likely a conjecture as the limited evidence available to us will allow and coincides with West's suggestion that the Greek and Hurrian myths "represent common descendants of a version itself derived from Mesopotamia."[15] Where the Babylonian *Enuma Elish* would appear in this line of derivation would depend on its early or late dating, and in any case is not as important as the recognition that the Greek *Theogony* occupies a relatively late position in a complex, widespread, and interrelated theogonic tradition encompassing western Asia and the Mediterranean.

FIRE AND WATER

The project of identifying or refuting lines of connection between myths of successive or separate cultures, by far the major occupation of scholars who have studied Hesiod cross-culturally, takes on a much different (in fact, almost diametrically opposed) aspect when the subject is approached from a psychoanalytic viewpoint. The accusation of "reductionism" so often made against psychoanalytic studies would seem more applicable to an approach that reduces the explanation of cross-cultural similarities in myth to one of two possibilities: culture A copied X from culture B, or culture A did not copy X from culture B (in which case the similarity is explained by a suspiciously Jungian reference to "general" or even "universal" concepts). Chinese and Americans both enjoy Chinese food, but to show how America learned of Chinese cuisine is not the same thing as explaining why it was adopted or why it is enjoyed.

The proposition that one (perhaps the most important) reason why myths are invented, borrowed, and retained is their success in responding to the emotional needs of a culture leads to certain conclusions:

1. The similarity of isolated elements in the myths of different cultures is potentially as significant as the repetition of complex patterns. Either case is as likely to reveal a common response to a common need.

2. The complexity of similar patterns in different cultures is a major determinant of the possibility of transmission from one to the other, but transmission only occurs *freely* (that is, without

compulsion) when the transmitted myth responds to the needs of its adoptive culture better than other alternatives. This may help explain why a conquering people so often assumes the myths of the conquered.

3. The appearance of similar elements or patterns in cases where transmission is impossible does not happen by chance (nor because of a "collective unconscious"), but may result from the existence of independent but similar psychocultural situations. This is one reason why theogonic elements similar to Hesiod's version appear in such distant areas as subsaharan Africa, Polynesia, and the Orient.

4. That there is more similarity than difference in myths worldwide follows from the fact that there is more similarity than difference in virtually all cultures in regard to the conditions of growing up in a family with acknowledged parents and of attempting to establish satisfactory relationships with other persons within the cultural framework.

5. Like the apparently insignificant detail in a manifest dream that clarifies or reveals the latent meaning, an element, motif, or pattern in the myths of one culture may throw unexpected light on the meaning of myths in another culture. This is not a license for the Jungian attribution of any meaning to any concept anywhere—cultures *are* different, and even if the primary emotional concerns embodied in myth are similar for all humans, the modalities in which they are expressed are largely culture-specific—but cross-cultural reference is valuable when it supplies a missing link to, or verifies or illuminates, an argument already probable on the basis of internal considerations.

An interesting example of the occurrence of a similar mythic pattern in two cultures that share a common background is found in the comparison of Greek and Hindu concepts of *ambrosia,* a special food eaten by the gods and providing them with immortality. Both cultures are Indo-European and the original idea of a magical food of the gods must be derived from an early common source; the concept is ubiquitous in Indo-European cultures, and the Greek word *ambrosia* is cognate with Sanskrit *amrta* (the literal meaning of both words is "immortality"). Nevertheless it is unthinkable that the complexity and force of these concepts as they developed independently can be explained by derivation or influence.

There are actually two Sanskrit words for ambrosia, *amrta* and *soma*. Soma is the name of the moon and of a god, but both of these usages are derived from its two primary meanings: the name of a plant whose juice is offered (and sometimes drunk) during the Vedic oblation ritual, and the name of the elixir that provides immortality.[16] What men offer in sacrifice is carried to the gods by fire and smoke and becomes what gods eat; amrta and soma are usually synonymous, but if a distinction is made between them it is that amrta is soma after the sacrificial transformation has occurred. Amrta and soma are thus, respectively, the narrow and broad definitions of the same thing. It might be said that amrta represents a particular form of soma, but this is probably too limiting; the two words share certain extended meanings and associations (for example, with milk or rain).

The god principally associated with soma is Agni, the Hindu god of fire. As the fire that consumes the sacrifice, whether liquid or solid, Agni is called the "Oblation-Eater," and as the "Oblation-Bearer" he is the smoke rising from the sacrifice to feed the gods and give them immortality. But in addition to carrying the sacrificial offerings up to heaven, he also makes the journey from heaven to earth, sometimes in the form of a bird, carrying fire or soma in his beak or in a hollow reed.

The elemental opposition of fire and water that appears in the oblation sacrifice is conspicuous throughout the myths of Agni and soma. Agni seems most at home in water, as in the many myths in which he flees from the gods and hides in water, often in order to dictate to the gods a redistribution of the sacrificial portions. The notion of fire-in-liquid is balanced by that of liquid-in-fire, especially the soma sacrifice, which must pass through fire to reach the gods but retains its liquid nature so that it can be drunk by them (but not by mortals). In the several versions of the "submarine mare" myth we find liquid-in-fire-in-liquid: when a great fire threatened to destroy the universe, Brahma put the fire in the body of a mare with fiery ambrosia in her mouth and then put the mare in the ocean to be kept until the final flood. Soma itself is first created from the ocean, when all the gods and demons churn its waters with the uprooted mountain Mandara; a huge fire caused by friction from the churning burned the herbs on the mountain, and their juices (called "liquid gold") flowed into the ocean which, mixed with the soma juice, turned first to milk, then to clarified butter (the two usual oblation liquids), and finally produced for the gods a white bowl of ambrosia.

The underlying meaning of fire/water and ambrosia is its analogy with semen, an equivalence that appears explicitly on many occasions, especially in the earliest Hindu myths (written versions of the Rg Veda, Brahmanas, and Upanishads are generally dated 1200–700). In a Rg Veda creation myth, with Sky as father and Earth as mother, Agni makes the semen of the creator god. In the Brahmanas, the semen of Prajapati, lord of creatures, is cast into the sacrificial fire in place of the usual liquid oblation (or, conversely, Prajapati produces milk and clarified butter and fire through manipulating his own body by "rubbing" or "churning"); in another variant, found in the Jaiminiya Brahmana, Tvastr throws soma into the sacrificial fire and Vrtra is born. The most explicit statement occurs in the Brhadaranyaka Upanishad: "Now, whatever is moist he [Brahma, the Creator] created from semen, and that is soma. All this universe is food and the eater of food [i.e., soma and fire]. For soma is food, and Agni is the eater of food."[17]

Semen is the combination of fire and water, a liquid that contains the spark of life.[18] The semen of the gods is always fiery: in the Kalika Purana, the earth conceives from the "fiery semen" of Vishnu; in the Shiva Purana the burning semen of Shiva is passed from Agni to the gods, the wives of six of the Seven Sages, the mountain Himalaya, and the river Ganges, none of whom can bear its "feverish burning" until finally the son of Shiva is born.

TANTALOS AND PROMETHEUS

Even this brief sketch of the Hindu concept recalls many Greek parallels. Most obvious is the function of Zeus' rain and lightning, water and fire, as the two means by which the sky god impregnates the earth goddess.[19] Or the nine years' sojourn of Hephaistos, the Greek Agni, in the cavern of Thetis under the ocean.[20] But we should begin with the actual occurrence in Greek myth of ambrosia, the equivalent of amrta and soma.

The key Greek myth concerning ambrosia is the story of Tantalos, who lived in that early time (perhaps the golden age) when men lived and dined together. Tantalos wanted to prove himself equal or superior to the gods, and the close relations then of gods and men provided him with the opportunity for a great crime, as a result of which he was punished with eternal hunger and thirst in Tartaros. He is said to have revealed the gods' secrets, or to have served his cooked son Pelops to the gods when they came to his house for dinner, or to have stolen ambrosia. The usual explanation of these crimes is quite general and obvious: men who want to be like gods, men who overstep the boundaries between men and gods, are guilty of *hybris,* and so the crimes of Tartaros are variant violations of the Delphic prescription "nothing in excess."

We can be more specific, however, about this "infringement of Zeus' prerogative."[21] From a psychoanalytic viewpoint, the crimes of Tantalos are oedipal transgressions,[22] similar to the offenses of the other three sexual criminals who receive special punishment in Tartaros. Sisyphos also was guilty of revealing the gods' secrets, and in his case the sexual and voyeuristic nature of the crime is clear, while Ixion and Tityos each tried to have a sexual relationship with one of Zeus' wives, either Hera or Leto. The second crime of Tantalos is both oedipal and counter-oedipal; like Ouranos and Kronos, he tries to kill his potential successor and furthermore he does this in order to prove his superiority over Zeus,[23] who, we should remember, is the real (as well as symbolic) father of Tantalos.

Tantalos' third crime, the theft of ambrosia, fits this general pattern, as an hybristic and oedipal attack on the prerogative of his father Zeus. At this point it would seem both appropriate and justifiable to introduce the Hindu analogy; soma and ambrosia, the food of the gods and the source of their immortality, are also symbolic manifestations of paternal sexuality, as the Hindu myths explicitly state. What Tantalos wants, when he steals ambrosia (and in his other crimes as well), is to acquire the sexual power and freedom of his father Zeus.

This interpretation can be argued by a Greek analogy as well as by comparison to the Hindu myths. The other great example in Greek myth of the usurpation of a divine (that is, paternal) prerogative is the theft of fire from Zeus by the Titan Prometheus. We would already expect, from the Hindu parallels, that the divine fire signifies paternal sexuality, and this meaning is repeatedly confirmed in Greek philosophy and myth (to cite just one example, when Zeus is deceived into making love to Semele in his true form, the hapless girl is consumed in the god's fiery sexuality).[24] The theft of fire is a sexual crime, and therefore Prometheus receives virtually the same punishment as the giant Tityos received for his attempted rape of Zeus' wife; both are bound in chains while birds (an eagle or two vultures) eat their livers. Thus the sexual nature of Prometheus' crime, like the overtly sexual crimes of the other sufferers in Tartaros, confirms the sexual nature of Tantalos' crime, and the Hindu associations of soma and fire with semen and with each other further strengthen this interpretation.

The similarities between Tantalos and Prometheus extend beyond the obvious connection between ambrosia and fire, and supplement their roles as oedipal pretenders. In Hesiod's account (*Theogony* 507–616), the quarrel between Zeus and Prometheus began at Mekone, where gods and men met to make a decision concerning the distribution of sacrifices. Prometheus cut up a sacrificed ox and placed before men the meat covered by the skin and stomach, while before Zeus he put the bones "rightly arranged and covered with shining fat" (541). Although Hesiod says that Zeus "recognized the trick" (551) but acted as if he did not, commentators agree that in the original version Zeus really was deceived and that the Hesiodic account is an attempt to rescue Zeus from the charge of being duped.[25] In his anger Zeus took back from men the gift of fire, but Prometheus again deceived him by stealing fire and carrying it to men in a hollow reed. As a result Zeus punished mankind by the creation of Pandora, the first woman, and condemned Prometheus to be tortured by the eagle eternally.

The meeting at Mekone, as West notes, "must be the one that took place at the end of the period when men and gods lived and ate together."[26] Kirk agrees that men and gods "met at Mekone for the last time," adding "Their decision to separate must have been caused by the end of the golden age, the displacement of Kronos and the new rule of Zeus," and he also connects the meeting at Mekone with the dinner of Tantalos (along with the weddings of Peleus and Thetis and Kadmos and Harmonia) as examples of the relationship between men and gods in a golden age.[27] All three of Tantalos' crimes could only occur in the hypothetical conditions of a golden age if, as Kirk indicates, one of the characteristics of this era was the intimate association of gods with men. The same is true of the criminal Ixion, who conceived his passion for Hera during his frequent visits to Olympos.

Neither Kirk nor West notices, however, the similarity that exists between the deceptions employed by Prometheus and Tantalos. Each of them chooses the communal meal for his crime, and each conceals something beneath the surface of the food in an ambiguously successful attempt to deceive the gods; Zeus may recognize Prometheus' trick but chooses the wrong portion anyway, while the other gods recognize Tantalos' trick except for Demeter, who eats a shoulder of Pelops.

The myths of Prometheus and Tantalos, then, are virtual doubles of one another; each of them is punished for having stolen the sexual possession of the gods and also for having deceived the gods by a meal with hidden contents. The difference between them lies in the permanent punishment of the mortal Tantalos and the eventual victory of the god Prometheus, a victory, moreover, that consists precisely in reminding Zeus that only by a limitation of his sexual activity (in fact, by giving up a desired female to another male) will he avoid being overthrown by an oedipal rival, the son who is destined to be greater than his father.[28]

At this point we could once more turn to the Hindu myths for comparison. The theft of fire from the gods, as we have seen, is often accompanied by a dispute concerning the distribution of the parts of a sacrifice; a Rg Veda version in which Agni claims for himself the "nourishing part of the offering"[29] is particularly reminiscent of the Promethean division. The punishments of both Prometheus and mankind also have Hindu parallels. Although the conception of the liver as the organ of desire does not appear in Greek literature until 200 years after Hesiod, this does not mean that it did not exist before Aeschylus; if it did, the particular torment of Prometheus may be compared to Agni, who appears "tortured with desire" in the *Mahabharata* and is punished with "feverish burning" of a clearly sexual nature for having stolen the semen of Shiva in the *Shiva Purana*. Mortal men, on the other hand, are punished by Zeus through the creation of Pandora, the first woman and the source of all evils for men; similarly we read in the *Mahabharata* that "there is nothing more evil than women" and that God "created women by a magic ritual in order to delude mankind."[30]

There is, of course, not much in those sections of Greek myth concerned principally with the gods that cannot find a parallel somewhere in the interminable Hindu myth cycles. Still I cannot resist mentioning one more, in connection with Hesiod's account of the birth of Aphrodite from the severed phallus of Ouranos, which Kronos threw into the ocean. Aphrodite's name means "born from foam," and the phallus of Ouranos is surrounded by foam; as West notes, "Aphrodite is formed in foam to explain her name."[31] Association of the goddess of desire with the phallus is not difficult to understand, but why the connection with foam? Hesiod may put Aphrodite in foam because he found foam in her name, but how is foam connected with Aphrodite in the first place? The association must result, I would think, from a prior connection with the phallus and consequently from a visual similarity between semen and the foam excreted by the sea.

Again in the *Mahabharata,* soma, a mythic counterpart of semen, is created by the gods in the form of the foam produced by churning the ocean with an uprooted mountain; the sexual symbolism of this cosmic penetration is obvious. The Sanskrit verb that means "churn" is *manth,* a word that embodies many of the associations we have been discussing. Its primary reference is "vigorous backwards and forwards motion of any sort"; it also refers to the production of fire from fire sticks, sexual activity, and stealing (especially the theft of soma), it is related to the name Mandara (the mountain used for churning soma), and it is cognate with the Greek Prometheus.[32] In addition, the name "Prometheus" could be related to the Hindu culture-hero Prthu, who steals the cow of immortality from the gods to help a mortal, and "restores food and establishes civilization."[33]

The derivation of both Greek and Hindu myths from a common Indo-European tradition in neolithic times helps to explain some of the striking similarities of symbolic patterns in the two cultural systems. However, the lapse of more than two millennia between the neolithic period and the early Iron Age, when the first written versions of these myths appeared in both India and Greece, makes it impossible to trace either the descent of separate traditions or connections between different traditions. Mesopotamian influence certainly affected both Greek and Hindu myth, and the pre-Aryan Harappa culture of the Indus valley must have influenced Hindu myth in much the same way as Minoan/Mediterranean myths were incorporated into Greek myth, but any specific certainty about these matters cannot be attained.

Worth noting, however, is a non-Greek, non-Indian myth that seems to predate Hesiod and has striking associations with the mythic configuration we have been discussing. A. Olrik collected and analyzed myths from the region of the Caucasus that tell of the punishment of an impious giant, chained to a mountain while a vulture eats his "bowels."[34] His crime is an attempt to steal the "water of life" (that is, immortality), and in his punishment this water flows just beyond his reach (like the punishment of Tantalos) or is swallowed by him but then removed from his bowels by the vulture. A connection with the myths of Tantalos, Tityos, and Prometheus is clear, but there are also similarities with the myths of Agni and soma. The water of life is equivalent to Tantalos' ambrosia, Prometheus' fire, and the soma/semen of Hindu myth; the bird who removes the swallowed "semen" is comparable to Agni, who frequently swallows the "seed of the gods" or, in the form of a bird, steals the semen swallowed or produced by others. Also the giant of the Caucasus, if ever freed from his punishment, will destroy the whole world in his rage, and a cosmic cataclysm by fire or flood figures importantly in Hindu, Norse, and Near Eastern myth and, in a muted form, in Greek myth. If Olrik is correct about the dating and precedence of the Caucasus myth, we may possibly see here a point of intersection in the mysterious journey of an involved mythic pattern.

At the level of psychological significance, it is of course unnecessary to demonstrate diffusion or dependence; the same emotional concerns appear in the myths of Japan and New Guinea as well as in Greece or India. It is the similarity in the specific modality of these appearances, in the mythic circumstances that embody these concerns, that we may attribute, at least in part, to the influence of one group upon another. Yet even in cases of elaborate similarity in myths we cannot leave out of account the possible impact of cultural similarity between groups—not only societal and familial universals and similarity in the current level of cultural development, but also similarity in the vicissitudes of past history.

THE *THEOGONY* OF HESIOD

Although Hesiod's *Theogony* may be the oldest *written* Greek literature we possess, there was probably a theogonic tradition in

Greek myth as old as the myths themselves. Striking similarities between the *Theogony* and various earlier Near Eastern theogonies suggest that Hesiod's version goes back in some parts at least half a millennium, to contacts between the Minoan-Mycenean world and eastern cultures, and in some cases the ultimate source may lie even earlier, in the largely uncharted migrations of the Indo-Europeans. Other theogonic poems almost certainly existed in Greece before Hesiod's, but these were oral literature and we know next to nothing about them.

Other Greek theogonies may still have existed at the time of Hesiod, but we cannot know whether the story of the world's beginning told in the *Theogony* represents the usual view held at the time, or whether it was merely one of several competing views. The scant hints we do have of a genuine mythic alternative to Hesiod's version amount to only a few scattered lines and passages, particularly in the *Iliad*. Whether the theogonic tradition before Hesiod was fluid or relatively fixed, and whatever the competition may have been like, the *Theogony* became for almost all later Greeks the true story of how the world and the gods began. The theogonic summary found at the beginning of the *Library* of Apollodoros, for example, differs from the *Theogony* in only a few details, although it was probably written almost a thousand years after Hesiod.

THEOGONY[35]

Let us begin to sing of the Muses of Helikon,
who hold the great and holy mount of Helikon
and dance on tender feet round the violet spring
and the altar of Kronos' mighty son.
5 Having washed their soft skin in Permessos'
spring, or Hippokrene, or holy Olmeios,
on Helicon's summit they lead the fair and
beautiful dances with rapid steps.
Setting out from there, concealed by air,
10 they walk at night, chanting their fair song,
singing of Zeus Aigiochos and mistress Hera
of Argos, who walks in golden sandals, and
Zeus Aigiochos' daughter, owl-eyed Athena,
and Phoibos Apollo and archeress Artemis,

15 and Poseidon earth-embracer, earth-shaker,
and revered Themis and glancing Aphrodite,
and gold-crowned Hebe and lovely Dione,
Leto, Iapetos, and crafty Kronos,
Eos, great Helios, and bright Selene,
20 Gaia, great Okeanos, and black Nyx, and
the holy race of other immortals who always are.

Once they taught Hesiod beautiful song
as he watched his sheep under holy Helicon;
this is the first thing the goddesses told me,
25 the Olympian Muses, daughters of Zeus Aigiochos:

"Rustic shepherds, evil oafs, nothing but bellies,
we know how to say many lies as if they were true,
and when we want, we know how to speak the truth."

This is what the prompt-voiced daughters of great Zeus said;
30 they picked and gave me a staff, a branch of strong laurel,
a fine one, and breathed into me a voice
divine, to celebrate what will be and what was.
They told me to sing the race of the blessed who always are,
but always to sing of themselves first and also last.
35 But what is this of oak or rock to me?
Hesiod, let us start from the Muses, who with singing
cheer the great mind of father Zeus in Olympos,
telling things that are and will be and were before,
with harmonized voice; the unbroken song flows
40 sweet from their lips; the father's house rejoices,
the house of loud-sounding Zeus, as the delicate voice
of the goddesses spreads, the peaks of snowy Olympos echo,
and the homes of the immortals; with ambrosial voice
they praise in song first the august race of gods
45 from the beginning, whom Gaia and wide Ouranos begot,
and those born from them, the gods, givers of good;
and second of Zeus, the father of gods and men,
[the goddesses sing, beginning and ending the song]
how he is best of gods and greatest in power;
50 next, singing of the race of men and mighty Giants
they cheer the mind of Zeus in Olympos, themselves
the Muses of Olympos, daughters of Zeus Aigiochos.
Mnemosyne, who rules the hills of Eleuther, having lain
with the father, Kronos' son, in Pieria, bore them to be

55 a forgetting of evils and a respite from cares.
For wise Zeus lay with her nine nights
apart from the immortals, going up to the holy bed;
but when a year went by, and the seasons turned round
as moons waned, and many days were completed,
60 she bore nine like-minded daughters, in whose
breasts and spirit song is the only care,
just below the summit of snowy Olympos. There
are their polished dance floors and lovely houses;
next to them the Charites and Himeros have homes
65 in joy; chanting from their lips a sweet song,
they sing, and praise the customs and noble ways of
all the immortals, chanting a most sweet song.
Then they went to Olympos, rapt in the lovely air,
the ambrosial song; the black earth echoed round
70 to their singing, and a sweet beat arose under their
feet as they went to their father; he was ruling the
sky, holding the thunder and fiery lightning-bolt himself,
having conquered father Kronos by might; in right detail
he dealt laws and appointed honors to the immortals.
75 These things the Muses sang, who hold Olympian homes,
nine daughters begotten by great Zeus,
Kleio, Euterpe, Thaleia, and Melpomene,
Terpsichore, Erato, Polymnia, Ourania,
and Kalliope, who is most eminent of all,
80 for she is companion of reverent kings.
Whomever of kings, favored by Zeus, the daughters
of great Zeus will honor and see being born,
they pour sweet dew on his tongue, and
from his lips flow honeyed words; his people
85 all look to him as he decides issues with
straight judgments; speaking unerringly he
quickly and wisely ends even great strife;
this is why there are sensible kings, since
they secure restitution for the wronged in
90 public and easily, persuading by soft words;
going to assembly, they pray to him as to a god,
with supplicant awe; in assembly he is pre-eminent.
Such is the holy gift of the Muses to men.
For from the Muses and far-shooting Apollo
95 are men on earth who sing and play the harp,
but kings are from Zeus; he prospers, whom the
Muses love; a sweet voice flows from his lips.

For if one has grief in his newly vexed spirit, and
his heart is withered in sorrow, and then a bard,
100 the Muses' servant, sings the fame of former men
and the blessed gods who hold Olympos, soon
he forgets his mind's burden and remembers none of
his cares; quickly the goddesses' gifts divert him.

Greetings, children of Zeus; grant me lovely song,
105 and praise the holy race of immortals who always are,
who were born from Gaia and starry Ouranos,
and from dark Nyx, and those salty Pontos raised.
Tell how at first gods and earth came to be,
and rivers and vast sea, violent in surge,
110 and shining stars and the wide sky above,
[and the gods born from them, givers of good]
how they divided their wealth and allotted honors
and how first they held valed Olympos.
Tell me these things, Muses with Olympian homes,
115 from the first, say which of them first came to be.

First of all Chaos came into being; but next
wide-breasted Gaia, always safe foundation of all
immortals who possess the peaks of snowy Olympos,
and dim Tartaros in a recess of the wide-pathed earth,
120 and Eros, most beautiful among the immortal gods,
limb-weakener, who conquers the mind and sensible thought
in the breasts of all gods and all men.

From Chaos were born Erebos and black Nyx;
from Nyx were born Aither and Hemera,
125 whom she conceived and bore, joined in love with Erebos.
Gaia first bore a child equal to herself,
starry Ouranos, to cover her all over, and
to be an always safe home for the blessed gods.
She bore the high Ourea, pleasing homes of divine
130 Nymphs, who dwell in the valed mountains.
She also bore the barren sea, violent in surge,
Pontos, without love's union; but next
she lay with Ouranos and bore deep-whirling Okeanos,
and Koios and Kreios and Hyperion and Iapetos,
135 and Theia, and Rhea and Themis and Mnemosyne
and gold-crowned Phoibe and attractive Tethys.

After them was born the youngest, crafty Kronos,
most terrible of children; he hated his lusting father.

Next she bore the Kyklopes with over-proud heart,
140 Brontes and Steropes and hard-hearted Arges,
who gave Zeus thunder and made the lightning-bolt.
They were like the gods in everything else,
but a single eye was in the middle of their foreheads;
they were given the name Kyklopes because
145 one round eye was in their foreheads;
strength, force, and skill were in their works.

Next others were born from Gaia and Ouranos,
three great and mighty sons, unspeakable
Kottos and Briareos and Gyges, rash children.
150 From their shoulders shot a hundred arms
unimaginable, and fifty heads on the shoulders
of each grew over their strong bodies;
great and mighty strength was in their huge shape.

For all who were born from Gaia and Ouranos were the
155 most terrible of children, and their father hated them
from the first; when any of them first would be born,
he would hide them all away, and not let them come up
to the light, in a dark hole of Gaia; the evil deed
pleased Ouranos. But she, vast Gaia, groaned within
160 from the strain, and planned an evil crafty trick.
Quick she made the element of grey adamant,
made a great sickle, and advised her sons,
speaking encouragingly, while hurt in her heart:

"Children of me and a wicked father, if you are willing
165 to obey, we may punish the evil outrage of your
father; since he first planned unseemly deeds."

She said this, but fear seized them all and none of them
spoke. But great and crafty Kronos was brave, and
quickly gave an answer to his dear mother:

170 "Mother, I would undertake and do this task,
since I have no respect for our father
unspeakable; since he first planned unseemly deeds."

He spoke, and vast Gaia was greatly pleased in her mind.
She placed and hid him in ambush, and put in his hands
175 a sickle with jagged teeth, and revealed the whole trick.
Great Ouranos came, bringing on night, and upon Gaia
he lay, wanting love and fully extended;
his son, from ambush, reached out with his left hand
and with his right hand took the huge sickle,
180 long with jagged teeth, and quickly severed
his own father's genitals, and threw them to fall
behind; they did not fall from his hand without result,
for all the bloody drops which spurted were
received by Gaia; as the years revolved,
185 she bore the strong Erinyes and great Giants,
shining in armor, holding long spears in their hands,
and the nymphs called Meliai on the endless earth.
As soon as he cut off the genitals with adamant,
he threw them from land into the turbulent sea;
190 they were carried over the sea a long time, and white
foam arose from the immortal flesh; within a girl
grew; first she came to holy Kythera, and
next she came to wave-washed Cyprus.
An awesome and beautiful goddess emerged, and
195 grass grew under her supple feet. Aphrodite
[foam-born goddess and well-crowned Kythereia]
gods and men name her, since in foam she grew;
and Kythereia, since she landed at Kythera;
and Kyprogenes, since she was born in wave-beat Cyprus;
200 and "Philommeides," since she appeared from the genitals.
Eros accompanied her, and fair Himeros followed,
when first she was born and went to join the gods.
She has such honor from the first, and this is her
province among men and immortal gods:
205 girls' whispers and smiles and deceptions,
sweet pleasure and sexual love and tenderness.

Great Ouranos, their father, called his sons Titans,
reproaching the sons whom he himself begot;
he said they strained in wickedness to do a
210 great wrong, but there would be revenge afterwards.

Nyx bore hateful Moros and black Ker and
Thanatos, she bore Hypnos and the tribe of Oneiroi.
Next Momos and painful Oizys were born to

the dark goddess Nyx, though she lay with no one,
215 and the Hesperides who keep, beyond famous Okeanos,
the beautiful gold apples and the fruit-bearing trees;
and she bore the Moirai and pitiless Keres,
[Klotho and Lachesis and Atropos, who give to
mortals at birth both good and evil to have]
220 who pursue the sins of men and gods;
the goddesses never end their terrible anger
until they inflict evil on anyone who sins.
And deadly Nyx bore Nemesis, a plague to mortal
men; after her she bore Apate and Philotes
225 and painful Geras and hard-hearted Eris.

And hateful Eris bore painful Ponos,
Lethe and Limos and the tearful Algea,
Hysminai, Machai, Phonoi, and Androktasiai;
Neikea, Pseudea, Logoi, and Amphillogiai,
230 Dysnomia and Ate, near one another,
and Horkos, who most afflicts men on earth,
when anyone willingly swears a false oath.
Pontos begot Nereus, truthful and never false,
eldest of his children; he is called the Old Man
235 since he is true and gentle; what is lawful
he remembers, and he knows just and gentle thoughts.
Then he begot great Thaumas and proud Phorkys,
from union with Gaia, and fair-cheeked Keto, and
Eurybia, who has in her breast a heart of adamant.

240   To Nereus were born numerous divine children
in the barren sea; their mother was fair-haired Doris,
daughter of Okeanos, the full-circling river:
Protho, Eukrante, Sao, Amphitrite,
Eudora, Thetis, Galene, and Glauke,
245 Kymothoe, swift Speio, lovely Thalia,
Pasithea, Erato, and rose-armed Eunike,
graceful Melite, Eulimene, Agaue,
Doto, Proto, Pherousa, and Dynamene,
Nesaia, Aktaia, and Protomedeia,
250 Doris and Panope and shapely Galateia,
lovely Hippothoe, rose-armed Hipponoe,
Kymodoke, who easily calms waves on the windy
sea and the blowing of windy gales,
with Kymatolege and fine-ankled Amphitrite,

255 and Kymo, Eione, and well-crowned Halimede,
Glaukonome, who loves smiles, and Pontoporeia,
Leiagora and Euagora and Laomedeia,
Poulynoe and Autonoe and Lysianassa,
Euarne of lovely shape and blameless form,
260 Psamathe of graceful body, divine Menippe,
Neso, Eupompe, Themisto, and Pronoe, and
Nemertes, who has the mind of her immortal father.
These were the daughters of blameless Nereus:
fifty girls, skilled in blameless works.

265   Thaumas married deep-flowing Okeanos'
daughter Elektra; she bore swift Iris
and the fair-haired Harpies, Aello and Okypete,
who fly as the birds and gusts of winds
on swift wings, rushing high in the air.

270   Keto bore to Phorkys the fair-cheeked hags,
grey from birth, who are called the Graiai
by immortal gods and men who go on earth,
fine-robed Pemphredo and saffron-robed Enyo,
and the Gorgons, who live beyond famous Okeanos,
275 at the limit toward Night, with the clear-voiced
Hesperides, Sthenno, Euryale, and unlucky Medousa;
she was mortal, but they were immortal and ageless,
both of them; the Dark-Haired god lay with her
in a soft meadow and flowers of spring.
280 And when Perseus cut off her head, out
jumped great Chrysaor and the horse Pegasos,
who has this name since by the springs of Okeanos
he was born, and the other holds a gold sword in his hands;
he flew off and left the earth, mother of flocks,
285 and came to the immortals; he lives in the house
of wise Zeus and carries his thunder and lightning.
Chrysaor begot three-headed Geryoneus, from union
with Kallirhoe, daughter of famous Okeanos.
Mighty Herakles killed Geryoneus by his
290 rolling-gaited cattle in sea-washed Erytheia
on the very day he drove the wide-faced cattle
to holy Tiryns, having crossed the ford of Okeanos
and killed Orthos and the herdsman Eurytion
in the misty stable beyond famous Okeanos.

295   She bore another unbeatable monster, in no way
      like mortal men or immortal gods, in a
      hollow cave, the divine and hard-hearted Echidna,
      half a nymph with glancing eyes and lovely cheeks,
      half a monstrous snake, terrible and great, a
300   shimmering flesh-eater in the dark holes of holy earth.
      There she has a cave, down under the hollow rock,
      far from the immortal gods and mortal men; there
      the gods allotted to her a famous house to live in.

      Grim Echidna watches in Arima under the earth,
305   an immortal and ageless nymph for all days.
      They say that Typhoeus was joined in love with her,
      the arrogant and lawless monster with the glancing girl;
      she conceived and bore strong-hearted children:
      first she bore Orthos, the dog of Geryoneus;
310   next she bore the unfightable and unspeakable
      flesh-eating Kerberos, bronze-voiced dog of Hades,
      fifty-headed, pitiless and strong;
      third she bore the ill-intended Hydra of
      Lerna, whom the white-armed goddess Hera raised
315   in her infinite anger against mighty Herakles;
      she died by the unfeeling bronze sword of Herakles,
      son of Zeus and stepson of Amphitryon, with war-loving
      Iolaos, by the plans of army-leading Athena.
      She bore Chimaira, who breathes furious fire,
320   terrible and great, swift-footed and strong,
      with three heads—one of a hard-eyed lion,
      one of a goat, one of a snake, a strong serpent;
      [a lion in front, a snake behind, a goat in between,
      breathing the terrible strength of blazing fire]
325   Pegasos and noble Bellerophon killed her.
      And she bore the deadly Sphinx, destroyer of Kadmeians,
      from union with Orthos, and the Nemeian lion
      whom Hera, noble wife of Zeus, raised and
      settled in the hills of Nemeia, a plague to men.
330   There he lived and ravaged the tribes of men,
      master of Nemeian Tretos and Apesas, but
      the great strength of Herakles overcame him.

      Keto joined in love with Phorkys and bore her youngest,
      a terrible serpent in the recesses of dark earth,

335 at the great limits, who guards the all-golden apples.
And this is the progeny from Keto and Phorkys.

Tethys bore to Okeanos the swirling Rivers,
Neilos, Alpheios, and deep-whirling Eridanos,
Strymon, Maiandros, and fair-flowing Istros,
340 Phasis, Rhesos, and silver-swirling Acheloos,
Nessos, Rhodios, Haliakmon, Heptaporos,
Granikos, Aisepos, and divine Simois,
Peneios, Hermos, and fair-flowing Kaikos,
great Sangarios, Ladon, and Parthenios,
345 Euenos, Aldeskos, and divine Skamandros.
And she bore a holy race of Kourai, who on earth
raise youths to manhood, with lord Apollo
and the Rivers, holding this duty from Zeus:
Peitho, Admete, Ianthe, and Elektra,
350 Doris, Prymno, and Ourania of divine form,
Hippo, Klymene, Rhodeia, and Kallirhoe,
Zeuxo, Klytia, Idyia, and Pasithoe,
Plexaura, Galaxaura, and beautiful Dione,
Melobosis, Thoe, and fair-figured Polydora,
355 Kerkeis, beautiful of form, and cow-eyed Plouto,
Perseis, Ianeira, Akaste, and Xanthe,
lovely Petraia, Menestho, Europe,
Metis, Eurynome, and saffron-robed Telesto,
Chryseis, Asia, and desirable Kalypso,
360 Eudora, Tyche, Amphirho, and Okyrhoe,
and Styx, who is most eminent of all.
These were born from Okeanos and Tethys,
the eldest daughters; but there are also many others,
for Okeanos has three thousand slender-ankled daughters
365 who, scattered over the earth and watery depths,
serve everywhere alike, glorious divine children.
There are as many other rivers, noisily flowing
sons of Okeanos, whom mistress Tethys bore;
it is hard for a man to say the names of them all,
370 but individuals know the ones by which they live.

Theia bore great Helios and bright Selene
and Eos, who shines upon all on earth and
upon the immortal gods who hold the wide sky,
after Theia was won in love by Hyperion.

375   Divine Eurybia joined in love with Kreios and
       bore Astraios and great Pallas and Perses,
       who stands out among all for his knowledge.
       To Astraios Eos bore the strong-hearted winds,
       cleansing Zephyros and swift-running Boreas,
380   and Notos, a goddess united in love with a god;
       after these Erigeneia bore the star Eosphoros
       and the shining Stars the sky wears as a crown.
       Styx, daughter of Okeanos, lay with Pallas and bore
       Zelos and fine-ankled Nike in the house;
385   and she bore famous children, Kratos and Bia,
       whose house is not apart from Zeus; they neither sit
       nor go, except where the god should lead them,
       but always are stationed by deep-thundering Zeus.
       This is what immortal Styx, daughter of Okeanos, planned
390   on that day when the Olympian lightning-holder
       called all the immortal gods to vast Olympos
       and said whichever gods with him would fight the Titans
       would not lose their rights, but each would have
       the honor he held before among the immortal gods.
395   He said that whoever held no honor or right under Kronos
       would enter upon honor and rights, as is just.
       First immortal Styx came to Olympos
       with her children, by the advice of her father;
       Zeus honored her and gave outstanding gifts.
400   He set her to be the gods' great oath and
       gave to her children to live with him for all days.
       Just as he promised, to all without fail he
       fulfilled; as for himself, he rules with great power.

       Phoibe came to Koios' bed of much desire;
405   the goddess, pregnant by the god's love,
       bore dark-robed Leto, always sweet
       and gentle to men and immortal gods,
       sweet from the first, most mild in Olympos.
       She also bore remarkable Asteria, whom Perses
410   led to his great house to be called his wife.
       She conceived and bore Hekate, whom above all
       Zeus, Kronos' son, honored; he gave her notable gifts,
       to have a share of the earth and barren sea.
       She also has a share of honor from the starry sky,
415   and is honored most of all by the immortal gods.
       For even now, whenever someone of men on earth

sacrifices fine things and prays in due ritual,
he invokes Hekate; much honor comes to him
very easily, whose prayers the goddess favorably
420 receives, and she grants him wealth, since this is
her power. For as many were born of Gaia and Ouranos
and obtained honor, of them all she has her due;
Kronos' son neither wronged her nor took away
what she received among the Titans, the former gods,
425 but this she keeps, as was the division at the beginning.
Nor, since she is an only child, does the goddess obtain
less honor and privileges on earth and sky and sea,
but rather she has still more, for Zeus honors her.
Greatly she assists and benefits whom she will;
430 she sits by reverent kings in judgment, and he is
eminent among the people in assembly, whom she wishes;
whenever men arm for man-killing war, then
the goddess is there, and to whom she wishes
she gladly grants victory and extends glory.
435 She is good to stand by cavalry, by whom she wishes;
she is also good when men compete in the contest;
then also the goddess assists and benefits them;
one who wins by might and strength bears off the fine
prize easily and happily, and brings glory to his parents.
440 To those who work the grey sea's discomfort
and pray to Hekate and loud-sounding Earth-Shaker,
the noble goddess easily grants much catch, and
easily takes it back when it appears, if her heart wishes.
She is good, with Hermes, to increase the stock in barns;
445 herds of cattle and wide herds of goats and
flocks of wooly sheep, if her spirit wishes,
she increases from few and from many makes less.
So even though being her mother's only child, she
is honored with privileges among all the immortals.
450 Kronos' son made her guardian of the young, who after
her saw with their eyes the light of much-seeing Eos.
So always she guards the young, and these are her honors.

Rhea lay with Kronos and bore illustrious children:
Hestia, Demeter, and gold-sandaled Hera and
455 strong Hades, who lives in a palace under the ground
and has a pitiless heart, and loud-sounding Earth-Shaker
and wise Zeus, the father of gods and men,
by whose thunder the wide earth is shaken.

Great Kronos would swallow these, as each
460 would come from the holy womb to his mother's knees,
intending this, that none of Ouranos' proud line but
himself would hold the right of king over the immortals.
For he learned from Gaia and starry Ouranos
that it was fate that his own son would overthrow him,
465 although he was powerful, by the plans of great Zeus.
So he kept no blind man's watch, but alertly
swallowed his own children; incurable grief held Rhea.
But when she was about to bear Zeus, father of gods
and men, she begged her own dear parents,
470 Gaia and starry Ouranos, to help her think
of a plan, by which she might secretly have
her son, and make great crafty Kronos pay the
Erinyes of her father and the children he swallowed.
They heard and obeyed their dear daughter
475 and told her what was destined to happen
concerning king Kronos and his strong-hearted son.
They sent her to Lyktos, to the rich land of Crete,
when she was about to bear her youngest son,
great Zeus; vast Gaia received him from her
480 in wide Crete to tend and raise.
Carrying him through the swift black night, she came
first to Lyktos; taking him in her arms, she hid him
in a deep cave, down in dark holes of holy earth,
on Mount Aigaion, dense with woods.
485 Rhea wrapped a huge stone in a baby's robe, and fed it
to Ouranos' wide-ruling son, king of the earlier gods;
he took it in his hands and put it down his belly,
the fool; he did not think in his mind that instead
of a stone his own son, undefeated and secure, was left
490 behind, soon to overthrow him by force and violence and
drive him from his honor, and rule the immortals himself.

Swiftly then the strength and noble limbs
of the future lord grew; at the end of a year,
tricked by the clever advice of Gaia,
495 great crafty Kronos threw up his children,
defeated by the craft and force of his own son.
First he vomited out the stone he had swallowed last;
Zeus fixed it firmly in the wide-pathed earth
at sacred Pytho in the vales of Parnassos,
500 to be a sign thereafter, a wonder to mortal men.

He released from their deadly chains his uncles,
Ouranos' sons, whom their father mindlessly bound.
They did not forget gratitude for his help,
and gave him thunder and the fiery lightning-bolt
505 and lightning, which vast Gaia earlier had hidden;
relying on these, he is king of mortals and immortals.

Iapetos married the fine-ankled daughter of Okeanos,
Klymene, and went up to the same bed;
she bore him a son, strong-hearted Atlas, and
510 she bore all-eminent Menoitios, and Prometheus
subtle and devious, and wrong-thinking Epimetheus,
who was from the first an evil for men who work for food;
he first received from Zeus the molded woman,
the virgin. Wide-seeing Zeus sent arrogant Menoitios
515 down to Erebos, striking him with a smoking thunderbolt,
for his recklessness and excessive pride.
And Atlas, standing at the limits of the earth,
before the clear-voiced Hesperides, under strong compulsion,
holds the wide sky with head and untiring arms;
520 for this is the fate wise Zeus allotted him.
He bound devious Prometheus with inescapable
harsh bonds, fastened through the middle of a column,
and he inflicted on him a long-winged eagle, which ate
his immortal liver; but it grew as much in all
525 at night as the long-winged bird would eat all day.
Herakles, the mighty son of fine-ankled Alkmene,
killed it and freed from evil suffering the son
of Iapetos and released him from anguish
by the will of high-ruling Olympian Zeus,
530 so that the glory of Theban-born Herakles
would be more than before on the nurturing earth;
thinking of this, he honored his famous son, and
though he was angry quit the rage he had ever since
the Titan matched wits with Kronos' mighty son.
535 For when gods and mortal men made a settlement
at Mekone, then he cleverly cut up a big ox and
set it before them, trying to deceive the mind of Zeus.
For Zeus he set out meat and innards rich with fat
on the skin, covering it with the stomach of the ox;
540 but for men he set the white ox bones, with crafty skill
arranging them well and covering them with shining fat.
Then the father of men and gods said to him:

"Son of Iapetos, distinguished of all gods,
sir, how unjustly you divided the portions."

545   Thus Zeus, knowing deathless plans, spoke and mocked him.
But clever Prometheus answered him, gently
smiling, and did not forget his crafty trick:

"Zeus, most honored and greatest of eternal gods,
take of these whichever the spirit within tells you."

550   He spoke with the trick in mind; but Zeus, knowing deathless
plans, knew and did not miss the trick; in his heart
he foresaw evils which were going to happen to mortal men.
With both hands he lifted up the white fat,
but he was angry in mind and rage came to his spirit,
555 when he saw the white ox bones in the crafty trick.
Therefore the tribes of men on earth burn to the
immortals white bones on reeking altars.
Greatly angry, cloud-gatherer Zeus said to him:

"Son of Iapetos, knowing thoughts beyond all,
560 sir, you still have not forgotten your crafty trick."

So spoke angry Zeus, who knows deathless plans;
from then on, never forgetting the trick, he would
not give the strength of untiring fire to ash trees
for mortal men, who live on the earth.
565 But the great son of Iapetos deceived him
and stole the far-seen light of untiring fire
in a hollow narthex; this bit deep in the spirit
of high-thundering Zeus and his heart was angry
when he saw the far-seen light of fire among men.
570 In return for fire, he quickly made an evil for men;
for the famous Lame One made from earth the likeness
of a modest virgin, by the plans of Kronos' son.
Owl-eyed Athena sashed her and dressed her
in silver clothes; she placed with her hands a
575 decorated veil on her head, marvelous to see;
[and lovely fresh garlands, the flowers of plants,
Pallas Athene put around her head]
and she placed on her head a golden crown
which the famous Lame One had made himself,
580 shaping it with his hands, to please father Zeus.

On it he carved many designs, a marvelous sight;
of all dread beasts the land and sea nourish,
he included most, amazingly similar to living
animals with voices; and beauty breathed over all.

585   But when he made the lovely evil to pay for the good,
he led her where the other gods and men were;
she delighted in the finery from the great father's
owl-eyed daughter; awe filled immortal gods and mortal
men when they saw the sheer trick, irresistible to men.
590 For from her is the race of female women,
[from her is the deadly race and tribes of women]
a great plague to mortals, dwelling with men,
not suited for cursed Poverty, but for Wealth.
As when bees in covered hives feed
595 the drones, companions of evil works,
the bees work until sunset, all day
and every day, and make the pale combs,
while the drones stay inside, in the covered hives,
reaping the work of others into their own stomachs;
600 similarly for mortal men, high-thundering Zeus
made an evil: women, the partners of evil works.
He gave a second evil to balance a good,
since whoever escapes marriage and women's harm,
by refusing to marry, comes to deadly old age
605 with no son to tend him; not lacking livelihood
while he lives, when he dies distant kin divide
his estate. But even the man whose fate is to marry
and acquires a good wife, suited to his wants,
for him from the first good and evil are balanced
610 always; but whoever acquires the wicked sort
lives with unending trouble in his mind and
spirit and heart, and the evil is incurable.
So it is impossible to cheat or surpass the mind of Zeus.
For not even Iapetos' son, good Prometheus,
615 escaped his heavy anger, but of necessity
great bondage holds him, though he knows many things.

When first the father was angry at heart with Obriareos
and Kottos and Gyges, he bound them in strong bondage;
when he noticed their great manhood, their looks
620 and size, he put them under the wide-pathed earth.
They lived there under the earth in pain,

at the farthest borders of the great earth,
suffering much and long, with great grief of heart.
But Kronos' son and the other immortal gods,
625 whom fair-haired Rhea bore from Kronos' embrace,
brought them up to the light, by Gaia's counsel.
For she told them everything in detail, how with
their help they would win victory and bright fame.
For a long time they fought in bitter exertion
630 against one another in harsh battles,
the Titan gods and those born of Kronos,
the proud Titans from lofty Othrys
and from Olympos the gods, givers of good,
whom fair-haired Rhea bore, having lain with Kronos.
635 With bitter war against one another
they fought continually for ten full years;
there was no end or relief from harsh strife
for either, the war's outcome was evenly balanced.
But when he gave them everything fitting,
640 nectar and ambrosia, which the gods eat themselves,
and the proud spirit grew in the breasts of all,
[when they tasted nectar and desirable ambrosia]
then the father of gods and men said to them:

"Hear me, good children of Gaia and Ouranos,
645 that I may say what the spirit in my chest commands.
For a long time now against one another
we have fought every day for victory and power,
the Titan gods and we born of Kronos.
Show your great strength and unbeatable arms
650 against the Titans in savage war;
remember our kindness, and how much you suffered
before you came to the light from grievous bondage
under the murky gloom, thanks to our plans."

When he had spoken, blameless Kottos replied:

655   "Divine one, you tell us what we know; on our own
we know your superior mind and thoughts, and
that you defended the immortals from icy harm;
by your counsels we came back from the murky gloom,
back from the unyielding bonds, obtaining
660 the unexpected, lord son of Kronos.
So now with firm mind and willing spirit

we will defend your power in hostile war,
fighting the Titans in harsh battles."

After he spoke, the gods who give good welcomed
665 the words they heard; their spirit longed for war
even more than before, and they roused grim conflict
that same day, all of them, female as well as male,
the Titan gods against those born of Kronos and
those Zeus brought to light from darkness
670 under the earth, dread and strong, with huge might.
A hundred arms shot from the shoulders
of each and all, fifty heads grew from the
shoulders of each, from their massive bodies.
They stood against the Titans in grim battle,
675 holding great rocks in their massive hands;
the Titans opposite strengthened their ranks
expectantly; both displayed the work of arms
and might together, and the vast sea echoed loudly
and the earth resounded greatly, and the wide sky
680 shook and groaned, and great Olympos was shaken
from its foundation by the immortals' charge; a heavy
tremor of feet reached dim Tartaros, and the loud
noise of unspeakable rout and violent weapons.
So they hurled at each other the painful weapons;
685 shouts from both sides reached starry Ouranos,
as they came together with a great outcry.

Zeus no longer restrained his might, but now his
heart was filled with wrath, and he revealed all
his strength; from the sky and Olympos both,
690 he came throwing a lightning-flurry; the bolts
flew thick with thunder and lightning
from his massive hand, whirling a holy flame,
one after another; the life-giving earth resounded
in flames, the vast woods crackled loudly about,
695 the whole earth and Okeanos' streams and the
barren sea were boiling; the hot blast enveloped
the chthonic Titans, the flame reached the upper
air in its fury; although they were strong, the blazing
glow of thunder and lightning blinded their eyes.
700 The awful heat seized Chaos; it seemed,
for eyes to see and ears to hear the sound,
just as if earth and wide sky from above came
together; for so great a noise would arise

from the one fallen upon and the other falling down;
705 such a noise arose from the strife of clashing gods.
The winds stirred up earthquake and dust and
thunder and lightning and blazing lightning-bolt,
the weapons of great Zeus, and brought the shout
and cry into the midst of both sides; a great din
710 arose from fearful strife, and might's work was revealed.

But the tide of battle turned; before, in mutual
collision, they fought continuously in grim battles;
but now in the front ranks they roused dread war,
Kottos and Briareos and Gyges, hungry for war.
715 They threw three hundred rocks from massive hands
at once, and with their missiles overshadowed
the Titans; they sent them under the wide-pathed
earth, and bound them in cruel bonds,
having defeated them by force, despite their daring.
720 as far below the earth as sky is above the earth;
for it is that far from the earth to dim Tartaros.

A bronze anvil falling for nine nights and days
from the sky would reach the earth on the tenth;
and a bronze anvil falling for nine nights and days
725 from the earth would reach Tartaros on the tenth.
Around it runs a bronze fence; and about its
neck flows night in a triple row; while above
grow the roots of earth and the barren sea.

There the Titan gods under the dim gloom
730 are hid away by the plans of cloud-gatherer Zeus,
in a moldy place, the limits of vast earth.
For them is no escape, since Poseidon put in
bronze doors, and the fence runs on both sides.

[There Gyges, Kottos, and great-spirited Obriareos
735 live, the faithful guards of Zeus Aigiochos.

There dark earth and dim Tartaros
and the barren sea and starry sky
all have their sources and limits in a row,
terrible and dank, which even the gods abhor;
740 the chasm is great, and not until a year's end
would a man reach the bottom, if first he were within

the doors, but terrible gust after gust would carry him
here and there; it is awful even for the immortal gods]
[this is monstrous; and the terrible house
745 of dim Nyx stands covered in dark clouds]

    In front the son of Iapetos holds the wide sky
with his head and untiring arms, standing
immobile, where Nyx and Hemera come near and
address one another, passing the great threshold
750 of bronze; one will go down in, the other comes from
the door, and the house never holds both within,
but always one is out of the house and
traverses the earth, while the other is in the house
and awaits the time of her journey, when it will come;
755 one holds much-seeing light for those on earth,
the other, who holds in her arms Hypnos, brother of
Thanatos, is deadly Nyx, covered in misty cloud.

    There the children of dark Nyx have their homes,
Hypnos and Thanatos, awful gods; never does
760 shining Helios look on them with his beams,
as he goes up to the sky or comes down from the sky.
The former crosses the earth and wide backs of
the sea harmless and gentle to men, but the
other's heart is iron, and his bronze heart is
765 pitiless in his chest; he holds whomever he once
seizes of men; he is hateful even to the immortal gods.

    There in front the echoing homes of the nether god
[of mighty Hades and awesome Persephone]
stand, and a terrible dog is on guard in front,
770 unpitying possessor of an evil trick; on those
going in he fawns with his tail and both ears, but
does not let them go back out and, waiting,
eats whomever he catches going out the doors.
[of mighty Hades and awesome Persephone]

775   There dwells a goddess hated by the immortals,
terrible Styx, eldest daughter of back-flowing
Okeanos; away from the gods she lives in a noble
house, roofed with great rocks; on all sides
it reaches up to the sky with silver pillars.
780 Rarely does Iris, swift-footed daughter of Thaumas,

come as messenger over the sea's wide backs.
Whenever conflict and strife arise among the immortals
and one of those who have Olympian homes should lie,
Zeus sends Iris to bring the gods' great oath
785 from afar in a golden pitcher, the famous cold
water which trickles down from a high steep
rock; far below the wide-pathed earth it
flows from the holy river through black night;
a branch of Okeanos, a tenth part is allotted to it;
790 nine parts winding around the earth and sea's wide
backs in silver eddies fall into the sea, but the
tenth flows out from the rock, a great woe to the gods.
Whoever pours libation and breaks his oath, of the
immortals who hold the peaks of snowy Olympos,
795 lies unbreathing until the year's end;
he never comes near ambrosia and nectar
for food, but lies unbreathing and unspeaking
on a covered bed, and an evil coma covers him.
But when he ends being sick for a great year,
800 another harsher ordeal succeeds the first;
for nine years he is parted from the gods who always
are, and never joins in council and feasts,
for nine full years; in the tenth he rejoins the
meetings of the immortals who have Olympian homes.
805 The gods made the eternal and primal water of Styx
such an oath; it emerges through a forbidding place.

    There dark earth and dim Tartaros
and the barren sea and starry sky
all have their sources and limits in a row,
810 terrible and dank, which even the gods abhor.
There are shining gates and a bronze threshold
with never-ending roots, unmovable and
natural; beyond and far from all the gods
live the Titans, past gloomy Chaos.
815 But the famous helpers of loud-thundering Zeus
live in houses on Okeanos' foundations,
Kottos and Gyges; but the deep-roaring Earth-Shaker
made Briareos his son-in-law for his courage,
and gave him his daughter Kymopoleia to marry.

820   But when Zeus drove the Titans from the sky,
vast Gaia bore her youngest child Typhoeus

from the love of Tartaros, through golden Aphrodite;
his hands are strong, to do his work, and the
mighty god's legs never tire; from his shoulders
825 grew a hundred snake-heads, a dread serpent's
with dark and lambent tongues; his eyes
under the brows on the awesome heads shot fire;
[from all the heads fire blazed as he glowered]
from all the dread heads came voices which
830 spoke all unspeakable sounds; at one time,
they made sounds the gods understand; at another,
the sound of a proud bellowing bull, unstoppable
in wrath; at another, a lion with ruthless spirit;
again, sounds like a pack of dogs, marvelous to hear;
835 again, he would hiss and high mountains re-echoed.
A thing past help would have happened that day
and he would have ruled over immortals and mortals,
if the king of men and gods had not thought quickly.
He thundered hard and strong, and all the earth
840 resounded horribly, and the wide sky above and
sea and Okeanos' streams and earth's lowest parts.
Great Olympos tottered under the immortal feet
of the lord setting out, and the earth groaned.
Heat from both of them seized the violet sea,
845 from thunder and lightning, from the monster's fire,
from searing winds and from the fiery lightning-bolt.
The whole earth was boiling, and the sky and sea;
great waves raged around and over the coasts from
the immortals' attack, and endless rumbling arose;
850 Hades, lord of the dead below, trembled, and so
did the Titans around Kronos in Tartaros,
from the endless noise and awful war.

When the anger of Zeus reached its height,
he seized his weapons, thunder and lightning and
855 lightning-bolt, leaped from Olympos, and struck;
he burned all the dread monster's unspeakable heads.
When he had whipped him and broken him with blows,
he threw him down crippled, and great Gaia groaned.
Fire poured from the thunderstruck lord
860 in the dark rugged glens of the mountain where
he was hit, and the vast earth burned widely
from unspeakable heat, and melted as tin
is melted in well-bored crucibles by workmen's

skill, or as iron, hardest of all things, is
865 melted by burning fire in mountain glens
in the holy earth, by the arts of Hephaistos;
so the earth melted in the glare of blazing fire.
And Zeus, vexed in spirit, threw him into wide Tartaros.

From Typhoeus is the strength of wet-blowing winds,
870 except Notos and Boreas and clearing Zephyros;
these are a sort from the gods, a great help to mortals.
But the other winds blow false on the sea;
some fall upon the misty sea, a great plague
to mortals, and they rage with evil storm;
875 they blow unpredictably, scattering ships and
killing sailors; there is no defense against
their harm for men who meet them on the sea.
And other winds on the vast flowering earth
destroy the beautiful fields of earthborn men,
880 filling them with dust and terrible tumult.

But when the blessed gods had finished their work
and decided the matter of rights with the Titans
by force, they urged wide-seeing Olympian Zeus
to be king and rule the immortals, by Gaia's
885 advice; and he divided their honors among them.

Zeus, king of gods, made Metis his first wife,
she who knows most of gods and mortal men.
But when she was about to bear the owl-eyed
goddess Athena, then he deceived her mind with a
890 trick of wily words, and put her down in his belly,
by the advice of Gaia and starry Ouranos. Thus
they advised him, so that no other of the eternal
gods would hold the office of king but Zeus.
For from her wise children were fated to be born:
895 first a daughter, owl-eyed Tritogeneia,
like her father in strength and wise counsel,
but then she was going to bear a son
proud of heart, king of gods and men;
but first Zeus put her into his own belly,
900 so the goddess might advise him on good and evil.

Second, he married sleek Themis, who bore the Horai,
Eunomia and Dike and blooming Eirene,

who tend the works of mortal men, and the
Moirai, to whom wise Zeus gave most honor,
905 Klotho and Lachesis and Atropos, who give
mortal men to have both good and evil.

Eurynome, Okeanos' daughter of fairest form,
bore to him the three fair-cheeked Charites,
Aglaia, Euphrosyne, and lovely Thalia;
910 limb-loosening desire poured from their glancing
eyes; beautifully they glanced under their brows.

Next he came to the bed of nurturant Demeter;
she bore white-armed Persephone, whom Aidoneus
seized from her mother; but Zeus allowed it.

915   Then he loved fair-haired Mnemosyne, who bore
the nine Muses with golden headbands,
whose delight is banquets and the pleasure of song.

And Leto, joined in love to Zeus Aigiochos,
bore Apollo and archeress Artemis, beautiful
920 children beyond all of Ouranos' descendants.

Lastly he made Hera his blooming wife;
she bore Hebe and Ares and Eileithyia,
having joined in love with the king of gods and men.

He himself bore from his head owl-eyed Athena,
925 the awesome, fight-rousing, army-leading, unweary
mistress whose delight is din and wars and battles;
but Hera, who was angry and at odds with her husband,
without love's union bore famous Hephaistos,
excellent in arts beyond all of Ouranos' descendants.

930   From Amphitrite and loud-sounding Earth-Shaker
was born great and mighty Triton, who in the sea's
depth lives with his mother and lord father in
golden homes, an awful god. But to Ares, piercer
of shields, Kythereia bore Phobos and Deimos,
935 terrible ones who rout the dense ranks of men in
cold war with city-destroying Ares, and she bore
Harmonia, whom high-spirited Kadmos took as his wife.

And the Atlantid Maia bore to Zeus glorious Hermes,
herald of the gods, after going up to his holy bed.

940   And the Kadmeid Semele bore an illustrious son, much-
cheering Dionysos, after joining Zeus in love,
mortal with immortal; now they both are gods.

And Alkmene bore mighty Herakles, having
joined in love with cloud-gathering Zeus.

945   And Hephaistos, the famous lame god, made Aglaia,
youngest of the Charites, his blooming wife.

And gold-haired Dionysos took auburn Ariadne,
daughter of Minos, as his blooming wife;
Kronos' son made her immortal and ageless for him.

950   The strong son of fair-ankled Alkmene, mighty
Herakles, having finished his painful labors, took
Hebe, child of great Zeus and gold-sandaled Hera,
as his modest wife in snowy Olympos; he is
happy, who finished his great work and lives with
955   the immortals, carefree and ageless for all days.

To untiring Helios the famed Okeanid Perseis
bore Kirke and the king Aietes.
Aietes, son of Helios who shines on mortals,
by the gods' plans married fair-cheeked Idyia,
960   the daughter of the perfect river Okeanos;
she bore to him fine-ankled Medeia, conquered
in love thanks to golden Aphrodite.

Farewell now, you who have Olympian homes,
you islands, mainland, and salty sea within;
965   now, sweet-voiced Olympian Muses, daughters of
Zeus Aigiochos, sing the band of goddesses,
immortals who went to bed with mortal men
and bore children similar to gods.

The divine goddess Demeter, joined in dear love
970   with the hero Iasion in a thrice-plowed field,

in the rich land of Crete, bore kindly Ploutos,
who goes over the whole earth and the sea's wide
backs; who meets him and takes him in his arms,
the god makes rich and grants him much prosperity.

975   Harmonia, daughter of golden Aphrodite, to Kadmos
bore Ino and Semele and fair-cheeked Agaue
and Autonoe, whom long-haired Aristaios married,
and Polydoros in well-crowned Thebes.

Kallirhoe, Okeanos' daughter, joined in golden
980 Aphrodite's love to strong-hearted Chrysaor,
bore a son, the strongest of all mortals,
Geryoneus, whom mighty Herakles killed in
sea-swept Erytheia for his rolling-gaited cattle.

And Eos bore to Tithonos bronze-crested Memnon,
985 king of the Aithiopes, and the lord Emathion.
And to Kephalos she bore a glorious son, valiant
Phaethon, a man like the gods; when he was young
in the delicate flower of famous youth, a child
of tender thoughts, laughter-loving Aphrodite
990 snatched him up and took and made him innermost
keeper of her holy temples, a godlike daimon.

Aison's son, by the plans of the eternal gods,
took from Aietes, god-raised king, his daughter,
having finished the many painful labors
995 which the great and arrogant king assigned,
Pelias, violent and impetuous doer of wrong;
having finished these, Aison's son came to Iolkos
after much labor, bringing the glancing girl
on the swift ship, and made her his fresh bride.
1000 Tamed by Iason, shepherd of the people, she
bore a son Medeios, whom Phillyra's son Cheiron
raised in the mountains; great Zeus' will was done.

As for the daughters of Nereus, old man of the sea,
the divine goddess Psamathe bore Phokos from the
1005 love of Aiakos, thanks to golden Aphrodite;
and the silver-shod goddess Thetis, tamed by Peleus,
bore Achilleus, the lion-spirited manslayer.

And well-crowned Kythereia bore Aineias, having
joined in dear love with the hero Anchises
1010 on the peaks of windy Ida with many glens.

And Kirke, daughter of the Hyperionid Helios,
in the love of patient-minded Odysseus bore
Agrios and Latinos, blameless and strong;
[and she bore Telegonos thanks to golden Aphrodite]
1015 far away in a niche of holy islands
they ruled over all the famous Tyrsenians.

The divine goddess Kalypso, joined to Odysseus
in dear love, bore Nausithoos and Nausinoos.

These are the immortals who went to bed with
1020 mortal men and bore children similar to gods.
[Now, sweet-voiced Olympian Muses, daughters of
Zeus Aigiochos, sing of the race of women]

THE *LIBRARY* OF APOLLODOROS

We do not know who wrote the collection of Greek myths usually
referred to as the *Bibliotheke,* or *Library,* of Apollodoros the
Athenian, nor do we know when it was written, although most
scholars would date it to the first or second century A.D. There are
many references in ancient writings to the work of an eminent
Athenian grammarian named Apollodoros who lived in the second
century B.C., but it seems for various reasons impossible that this
Apollodoros was the author of the *Library,* which as far as we
know, is mentioned by no dated author earlier than Photius in the
ninth century A.D.

The mystery of its date and the anonymity of its author are,
in a sense, appropriate for the *Library.* No matter when it was actually written, it represents that hypothetical point in history when
Greek myth became a mythological system, fixed for all time.
Some, including perhaps the Greeks themselves, might identify
this point as the time of Hesiod and Homer, or even long before;
others might date it to the end of the fifth century, when the de-
mise of Greek tragedy crystallized the myths in their most familiar,
although often contradictory, variants. But for Apollodoros as much

as for Hesiod, the events related in myth are real and antedate all reports of them. Although the almost twenty sources cited by him range from Hesiod and Homer in the eighth century to Castor in the first century, the passage of time does not mean that myths change; it merely allows different versions to arise of what actually happened in that period before Hesiod when the events of myth took place.

The personality of the author of the *Library,* like the date at which he wrote, is completely transcended by his subject. Although preceded by a long tradition of scholarly writing on Greek myth, works which attempted either to interpret myths (e.g., Herodoros, Euhemeros, Palaiphatos) or to insert them into the history of cities or peoples (e.g., Hekataios, Akousilaos, Pherekydes), the *Library* has no purpose other than the orderly account of the totality of Greek myths in and for themselves. There is no attempt to evaluate or criticize or interpret the mythical material, nor is there any perceptible literary or artistic intention.

The following excerpts from the *Library* are taken from Book One and correspond in general to the material covered by Hesiod's *Theogony.*[36]

> 1.1.1   Ouranos [Sky], the first ruler of the whole world, married Gaia [Earth]. His first children were Brireus, Gyes, and Kottos, who are called the Hundred-Handed and were unsurpassed in size and power, each having one hundred hands and fifty heads.
>
> 1.1.2   After these, Gaia bore to him the Kyklopes, each with one eye on his forehead, Arges, Steropes, and Brontes. Ouranos however bound these and threw them into Tartaros (this is a dark place in Hades, as far away from earth as earth is from sky).
>
> 1.1.3   Ouranos again had children by Gaia: the sons, called Titans, were Okeanos, Koios, Hyperion, Kreios, Iapetos, and Kronos, the youngest; the daughters, called Titanides, were Tethys, Rhea, Themis, Mnemosyne, Phoibe, Dione, and Theia.
>
> 1.1.4   Gaia, angered by the loss of her children who had been thrown into Tartaros, persuaded the Titans to attack their father and gave an adamantine sickle to Kronos. All but Okeanos took part in the attack, and Kronos cut off his father's genitals and threw them into the sea; Alekto, Tisiphone, and Megaira, the Erinyes [Furies], were

born from the drops of flowing blood. After deposing Ouranos, they brought back their brothers who had been thrown into Tartaros and entrusted the rule to Kronos.

1.1.5   But he bound them and imprisoned them again in Tartaros, and married his sister Rhea. Since both Gaia and Ouranos prophesied to him that his rule would be usurped by his own son, he would swallow his children as they were born. He swallowed Hestia, the firstborn, then Demeter and Hera, and after them Plouton and Poseidon.

1.1.6   Angered by this, Rhea went to Crete when she happened to be pregnant with Zeus. The baby was born in a cave of Dikte and entrusted by his mother for nurturance to the Kouretes and the nymphs Adrasteia and Ida, daughters of Melisseus.

1.1.7   The nymphs therefore nursed the child with the milk of Amaltheia, while the Kouretes, in arms, guarded the baby in the cave by striking their shields with their spears, so that Kronos would not hear the child's voice. Rhea meanwhile wrapped a stone in a blanket as though it were a newborn child and gave it to Kronos to swallow.

1.2.1   When Zeus was full-grown, he acquired the assistance of Metis, the daughter of Okeanos; she gave Kronos a drug to swallow, by which he was compelled to disgorge first the stone, then the children he had swallowed. With their help Zeus carried on the war against Kronos and the Titans. After they had fought for ten years, Gaia prophesied victory to Zeus if he would have as allies those who had been thrown into Tartaros. He therefore killed Kampe, the custodian of their chains, and released them. The Kyklopes then gave Zeus thunder and lightning and the thunderbolt; and they gave a helmet to Plouton and a trident to Poseidon. Armed with these they conquered the Titans, shut them up in Tartaros, and appointed the Hundred-Handed as guards. As for themselves, they cast lots for the rule; Zeus obtained the kingship of the sky, Poseidon that of the sea, and Plouton that of Hades.

1.2.2   These are the descendants of the Titans: the children of Okeanos and Tethys were Asia, Styx, Elektra, Doris, Eurynome, and Metis, the Okeanides; the children of Koios and Phoibe were Asteria and Leto; the children of Hyperion and Theia were Eos [Dawn], Helios [Sun], and Selene [Moon]; the children of Kreios and Eurybia, daughter of Pontos [Sea], were Astraios, Pallas, and Perses.

1.2.3   The children of Iapetos and Asia were Atlas, who holds the sky on his shoulders, Prometheus, Epimetheus, and Menoitios, who was struck by Zeus' thunderbolt during the Titanomachy [Titan War] and thrown down to Tartaros.

1.2.4   The child of Kronos and Philyra was Cheiron, a centaur of double nature; the children of Eos and Astraios were the winds and stars; the child of Perses and Asteria was Hekate; the children of Pallas and Styx were Nike, Kratos, Zelos, and Bia.

1.2.5   The water of Styx, which flows from a rock in Hades, was made by Zeus into an object by which oaths were sworn; he gave this honor to Styx because she and her children had fought against the Titans with him.

1.2.6   The children of Pontos and Gaia were Phorkys, Thaumas, Nereus, Eurybia, and Keto. The children of Thaumas and Elektra were Iris and the Harpies, Aello and Okypete; the children of Phorcys and Keto were the Phorkides and the Gorgons (of whom we shall speak when we relate the adventures of Perseus).

1.2.7   The children of Nereus and Doris were the Nereids, whose names were Kymothoe, Speio, Glaukonome, Nausithoe, Halia, Erato, Sao, Amphitrite, Eunike, Thetis, Eulimene, Agaue, Eudora, Doto, Pherousa, Galateia, Aktaia, Pontomedousa, Hippothoe, Lysianassa, Kymo, Eione, Halimede, Plexaura, Eukrante, Proto, Kalypso, Panope, Kranto, Neomeris, Hipponoe, Ianeira, Polynome, Autonoe, Melite, Dione, Nesaia, Dero, Euagore, Psamathe, Eumolpe, Ione, Dynamene, Keto, and Limnoreia.

1.3.1   Zeus married Hera and became the father of Hebe, Eileithyia, and Ares, but he had sexual relations with many women, both mortal and immortal. His daughters by Themis, the daughter of Ouranos, were the Horai: Eirene [Peace], Eunomia [Order], and Dike [Justice]; and the Moirai: Klotho, Lachesis, and Atropos. By Dione he had Aphrodite; by Eurynome, daughter of Okeanos, he had the Charites: Aglaia, Euphrosyne, and Thaleia; by Styx he had Persephone; by Mnemosyne he had the Muses: first Kalliope, then Kleio, Melpomene, Euterpe, Erato, Terpsichore, Ourania, Thaleia, and Polymnia.

1.3.5   Hera gave birth to Hephaistos without having had sexual intercourse, but Homer says that she bore him to Zeus. When Hephaistos came to help his bound mother, Zeus threw him out of the sky; for Zeus had hung Hera from Olympos when she sent a storm against Herakles, who was at sea after capturing Troy. Hephaistos fell on Lemnos and his feet were crippled, but Thetis saved him.

1.3.6   Although Metis changed into many shapes in order to avoid a sexual encounter, Zeus had intercourse with her. When she became pregnant, he quickly swallowed her since she said that, after the daughter to whom she was about to give birth, she would bear a son who would be the ruler of the sky. This is what Zeus feared when he swallowed Metis. When it was time for the birth to take place, Prometheus [or, as others say, Hephaistos] struck the head of Zeus with an axe; and Athena leaped up from the top of his head with her weapons, at the river Triton.

1.6.1   Gaia, who was angry because of the Titans, gave birth to the Giants by Ouranos; these were insuperable in size and strength, and frightening in appearance, with long hair falling from their heads and chins, and the scales of dragons for feet. They were born, as some say, in Phlegrai, but others say that they were born in Pallene. They would throw rocks and flaming oaks at the sky. Porphyrion surpassed the rest, and so did Alkyoneus, who was immortal while fighting in the land where he was born. He also drove the cattle of Helios from Erytheia. The gods had an oracle that none of the Giants could be killed by the gods, but would die if a certain mortal were the ally of the gods. Gaia learned this and searched for an herbal drug so that they could not be killed by a mortal. Zeus commanded Eos, Selene, and Helios not to shine, and he was the first to pick the herb; he then had Athena summon Herakles to be his ally. Herakles first shot Alkyoneus, but when he fell on the ground he began to revive; at Athena's suggestion, Herakles dragged him out of Pallene and thus he died.

1.6.2   Porphyrion attacked both Herakles and Hera in the battle. But Zeus caused him to lust after Hera; when he tore her clothes, wanting to rape her, she called for help. Zeus struck him with a thunderbolt and Herakles killed him with an arrow. As for the rest, Apollo shot Ephialtes with an arrow in the left eye, and Herakles shot him in the right eye; Dionysos killed Eurytos with his thyrsos; Hekate killed Klytios with torches; Hephaistos killed Mimas with searing metal; Athena threw the island of Sicily on Enkelados as he fled and stripped off the skin of Pallas to protect her in battle; Poseidon, having pursued Polybotes through the sea until he came to the island of Kos, tore off the part of the island called Nisyron and threw it on him; Hermes, wearing the cap of Hades, killed Hippolytos in the battle; Artemis killed Aigaion; the Moirai, fighting with bronze clubs, killed Agrios and Thoas; Zeus killed the rest by striking them with thunderbolts, and Herakles shot them all with arrows as they died.

1.6.3   When the gods had conquered the Giants, Gaia became angrier; she had intercourse with Tartaros and gave birth in Kilikia to Typhon, who had the combined nature of man and beast. In size and strength he surpassed all the sons of Gaia; from the thighs upward, he had a human shape of such immense size that he towered over all the mountains and his head often touched the stars. One of his hands stretched toward evening and the other stretched toward dawn; from them projected a hundred serpent's heads. From the thighs downward, he had great coils of vipers which hissed loudly and, when uncoiled, reached up to his head. Wings covered his entire body, squalid hair on his head and jaw blew in the wind, and he flashed fire from his eyes. This was the appearance and size of Typhon when, hissing and shouting and throwing burning rocks, he made his way to the sky itself; from his mouth he sent a great spray of fire. When the gods saw him rushing toward the sky, they fled to Egypt and, being pursued, changed their shapes into animals. Zeus struck Typhon with thunderbolts when he was far off; when he was close, he struck him down with an adamantine sickle, and pursued him as he fled to Mount Kasios, which is situated above Syria. There Zeus saw that he was wounded and wrestled with him. But Typhon entangled him in his coils and held him; seizing the sickle and cutting the sinews of his hands and feet, he hoisted him on his shoulders and brought him through the sea to Kilikia where he put him down in the Korykian cave. Having hidden the sinews in a bearskin he left them there also, and stationed as a guard the she-serpent Delphyne, a virgin who was half-beast. Hermes and Aigipan, however, stole the sinews and fitted them to Zeus without being seen. He, having recovered his former strength, suddenly came riding in a chariot of winged horses from the sky and, throwing thunderbolts, pursued Typhon to the mountain called Nysa, where the Moirai deceived him in his flight, for he tasted the ephemeral fruit, having been persuaded that his strength would be increased. Therefore, again being pursued, he came to Thrace, and while fighting around Haimos he threw whole mountains. When these were thrust back at him by the thunderbolt, a quantity of blood streamed out from the mountain, and they say that the mountain is called Haimos for this reason. When he hastened to flee through the Sicilian sea, Zeus threw Aitna, a mountain in Sicily, on him. This mountain is of great size and to this day they say that eruptions of fire from it are due to the thunderbolts that were thrown.

1.7.1 I have now said enough about that matter. Prometheus, having made men from water and earth, also gave them fire, hiding it in a fennel-stalk without the knowledge of Zeus. When Zeus learned of this, he ordered Hephaistos to nail Prometheus's body to Mount Caucasus, a Skythian mountain on which he was fastened and confined for many years. Each day an eagle flew down and fed on the lobes of his liver, which grew during the night. Prometheus paid this penalty for the stolen fire until Herakles later released him.

CHAPTER FOUR

ORIGIN AND
SUCCESSION

THE BEGINNING

Children have a natural and easily observable curiosity about the process of birth; this curiosity, as well as the likelihood of its repression, is intensified by its inevitable connection with the child's curiosity about parental sexuality. The question "Where do babies come from?" is really a generalized combination of two questions of great emotional importance to the child: "Where did *I* come from?" and "How did my parents produce me?" The generalization itself is already a first indication of repression.

Where in myth might we expect to find a representation of the answers to these questions, which would necessarily include also the child's memories of his own beginning and earliest existence? In general, everywhere—every birth of a hero reflects the individual's repressed curiosity and ideas about the circumstances of his own birth. But specifically and especially it will be in stories of the beginning—of the world, of gods, of men—that we may expect to find a mythical version of the first great subject of infantile sexual curiosity, the beginning of the individual.

For the ancient Greeks the true story of the origin of the world begins with the spontaneous emergence of four uncaused entities—Chaos, Gaia (Earth), Tartaros, and Eros (Desire)—in lines 116–20 of Hesiod's *Theogony:*

> First of all Chaos came into being; but next
> wide-breasted Gaia, always safe foundation of all

126

> immortals who possess the peaks of snowy Olympos,
> and dim Tartaros in a recess of the wide-pathed Earth,
> and Eros, most beautiful among the immortal gods

Both Plato and Aristotle refer to this passage but omit the mention of Tartaros, and many modern editors regard the line in which Tartaros appears (119) as a later interpolation. It appears in other ancient sources, however, and in our manuscripts; the difficulty concerning it may lie in the lack of any immediately evident reason for the inclusion of Tartaros in a list of cosmogonic entities. The relevance of Chaos and Earth in such a list, on the other hand, is virtually self-evident. The concept of a primordial Chaos is reminiscent of the boundless and featureless watery waste called Nun in Egyptian cosmogony, the primeval expanse called Tiamat in Babylonian myth, and the formless void and abyss of Genesis. Similarly, the early and necessary existence of Earth is found in all Near Eastern cosmogonies: for example, the *Pyramid Texts* of the Egyptian Old Kingdom, the production of Earth and Sky from primordial waters in the Babylonian *Enuma Elish,* and the appearance of Earth at the beginning of both the Priestly and Yahwist accounts in Genesis (1.1, 2.4). While Hesiod's inclusion of Eros has no clear parallel in other cosmogonies (although a somewhat similar function is performed by the fire-god Agni in Vedic myth),[1] nevertheless it is easy to see in the figure of Eros a kind of demiurgic principle whose purpose is to keep the process of creation going, a function that falls somewhere between the activity of the creator-gods of the Near East and the fundamental principle or structure of the universe, which the first Greek philosophers in Ionia (like their counterparts today) were seeking to identify. For once Eros has come into existence, all further production is reproduction, with or without the benefit of sexual intercourse. It is only the first four entities, from Chaos to Eros, that come into being without coming from something else; immediately after the appearance of Eros the first suggestions of begetting and coupling occur, as Chaos produces Erebos (Darkness) and Nyx (Night), they mate to produce Aither (Upper Air) and Hemera (Day), and Gaia begins having children, at first by herself and then through intercourse with her son Ouranos.

Let us return now to the four uncaused primal entities, Chaos through Eros, and see if an understanding of the passage in which they occur can be achieved by regarding them not as mythical versions of a cosmic reality but rather as cosmic symbols of a psychological reality. We should expect to find at the very start of a cosmogonic myth what is often implicit in other sorts of myth, a curiosity about origins and a search for the beginning of whatever matters for the individual or the culture (as in the many etiological myths explaining the origin of a ritual, a family, a state, or some aspect of social organization). Translated into philosophical terms, this curiosity became one of the leading motives behind the beginning of Greek philosophy in the sixth century. The first philosophers were greatly concerned with the search for the original substance, or fundamental principle, of the universe; Thales thought it was water, Anaximander identified it as the "unlimited" which contained the great oppositions (moist/dry, warm/cold, etc.), Anaximenes believed it was air and that all change was caused by air dilating and condensing, Heraklitos opted for fire, Pythagoras for number, Parmenides for the One, and Empedokles for a set of four primal substances (earth, air, fire, water). Although these first philosophical enquiries represent a different kind of conceptualization from the mythical quest for origins, the original motive may well have been the same for both. It may seem that the crucial difference between Greek myth and philosophy is the reliance of the latter on empirical observation and rational deduction; the theories of Thales, Anaximander, and Anaximenes at the beginning of Ionian science may be viewed as the logical result of the empirical knowledge that water solidifies and evaporates. But myths too have an empirical base, and so do dreams, in the concrete experience of emotional needs and the remembered childhood of every individual. Furthermore, myth is as logical as philosophy and science, although the logic of myth is that of unconscious thought. It might be possible to differentiate between myth and philosophy on the basis of primary process versus secondary process, but even this distinction cannot be systematically maintained; Lévi-Strauss has shown the pervasiveness of a kind of preconscious rationality in so-called primitive thought,[2] and it can hardly be argued that even modern philosophy and science are devoid of primary process thinking.

A more obvious difference between myth and philosophy is the mythic tendency to avoid abstraction, despite the presence in Hesiod's genealogies of such abstract entities as Deceit, Friendship,

Forgetfulness, Destruction, and Oath; these are quasi-philosophical intrusions into myth and have no subsequent role or importance in myth. In myths as in dreams, the thing symbolized is a concrete and experienced phenomenon, and in a myth of the beginning of the world what we should expect to find is a symbolic representation of the first and perhaps most important questions concerning origins in the life of every individual, those questions that Freud called the "sexual researches of childhood."

Cosmogonic, theogonic, and anthropogonic myths elaborate the typical objects of a young child's curiosity: Where did I come from? Why are there different sexes? Who are my parents and what are they like, both now and before I was born? And the earliest and most fundamental question of all: What is the difference between "me" and "not-me"? As the anthropologist Edmund Leach said, "the child's first and continuing problem is to determine the initial boundary,"[3] and it is precisely this problem reflected in the passage of Hesiod. As we shall see, the five lines which announce the mythical beginning of the world accurately and succinctly summarize the unconscious experience of the beginning of the individual's world.

MYTHIC SYMBIOSIS:
CHAOS AND GAIA

Why does the world begin with Chaos? The Greek word *chaos,* associated with the verb *chasko,* signifies a void, an abyss, unlimited space, infinite darkness, unformed matter; it does *not* signify disorder or confusion, the usual meanings of the English word "chaos." Since *chasko* means "gape," "open," "yawn," there may be the suggestion of something (a womb?) that opens to bring forth life, but in the actual occurrences of *chaos* in Greek literature we find much stronger connotations of impenetrable darkness and unmeasurable totality, of an immense opacity in which order is nonexistent or at least unperceived. Although it is difficult to see how any order can be prior to the existence of Chaos, some scholars have argued on the basis of its etymology that Chaos signifies "a moment of division or separation" and thus "implies a change that takes place in some already existing entity or situation."[4] This is certainly possible, but problems arise when it comes to identifying the "entity or situation": the usual explanation, derived from Near Eastern parallels, that Chaos represents the gap between Earth and Sky (before these two actually exist) is, as West says, "like the grin before the Cheshire Cat."[5] If we accept the view that some primal substance or situation antedates the existence of Chaos, we must remember that Chaos means "darkness" as well as "gap": although a change in a pre-existent situation may be implied, this change itself is lost in darkness and imperceptibility.[6]

Perhaps we can best arrive at a solution to the question of Chaos by turning momentarily to the second entity in Hesiod's list. Gaia, or Earth, is of course the mythological mother figure par excellence. In virtually all cosmologies (with the notable exception of the Egyptian), Earth is the primordial maternal symbol, and in Greek myth especially she plays an important role as the mother and wife of Ouranos (Sky), as mother of the Titans, and as grandmother of Zeus and the Olympian gods. Indeed, the connection between Earth and mother was so obvious and strong in Greek thought that Plato reversed the symbolism, saying that "the woman in her conception and generation is but the imitation of the earth, and not the earth of the woman" (*Menexenos* 238a).

If we remember that Gaia is both Earth and, as the Greeks called her, "Mother of all," and if we approach this myth of the beginning from the viewpoint of the individual's earliest experiences, we can surmise that Chaos represents a stage of life before any perception of the mother exists. This stage, comprising the first six months or so of a child's life, is regarded by modern psychoanalysis as crucially important for psychic development and its technical name is the symbiotic stage.[7] If we put our question like this—What is the meaning of a world that begins with an undifferentiated opacity followed by the emergence of Gaia (Mother/Earth) as the first recognizable entity?—the answer would be that Chaos, a state prior to perception, represents the situation of the child in the symbiotic state, defined by Mahler as the "state of undifferentiation, of fusion with mother, in which the 'I' is not yet differentiated from the 'not I.' "[8]

Symbiotic memories appear prominently elsewhere in Greek myth (and in all mythological systems), but we see them most often and obviously in myths of a primal paradise where there is no desire because there is no lack of gratification. This aspect of symbiosis, of which the Genesis Garden of Eden is probably the

best-known example, appears in Greek myth in such instances as
the Garden of the Hesperides, scene of Herakles' eleventh labor,[9]
and Hesiod's golden race, which begins the Five Ages (*Works
and Days* 109–20):

First a golden race of mortal men were
110 made by the immortals who have Olympian homes.
They lived in Kronos' time, when he ruled the sky;
they lived like gods with carefree hearts,
free and apart from trouble and pain; grim old age
did not afflict them, but with legs and arms always
115 strong they played in delight, apart from all evils;
They died as if subdued by sleep; and all good things
were theirs; the fertile earth produced fruit
by itself, abundantly and unforced; willingly and
effortlessly they ruled their lands with many goods,
120 rich in flocks and dear to the blessed gods.

Hesiod's account of the Golden Age, like the myths of the
Garden of Eden or the Garden of the Hesperides where, according
to Euripides, "streams flow with ambrosia" (*Hippolytos* 748–49)
is a fantasy of origin and of a lost and irrecoverable bliss. The
wide range of these "original paradise" myths, as well as their
emotional appeal, is due to their derivation from the universal human experience, unconsciously remembered, of primal gratification,
loss, and desire in earliest infancy.

While paradisal myths represent symbiosis through images of
instant and total gratification, a timeless and effortless Nirvana
without desire or the burdens of individuation, Hesiod's Chaos
portrays symbiosis under another aspect, as an undifferentiated
world in which the child cannot yet perceive the mother, or anything else, as separate. Structure and order exist, to be sure, but
they are as yet unknown to the child; they first enter perception
during the process of separation-individuation and the initial awareness of the difference between self and other. Therefore Chaos
may be regarded as a representation of the symbiotic phase as undifferentiation and imperception, as a formless totality; a change
has been caused in an already existing situation, but the child can
recognize neither the situation nor the change.

Although the end of symbiosis is due to developmental processes, the child knows nothing of this causality; he only knows

that one half of what had been the symbiotic unity is now another person, separate from himself. This "other person" is of course the mother; the child learns that she (who now embodies the world that has been lost, the other half of the self) is separate through her absence, and it is only through this awareness of her as separate that he comes to recognize himself as separate. This process is sometimes called "mirroring" by psychoanalysts; as if recognizing his image in a mirror, the child deduces his separateness from that of his mother. The transition from symbiosis to separation by this means appears in the Hesiodic myth as the emergence of Gaia, the mother who is the first object of the child's perception and the first structuring principle in the child's life.

MYTHIC INDIVIDUATION:
TARTAROS AND EROS

At this point in the mythological scenario, symbiosis has ended and separation-individuation, the state in which the rest of life is destined to be spent, has begun. This drastic change, which appears to us as a sign of the child's developing independence, must be seen by the child, however, as a loss. What was once part of the self is now a separate object; whether the mother who leaves the child's presence will ever return is from now on a question and a source of anxiety. What is from one perspective the birth of the individual, of an ego and a sense of identity, is from another the initial experience of loss, frustration, and anxiety. And it is also the occasion for the first emergence of desire—for mother, for security, and ultimately for restoration of the lost symbiotic state.

This experience of primal loss and the beginning of desire, based on the perception of the mother as separate at the end of symbiosis, appears in Hesiod as the appearance of Tartaros and Eros immediately after Gaia. Tartaros, like many cosmogonic phenomena, is both a location and also a (barely) anthropomorphized being, who mates and produces offspring but has no personality or career. Tartaros is not mentioned in the *Odyssey,* but appears in the *Iliad* as the lowest part of the underworld; Hesiod's description in the *Theogony* (720–25) is very similar to that of Homer in the *Iliad* (8.13–16):

> dim Tartaros
> far away, where the pit is deepest below the earth,
> where there are bronze gates and an iron threshold,
> as far below Hades's house as the sky is from earth.

In early Greek literature the underworld is usually called the "house of Hades (and/or Persephone)"; later (and once in Homer, *Iliad* 23.244) "home of" tends to be omitted, and the place as well as the god who rules it is called simply Hades. In the *Theogony* the underworld is everything below the surface of Earth, and Tartaros, the lowest part of the underworld, seems to be also the lowest part of Earth. Thus, while the Titans and the monster Typhoeus are said specifically to have been thrown into Tartaros by Zeus, the children of Ouranos are put by their father in a "dark hole" or "hiding-place" (Gk. *keuthmon*) of Earth (*Theogony* 158), and Zeus later rescues some of them from "under the Earth" (*Theogony* 621). Aeschylus also speaks of a "deep dark hole" (*keuthmon, Prometheus* 222), but of Tartaros rather than of Earth.

Unlike Apollodoros, who says that the three Kyklopes and the three Hundred-Handed were thrown into Tartaros but does not name the location of the Titans before they castrate their father, Hesiod seems to imply that all eighteen children of Ouranos are kept beneath the Earth, presumably in Tartaros. Hesiod's text, however, is vague on whether some or all of Ouranos' children were beneath the Earth (depending on whether the word "all" in *Theogony* 157 refers to all the children or all the Hundred-Handed), and vague also on whether the Kyklopes were imprisoned by Ouranos or Kronos or each in turn (depending on who is meant by "father" in *Theogony* 502).

Tartaros, then, is certainly the place where the Titans and Typhoeus are punished and presumably the place where the Titans, Kyklopes, and Hundred-Handed are put by Ouranos to prevent their birth; as West says, "Ouranos begets eighteen children, but prevents them from being born, apparently by continuing his intercourse with Gaia."[10] The Titans emerge after the castration of Ouranos until their defeat by Zeus again relegates them to Tartaros; the Kyklopes and Hundred-Handed may remain continuously in Tartaros until their release by Zeus or, as Apollodoros says and Hesiod may be interpreted to say, they may be freed by Kronos, imprisoned again by Kronos, and finally freed by Zeus.

In the *Theogony*, Tartaros is a place of punishment. The Titans are punished for what they did to their father and because they, like Typhoeus, lost to Zeus in the battle for cosmic supremacy. If the Titans are also put in Tartaros at birth, as both Hesiod and Apollodoros imply, this is a kind of proleptic punishment for what their father is afraid they will try to do (and, in fact, succeed in doing). Thus Tartaros appears as the place where losers in generational conflict are confined.

In subsequent literature, Tartaros was gradually localized as that part of the mythical underworld in which certain famous sinners suffer eternal punishment. Although the list was subject to substitution and amplification, there were four canonical sufferers in Tartaros: Tityos, Sisyphos, and Tantalos, whom Odysseus saw when he visited the underworld, and Ixion, whose crime and punishment are first mentioned by the poet Pindar (*Pythian* 2.21–48) and are summarized by Apollodoros.

> And I [Odysseus] saw Tityos, son of glorious Gaia,
> lying on the ground; he lay over nine acres, and
> two vultures, sitting on either side, tore at his liver,
> entering the bowels, and he could not ward them off with
> his hands; for he had attacked Leto, Zeus' noble bedmate,
> as she went to Pytho through beautiful Panopeus.
> *Odyssey* 11.576–92

> Soon afterward he [Apollo] also killed Tityos, who was the son of Zeus and Elare, the daughter of Orchomenos. Zeus had had intercourse with Elare and then had concealed her under the earth in fear of Hera; he then brought into the light Tityos, the huge son with whom Elare had been pregnant. Tityos saw Leto when she came to Pytho and, conquered by desire, tried to seduce her. She, however, called on her children and they shot him with arrows. And he is punished even after death, for vultures eat his heart in Hades.   Apollodoros 1.4.1

> And I saw Tantalos, suffering strong pains,
> standing in a pool which came up near his chin;
> he appeared thirsty, but could get nothing to drink;
> whenever the old man bent down, wanting to drink,

the water was drained and disappeared, and at his feet
the black earth appeared, and a god made it dry.
High-branched trees over his head poured down fruit,
pears and pomegranates and apple trees with shining fruit,
sweet figs and olives ready to pick;
when the old man straightened up to reach with his hands,
the wind would throw the fruit toward shadowing clouds.

Odyssey 11.582–92

Some say that he is punished in this way because he revealed the mysteries of the gods to men, or because he wanted to share ambrosia with his comrades.

Apollodoros, *Epitome* 2.1

And I saw Sisyphos, suffering strong pains,
trying to lift a monstrous stone with both hands.
Bracing himself with hands and feet, he would
push the stone up to the crest; but when he was about
to throw it over the top, the weight would turn it back;
then again the pitiless stone rolled to the plain.
But he would strain and push again, while sweat
poured down from his limbs, and dust rose from his head.

Odyssey 11.593–600

Sisyphos, another son of Aiolos, founded Ephyra, now called Korinthos, and married Merope, a daughter of Atlas. Their son was Glaukos, and the son of Glaukos by Eurymede was Bellerophon, who killed the fire-breathing Chimaira. Sisyphos is punished in Hades by rolling a stone with his hands and head; he wants to throw it over, but after it is pushed by him it again falls backward. He undergoes this punishment because of Aigina, the daughter of Asopos, since he is said to have informed Asopos, when he was searching for his daughter, that Zeus had secretly carried her off. Apollodoros 1.9.3

Ixion fell in love with Hera and tried to rape her. When she disclosed this, Zeus wanted to learn if it were true, and so he made a cloud in the likeness of Hera and laid it at his side. Ixion then boasted of having had sex with Hera, and Zeus tied him to a wheel, on which he pays the penalty of being carried by the winds through the air. And the child of the cloud and Ixion was Kentauros.

Apollodoros, *Epitome* 1.20

The common characteristic of the crimes of all four of the inhabitants of Tartaros is that they attempted to satisfy a sexual desire for one of Zeus' mates or committed a symbolic equivalent of this desire. Tityos tried to rape Leto, the sixth of Zeus' seven wives (*Theogony* 918–20) and mother of Apollo and Artemis, but was shot by her children before he could succeed. Ixion attempted to rape Hera, the seventh and last of Zeus's wives, but was deceived by Zeus, who substituted a phantom Hera made out of cloud for his wife. In the cases of Tantalos and Sisyphos, however, straightforward oedipal assault is replaced by an infantile metaphoric equivalent: Tantalos is punished for having revealed to men the "mysteries of the gods," and Sisyphos is punished for having revealed the secret that Zeus had carried off Aigina. A parallel account is found in the myth of the Theban prophet Teiresias, who is punished with blindness, in one version, for having revealed the "secrets of the gods" (Apollodoros 3.6.7). If we knew nothing further about the exact content of these secrets, we might nevertheless suppose, on the hypothesis that myths represent the wish fulfillments of childhood fantasies, that the "secrets" of the gods are in fact the secrets of the parents, specifically the secrets of parental sexuality. The chief objects of a male child's sexual curiosity are the mother's body and the parents' sexual activity, and it is by wanting to look at these that the child's sexual curiosity and incestuous impulses are first expressed. It would seem therefore that the real crime of those who reveal the secrets of the gods is not so much the act of revealing but rather the prior observation of a forbidden sexual sight (a "primal scene fantasy"); telling the secrets to others is not the crime but is instead the proof that the crime has been committed.

The assumption that revealing the secrets of the gods is a symbolic representation of looking at a forbidden sexual scene is conformed in the case of Sisyphos, who tells Asopos that he saw Zeus' rape of Aigina. The same is true of Teiresias, blinded because he revealed the secret of Zeus' affair with Alkmene to her husband Amphitryon (or, in other variations of the same offense, because he saw a goddess and his mother naked, or because he offended Hera with the extent of his sexual knowledge).[11]

As for the crime of Tantalos,[12] we are never told the content of the secrets, or "mysteries," of the gods that he revealed to men. Nevertheless, it seems reasonable to suppose that these secrets must be similar to those revealed by Sisyphos and Teiresias, an assumption that is supported by the nature of the other crimes with which he was charged: both Apollodoros (*Epitome* 2.1) and Pindar (*Olympian* 1.59–64) say that he stole the ambrosia of the gods, and Pindar in the same poem also mentions, but says he does not believe, the common story that Tantalos was so obsessed with proving himself superior to the gods that he cut up his son Pelops and served him to the gods for dinner. If any of the gods ate a piece of Pelops, Tantalos figured, this would prove that he knew something that they did not know. All the gods recognized Pelops on their plates and refused to eat, with the exception of Demeter. Distraught because her daughter Persephone had disappeared, she was picking at her food absentmindedly and inadvertently ate Pelops' shoulder. The other gods, horrified at what had happened, punished Tantalos and put Pelops back together; they made an ivory shoulder to replace the missing part and restored him to life.[13]

The theft of ambrosia is an attempt to usurp a paternal prerogative. Ambrosia is the food of the gods, the source of their immortality (the literal meaning of Gk. *ambrosia*). Ambrosia is thus the sign of the difference between the gods and mortals; it is what gods have but men want (according to Athenaios [281b, citing the epic *Nostoi*], Tantalos is punished for wanting "to live in the same way as the gods"). From a psychological perspective, the wish of men (that is, children) to win the prerogative of the gods (that is, parents) is an oedipal desire; the paternal possession that the son wants, but fears he will be punished for wanting, is the mother (or, to put the same wish in other terms, the sexual power and freedom of the father). The oedipal nature of the theft of ambrosia is confirmed in three ways: (1) as a result of his crime Tantalos is punished in Tartaros, and his fellow prisoners there have all committed obviously oedipal crimes; (2) ambrosia is the Greek version of various divine substances in Indo-European mythology that symbolize semen and paternal sexuality;[14] (3) the crime of Tantalos is similar to the crime of the culture-hero Prometheus, who stole fire (another divine prerogative) and gave it to men. The punishment of Prometheus is almost exactly identical to the punishment suffered by the oedipal criminal Tityos in Tartaros; both have their livers eaten by a bird (Prometheus' eagle) or birds (Tityos' vultures), and the livers of both grow back regularly (that of Prometheus daily, that of Tityos monthly). On the assumption that similarity in punishment denotes similarity in crime, the theft of fire is then equivalent to Tityos' attempt to rape Zeus' wife.

The sexual significance of fire is widespread and well attested in mythology and folklore. In Greek myth and philosophy the cosmic symbol of the female sexual role is the earth, while male sexuality is represented sometimes by water, sometimes by its opposite, fire, and sometimes by a combination of the two. Thus philosophers from Anaximander and Heraklitos to Protagoras and Theophrastos spoke of fire and heat as the generative element in nature, often in the context of an activating principle working on an otherwise inert mixture of earth and water. Aristotle's comment (*Metaphysics* 278b22) that the hot and cold are active whereas the wet and dry (i.e., water and earth) are passive finds an interesting parallel in the myths that attribute the creation of the first men or the first woman from earth and water to the work of the fire-gods Hephaistos or Prometheus. Since earth is the great mother from whom all life springs, water represents the fructifying rain that falls from the sky, the semen of the sky-god falling upon the earth-goddess. This symbolism is vividly expressed in a fragment of the lost *Danaides* of Aeschylus:

> Eros makes holy Sky lie with Earth, Eros makes Earth
> want to lie with Sky; Rain falling from Sky's coming
> makes Earth pregnant. She bears flocks of sheep, and
> grain, so men may live; the forest comes to life,
> watered by this marriage.

In light of the seminal symbolism of rain, we might suppose that there is an association between the noun *ouranos* and the verb *ourein* (to urinate). Since in the unconscious as in many folk customs urine can symbolize semen,[15] the generational function of the paternal sky god is implied in his name itself, which could be translated "Urinator."

In myth the phallic significance of fire appears most clearly in the form of Zeus' lightning, the emblematic possession that establishes and ensures his rule over gods and men. That the lightning ultimately represents Zeus' overwhelming sexual power can be seen in the myth of Semele's death; tricked by Hera into demanding that her lover Zeus have sex with her in the same way that he did with his divine mate, she was instantly incinerated by

Zeus, who burst through the bedroom door hurling lightning bolts. The story is told by Apollodoros (3.4.3) a bit differently from usual, since he has Semele die of fright:

> Zeus fell in love with Semele and went to bed with her behind Hera's back. But she was deceived by Hera and, when Zeus agreed to do whatever she asked, she asked him to come in the same way he came when he was courting Hera. Zeus could not refuse, and so, arriving at her bedroom in a chariot, accompanied by thunder and lightning, he threw a thunderbolt. Semele died of fright and Zeus, seizing the six-month-old fetus from the fire, sewed it in his thigh. When Semele died, the other daughters of Cadmus began a rumor that Semele had had an affair with some mortal, had blamed it on Zeus, and for this reason had been incinerated. But in due time Zeus undid the stitches and gave birth to Dionysos, whom he gave to Hermes.

The sexualization of fire and water/lightning and rain as male means of procreativity is due of course to a simple question: If Sky is the father and Earth is the mother, how do they get together to produce offspring?

The other crime of Tantalos, that he killed and served his son Pelops to the gods, is clearly an oedipal offense also. The very act by which Tantalos eliminates the potential threat of his own son is at the same time an effort to prove himself superior to Zeus, who is the real, as well as symbolic, father of Tantalos. In addition, the cannibalistic nature of his crime is reminiscent of Kronos, the paradigmatic oedipal god who, as we shall see, castrated his father Ouranos and then swallowed his children in an ultimately futile endeavor to prevent his own overthrow.

We have seen that the offenses of the four criminals in Tartaros are essentially the same; each of them represents the male child's impossible wish to replace the father in his mother's affection. If this is true, we should expect that the punishments suffered by the four will also be a set of variations on the same psychological theme. In one way or another, each of the crimes signifies oedipal striving, the epitome of impossible desire, and each of the punishments signifies frustration, of appetite or endeavor, and enforced immobilization. Furthermore, since the crimes are sexual offenses and the law of talion ("an eye for an eye") is dominant both in the unconscious and in early cultures, the four punishments must ultimately represent castration (Freud once said that "every punishment is ultimately castration").[16] The child's fear that his illicit desire will lead to his castration, a fear that compels him to give up the desire, is reflected in the punishment of those who do not relinquish their desire and are therefore symbolically castrated. To be frustrated in desire and effort is both the essence of castration and also the necessary sign and consequence of a desire that cannot and must not be fulfilled.

But at the same time as these punishments recapture the inevitable frustration of impossible desire, that desire itself is portrayed as never annulled. Perpetual frustration leads only to perpetual re-emergence of new desire: Tantalos forever hungers and thirsts; Sisyphos begins again to roll his stone uphill; Ixion spins on forever with no destination; the liver of Tityos is regenerated each month. The desire that led to punishment is thus reflected in the various modes of punishment and is characterized by the impossibility of gratification. The psychological significance of Hesiod's account of Tartaros as a primal cosmogonic entity is therefore found in the symbolic representations of the *frustration* of desire, while desire itself is invariably presented within an oedipal structure that guarantees its eternal persistence.

Tartaros, the traditional site of punishment for oedipal crimes, is protrayed in the Hesiodic myth as a place where the Titans, who overthrew their father Ouranos, are confined. On the other hand, it is also a primal entity following Chaos and Gaia, the pair who represent the symbiotic state and its end through perception of the mother as separate. Tartaros as a place of frustration and eternal loss would then represent that first and all-important loss in the life of every individual, the loss of the symbiotic state as manifested by separation from the mother. Since this is the precursor of all subsequent experiences of loss (all anxiety is ultimately separation anxiety), it is appropriate that it appears in the guise of oedipal loss, an experience that is isomorphic with the loss of symbiosis. The symbolic castration inflicted on the sufferers in Tartaros replicates the original loss suffered by the post-symbiotic child.

We come now to Eros, the last of the cosmogonic entities. It is immediately evident that this is not at all the cherubic Eros or Cupid of later mythology. Hesiod's Eros is virtually an abstraction, a figure of Desire as a basic principle of life and the cosmos.[17] The pair Tartaros and Eros would therefore signify respectively the *frustration* of desire and the *emergence* of desire, an opposition that defines the basic dialectic of development throughout all of life. In the broadest interpretation, Tartaros and Eros might be seen to represent the opposition between principles of death and life, as in Freud's final formulation (in *Beyond the Pleasure Principle*) of the two great classes of instincts as death instincts and life instincts, or as in the cosmic dualities of early Greek philosophers (e.g., Empedocles' Love and Strife).

But if Tartaros and Eros are Frustration and Desire, why does Tartaros appear before Eros? Should we not expect Eros to precede Tartaros, since desire must presumably precede its own frustration (as in the myths of the criminals in Tartaros)? A partial answer may be that, as we have seen, desire is portrayed as cyclical and eternal; its inevitable frustration leads to its inevitable re-emergence. Yet there is another mythical explanation, for which we may turn to Socrates' discussion in Plato's *Symposium* of the nature of Eros. As Socrates tells his listeners, he had once believed as they did that Eros was a great and powerful god who lacked nothing, but he had learned from the wise priestess Diotima that the truth was just the opposite; Eros was lacking in everything, since "Desire is always the desire of something, and that something is what is lacking" (*Symposium* 200e). In the Socratic myth, Eros is born from the intercourse of Lack and Resourcefulness in the Garden of Zeus; therefore, as Diotima says (203c–d, tr. Jowett):

> it has been his fate to be always needy; nor is he delicate and lovely as most of us believe, but harsh and arid, barefoot and homeless, sleeping on the naked earth, in doorways, in the very streets beneath the stars of heaven, and always partaking of his mother's poverty.

Viewing Diotima's instruction to Socrates in the light of childhood development, we may recall that, whatever its real causes, separation-individuation is for the child the occasion for the emergence of desire for what has been lost: the mother, the breast, the world that was once part of the undifferentiated symbiotic state. Tartaros must therefore precede Eros, as loss precedes desire, since desire begins originally in the perceived lack of what was once a source of gratification, although this gratification is not perceived as such until lost. The oedipus complex itself, the nuclear complex of the myths of Tartaros, is therefore a reformulation of the dialectic of inevitable loss and impossible desire that began in the first year of life.

We may now summarize the psychological meaning of Hesiod's brief account of the world's beginning as follows: the amorphous undifferentiated totality of symbiotic existence (Chaos) is brought to an end by the perception of the mother (Gaia) as separate; but she is known only at the price of being lost; it is on the basis of this loss (Tartaros) that desire (Eros, the Socratic child of Lack) comes into being.

THE FIRST GENERATION

In the abridged version of Apollodoros, the world began with the marriage of Ouranos and Gaia; their children were the three Hundred-Handed, then the three Kyklopes, and then thirteen Titans. At this point Gaia persuaded her children to attack their father; all but Okeanos took part in the attack, and Kronos castrated Ouranos and threw his genitals into the sea. The three Erinyes (Furies) were born from drops of Ouranos' blood, and the Hundred-Handed and Kyklopes were brought up from Tartaros, where Ouranos had imprisoned them.

Hesiod's account is more elaborate. After the appearance of Eros, both Chaos and Gaia produced children parthenogenically (i.e., without a sexual partner). From Chaos were born Erebos and Nyx (Night), and these two were, respectively, father and mother of Aither and Hemera. Night alone then produced a brood of 15 abstractions, both singly and in groups: Moros (Doom), Ker (Destiny), Thanatos (Death), Hypnos (Sleep), Momos (Blame), Oizys (Pain), Nemesis (Retribution), Apate (Deceit), Philotes (Love), Geras (Old Age), Eris (Strife), Oneiroi (Dreams), Hesperides (Daughters of Night), Moirai (Fates), and Keres (Destinies). Eris, the last-born daughter of Night, then produced by herself a further list of fourteen abstractions (Labor, Quarrels, Murders, Famine, Oath, etc.).

Meanwhile Gaia was giving birth to Ouranos, then the Ourea (Mountains), then Pontos (Sea) before finally joining with Ou-

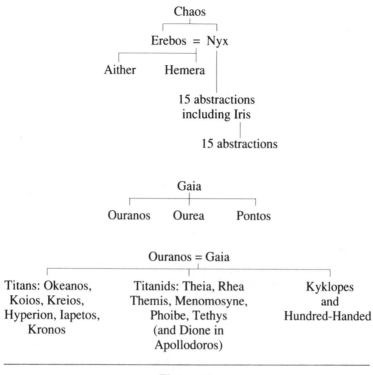

Chaos

Erebos = Nyx

Aither   Hemera

15 abstractions
including Iris

15 abstractions

Gaia

Ouranos   Ourea   Pontos

Ouranos = Gaia

| Titans: Okeanos, Koios, Kreios, Hyperion, Iapetos, Kronos | Titanids: Theia, Rhea Themis, Menomosyne, Phoibe, Tethys (and Dione in Apollodoros) | Kyklopes and Hundred-Handed |

Figure 4.1

ranos to produce the twelve Titans (Hesiod's list is similar to that
of Apollodoros except that Dione is added by the latter), the Kyklopes, and the Hundred-Handed (see Fig. 4-1).

The birth of four other abstract entities is mentioned later
by Hesiod (*Theogony* 383–85), who makes the river Styx and
the second-generation Titan, Pallas, mother and father of Zelos
(Glory), Nike (Victory), Kratos (Power), and Bia (Force).
This family is also described by Apollodoros (1.2.4), but he
omits all of Hesiod's other abstractions and, in fact, never even
mentions Nyx, let alone her offspring. The probably explanation
for this is that Apollodoros was simply not interested in anything
that did not play a mythological role, while Hesiod was concerned
with explaining the origin of whatever existed that significantly
affected the life of man. Since Apollodoros knew that Nike was

worshipped as a goddess and that Kratos and Bia appeared as
characters in Aeschylus' tragedy *Prometheus Bound,* he included
them along with their brother Zelos but omitted all the others.

However Hesiod himself may have been motivated not only
by a desire for completeness but also by the intention of expressing
the obvious fact that conflict exists in a world comprised of strife
as well as love, ugliness as well as beauty, death as well as life.
This dualism appears in the structure itself of the *Theogony* (immediately after the awful children of Night and Strife, Hesiod
turns to "just and kindly" Nereus, then to "arrogant" Phorkys and
"hard-hearted" Eurybia, then to the fifty beautiful and charming
daughters of Nereus, then to the various monsters, then to the
noble rivers and the lovely ocean-nymphs) and may be seen as
expressing the fact of both external opposition (e.g., war and
peace, calm and storm, life and death, winter and summer) and
internal conflict (e.g., love and hate, desire and fear). It may be
relevant that Freud's entire theory of psychic dynamism is based
on the fact of internal conflict, and that in one of his last works
he gave the credit for discovering this dualism to early Greek
thinkers.[18]

The parthenogenic children of Gaia—Sky, Mountains, and
Sea—are clearly the most obvious constituents of the physical
world. That she would select her son Ouranos to be her husband
reflects the widespread mythic motif in which the life-giving and
maternal earth is fertilized and inseminated by the sky. This
union, represented in argicultural rituals at least as ancient and
universal as the myths, also symbolizes (although this is of course
not Hesiod's intention) the merger of the father/sky-worshipping
Indo-European (Mycenean) culture with the mother/earth-wor-
shipping Mediterranean (Minoan) culture. As Guthrie says, "the
worship of the earth as the Great Mother . . . was established
in the lands around the Aegean Sea long before invaders brought
with them the idea of a male father-god as the supreme deity, and
instead of supplanting her, the patriarchal Zeus and his brothers
soon found themselves compelled to come to terms."[19]

Since we have already discussed the symbolic manifestations
of the intercourse of Gaia and Ouranos in the form of rain and
lightning, we may now turn to their children and to the question
of why Ouranos refuses to allow them out of their mother's body.
West's explanation that "it was because of the children's fearsome

nature that Ouranos hated them and tried to suppress them"
seems to be contradicted by his subsequent statement that "the
story must have been that the Titans were kept in Gaia's womb by
Ouranos' unremitting embrace: that is why she is so distressed,
and why castration solves the problem."[20] If Gaia's children never
left her womb, how could Ouranos come to know and hate their
fearsome nature? The apparent contradiction is readily resolved,
however, once we realize that Ouranos' fear and suppression of
his children resulted not from their "fearsome" nature, but from
his own fearsome memory. As we shall see, Kronos and Zeus, the
son and grandson of Ouranos, treat their wives and children in
ways that are determined by their own experience, and the same
is true of Ouranos. If he does not allow his children to be born,
it is because he remembers that he is his wife's son; if he married
his mother, his sons will also want to marry theirs. Ouranos, by
virtue of his oedipal success, figures that his sons will want to do
the same, and the continuous intercourse that represents this success serves also to eliminate the threat potentially posed by his
children.

As to the nature of the children of Gaia and Ouranos, the
Titans may be children in the view of Ouranos, but from the view-
point of Zeus (the most important viewpoint of all), they represent the father, the parents, the "older generation of gods,"[21]
Hesiod's "the former gods" (*Theogony* 424, 486). Almost all human genealogies in Greek mythology can be traced back to two
Titans (Okeanos and Iapetos), and the punishment of the Titans
in Tartaros is due no more to their defeat *of* an older generation
(Ouranos) than to their defeat *as* an older generation (by Zeus).
The idea that the Titans represent an *older generation* is reinforced by the gigantic stature of all eighteen children of Ouranos,
and is perhaps supported by the physical peculiarities of their six
brothers, the Kyklopes and Hundred-Handed. The latter's proliferation of heads and arms may reflect the infant's original difficulty in discerning and assigning physical boundaries, and the
single huge eye of the Kyklopes may well represent the strongest
impression received by the infant's immature vision of a parent's
face a few inches from his own.[22]

THE FIRST REVOLT

When we first meet the Titans, however, they are the children
whom Ouranos fears, supposing (rightly) that they will attempt to
deprive him of his unlimited sexual prerogative. It is a clearly
oedipal conflict: the father, married to his own mother, tries to
prevent his sons from overthrowing him and usurping his privileges; mother and sons then conspire together to defeat the father;
the younger generation becomes the older, and the sons become
the new fathers. But if this is true, why don't the Titans seek to
marry their mother Gaia, just as Ouranos married his mother?
Isn't the ultimate goal of the oedipus complex the fulfillment of
the son's wish to become the sexual partner of his mother? Yet
there is no indication that the Titans want or attempt to marry
their mother; four of the Titan sons marry their sisters (Okeanos
marries Tethys; Hyperion, Theia; Kois, Phoibe; and Kronos,
Rhea), Kreios marries his half-sister Eurybia, and Iapetos marries his niece Klymene. Gaia does in fact marry another of her
sons after the overthrow of Ouranos, but her new husband is not
one of the Titans; he is her youngest parthenogenic son Pontos,
by whom she gives birth to three sons and two daughters (*Theogony* 233–39).

An answer to this problem, which will be repeated in the
case of Zeus, is that the succession myth presents a kind of pro-
gression in which each generation tries to get what it wants without repeating the mistakes of the previous generation. Thus the
Titans deposed their father and won his sexual power but, not
wanting to suffer the same fate as he had incurred, they chose to
exercise their new sexual freedom by marrying their sisters or
other relatives but *not* their mother.

In this respect the Titans bear a striking resemblance to the
Primal Horde hypothesized by Freud in his mythical anthropology
of the beginning of human society. In *Totem and Taboo* Freud
cites Darwin's theory that primitive humans lived in small groups
controlled by the strongest male, who jealously prohibited the
other males from sexual opportunity until finally he was overthrown and the process was repeated. Combining this theory with
Robertson Smith's studies of totemism and supplying a psychologi-

cal motivation, Freud created his own myth of the earliest state of society:

> One day the brothers who had been driven out came to-
> gether, killed and devoured their father and so made an
> end of the patriarchal horde. United, they had the courage
> to do and succeeded in doing what would have been im-
> possible for them individually. (Some cultural advance,
> perhaps, command over some new weapon, had given them
> a sense of superior strength.) Cannibal savages as they
> were, it goes without saying that they devoured their victim
> as well as killing him. The violent primal father had doubt-
> less been the feared and envied model of each one of the
> company of brothers: and in the act of devouring him they
> accomplished their identification with him, and each of
> them acquired a portion of his strength. The totem meal,
> which is perhaps mankind's earliest festival, would thus be
> a repetition and a commemoration of this memorable and
> criminal deed, which was the beginning of so many
> things—of social organization, of moral restrictions and of
> religion.
>   In order that these latter consequences may seem
> plausible, leaving their premises on one side, we need only
> suppose that the tumultuous mob of brothers were filled
> with the same contradictory feelings which we can see at
> work in the ambivalent father-complexes of our children
> and of our neurotic patients. They hated their father, who
> presented such a formidable obstacle to their craving for
> power and their sexual desires; but they loved and admired
> him too. After they had got rid of him, had satisfied their
> hatred and had put into effect their wish to identify them-
> selves with him, the affection which had all this time been
> pushed under was bound to make itself felt. It did so in
> the form of remorse. A sense of guilt made its appearance,
> which in this instance coincided with the remorse felt by
> the whole group. The dead father became stronger than
> the living one had been—for events took the course we so
> often see them follow in human affairs to this day. What
> had up to then been prevented by his actual existence was
> thenceforward prohibited by the sons themselves, in ac-
> cordance with the psychological procedure so familiar to
> us in psychoanalyses under the name of "deferred obedi-
> ence." They revoked their deed by forbidding the killing

of the totem, the substitute for their father; and they renounced its fruits by resigning their claim to the women who had now been set free. Thus they created out of their filial sense of guilt the two fundamental taboos of totemism, which for that very reason inevitably corresponded to the two repressed wishes of the oedipus complex. Whoever contravened these taboos became guilty of the only two crimes with which primitive society concerned itself.[23]

Like Freud's horde, the Titans overthrew their father, the jealous patriarch who denied to his sons any access to the sexual privilege he enjoyed; and then, having accomplished this, the Titans, like the horde, renounced the sexual object of their revolution. For Freud, the horde's motive was both psychological and practical: on one hand, guilt and remorse led them to identify with the dead father and to institutionalize his prohibitions; on the other hand, they sensed that the new society would be destroyed in fratricidal war unless a system of exogamy (the social extension of the incest taboo) was established:

> Sexual desires do not unite men but divide them. Though the brothers had banded together in order to overcome their father, they were all one another's rivals in regard to the women. Each of them would have wished, like his father, to have all the women to himself. The new organization would have collapsed in a struggle of all against all, for none of them was of such overmastering strength as to be able to take on his father's part with success. Thus the brothers had no alternative, if they were to live together, but—not, perhaps, until they had passed through many dangerous crises—to institute the law against incest, by which they all alike renounced the women whom they desired and who had been their chief motive for despatching their father.[24]

The second, utilitarian, motive appears much more operative in the myth of the Titans than the first, guilt and remorse. After all, Ouranos may have been castrated but he had not been killed. And yet murder can hardly be a necessary prerequisite for guilt. Every son, to more or less an extent, suffers guilt for the hostile (and ultimately fatal, in the logic of the unconscious) feelings he had entertained, and subsequently repressed, against his father.

The sexual nature of the conflict between the Titans and their father is made even clearer by the method and means of their attack. They do not kill him but castrate him, depriving him of his sexual sovereignty, and the means they employ is a jagged-toothed sickle (Gk. *harpe*) made of adamant (literally "the inflexible," presumably iron or whatever could be imagined as stronger than iron). A similar weapon will be used by Zeus against the monster Typhoeus, by Perseus against Medousa, and by Iolaos against the Hydra; in all three instances the conflict is sexual, and the sickle is used by the winner to separate the loser from his or her own sexuality.

Furthermore, Gaia is not entirely absent from the sexual objectives of her victorious Titan sons. Kronos, the leader of the Titans and the one who actually uses the sickle, will marry his sister Rhea, who is "practically indistinguishable from Gaia, and moreover blended with a very old and widely worshipped power, the Mother, who, if she is not herself the Earth, at least has close relations with earth-goddesses."[25] If Kronos is to be the new lord of the sky, as was his father, he must marry the woman who is a double of his mother Gaia. The same will be true in the next generation of the third sky-god Zeus, whose mates will include the earth-goddesses Demeter and Themis.

According to Hesiod, all the Titans but Kronos were afraid to take part in the attack on Ouranos. Apollodoros, on the other hand, says that all but Okeanos took part in the attack, under the leadership of Kronos. The reluctance of Okeanos is clarified by passages in the *Iliad* referring to "Okeanos whence the gods have risen" (14.201) and "Okeanos whence is risen the seed of all the immortals" (14.246).

Both Apollodoros and Homer seem to preserve a vestige of a lost theogony in which Okeanos and Tethys, not Ouranos and Gaia, were the primal parents. A close Near Eastern parallel occurs in the Akkadian-Babylonian *Enuma Elish,* in which the world begins with two water-deities, Apsu (sweet male waters) and Tiamat (bitter female waters); within their mingled waters the first gods come into existence, are threatened by Apsu, and eventually overthrow him. Apollodoros' exclusion of Okeanos from the insurgent Titans might represent a Greek variant of this tradition. Or there may have been a version in which Okeanos and Gaia were the first parents; a fragment of the early mythographer

Pherekydes names Okeanos and Gaia as the parents of the Eleusin-
ian culture-hero Triptolemos, and Hesiod himself has Gaia marry
not Okeanos but an older ocean-god, her son Pontos.

The immediate result of the castration of Ouranos is the appearance of several new divine beings. Apollodoros mentions only
the three Furies (Alekto, Tisiphone, and Megaira) born from the
blood of Ouranos, but Hesiod adds the Giants (Gigantes), the
Meliad (ash tree) nymphs, and, from the severed penis itself, the
goddess Aphrodite. The Giants will have a long gestation period,
since Gaia will keep them within her body until her later anger
with Zeus leads her to seek new champions to fight against him.

Hesiod's story of the birth of Aphrodite conflicts with Homer
and Apollodoros, both of whom make Aphrodite the daughter of
Zeus and Dione (hence Apollodoros' thirteenth Titan). Most
scholars regard the Hesiodic version as due to Near Eastern influence (for example, the Hurrian-Hittite myth in which the sky-god
Anu is castrated by Kumarbi, who bites off and swallows Anu's
genitals, from which subsequently three gods will be born),[26] and
there is certainly a strong resemblance between the frankly sensual
and often dangerous Aphrodite and the character of Sumerian
Inanna and the various Semitic Ishtars (although Aphrodite is
usually a very mild version of her bloodthirsty and carnal Near
Eastern counterparts). The complicated question of her origin,
however, need not detain us here;[27] insofar as the psychology of
the succession myth is concerned, Aphrodite is represented in the
myth invented or reported by Hesiod as having her origin in the
act of castration.

The transformation of a severed phallus into the goddess of
sexual desire is not as incongruous as it may first seem. If Athena,
the goddess of wisdom, will be born from the head of Zeus, is it
not appropriate that Aphrodite be born from a god's genitals?
This is, after all, her sphere of dominion. Furthermore, she represents the sexuality with which Ouranos had seemed to be exclu-
sively concerned, symbolized metonymically by his phallus. And
it is access to this sexuality that the Titans win, precisely through
the means of castration.

The sexual desire of Ouranos led to his castration, but this
in turn produced the goddess emblematic of sexual desire. The
presumption that Ouranos was involved in intercourse with Gaia
at the time of the attack—since the Titans were prevented from

emerging by the nonstop sexual activity of their father, Kronos must have made his sickle attack from inside Gaia's body—leads to a further symbolic meaning. Every sexual act that leads to orgasm is, at least for the male, the occasion for a "castration," the temporary impotence that necessarily follows orgasm. The fulfillment of sexual desire is equivalent to castration, and the resurgence of desire begins from castration (the birth of Aphrodite from the castration of Ouranos). It is difficult not to recall here an earlier episode in which also the symbol of desire was immediately preceded by an idea associated with castration, the appearance of Eros after Tartaros.

In several of his later writings, most notably *The Ego and the Id*, Freud noted that castration and death seemed virtually synonymous in the unconscious. An indication of this association occurs in the practice, in both French and Spanish, of referring to the state of post-orgasmic impotence as "the little death." Since death can signify castration, a paradoxical tie between sexual desire and castration underlies the common double-entendre between love and death (Fr. *l'amour* and *la mort*) in poetry and legend. When the metaphysical poet John Donne wrote in his "The Canonization," "We die and rise the same, and prove/ mysterious by this love," he meant by "die and rise" the same association between orgasmic castration and the beginning of desire as found in the emergence of Aphrodite from the castration of Ouranos.

The three Furies born from the blood of Ouranos are officially the avengers of those crimes, especially within the family, that threaten the traditional structures of home and society. Their particular concern with the punishment of parricide and matricide appears in their pursuit of Orestes and Alkmaion, each of whom killed his mother. Born themselves from the crime of sons against their father, the Furies are psychological symbols of *guilt*, especially that guilt that is attached to enacted or repressed hostile impulses against parents. Born from castration, they are themselves castrating spirits, as may be seen in the tirade directed against them by Apollo in Aeschylus' *Eumenides* (185–90):

> It is not fit that you inhabit this house,
> but rather where there are beheadings and eye-gougings
> and throat-slit judgments, and by castration the

virility of youths is ruined, and mutilations
and stonings, and men moan most pitiably,
impaled under the spine.

THE MONSTERS

After the account of Ouranos' castration, Apollodoros turns
straightaway to the steps taken by his successor Kronos to avoid
a similar fate. Hesiod, however, does not take up this subject until
he has completed the story of the children of Night, this time the
fatherless family of abstractions born to her and to her daughter
Eris. Hesiod goes on to tell of the children of Gaia and Pontos
and their descendants, including the fifty Nereid nymphs and the
monsters (233–336) and, since Kronos is the youngest Titan, he
recounts the children of Okeanos (337–70) and the other older
Titans (371–452) before finally coming to Kronos and resuming
the succession myth proper.

There are several points of psychological interest in this
array of progeny, principally the significance of the various marine
deities and of the monsters. We will defer the former subject until
the discussion of Poseidon, but we will treat the monsters now as a
group (see the genealogies in Fig. 4-2).

The union of Gaia and Pontos, perhaps a reminiscence of the
marriage of water and earth as primeval fertility principles, eventually produces most of the major monsters of Greek mythology. In
the *Theogony* the children of Phorkys and Keto ("sea monster"
or "whale") are the three Gorgons (Sthenno, Euryale, Medousa),
the two Graiai (Enyo, Pemphredo), Ladon (the hundred-headed
multilingual serpent who guards the apples of the Hesperides),
and Echidna, half beautiful nymph and half flesh-eating speckled
snake (who is called the daughter of Tartaros and Gaia by Apollodoros [2.1.2]). From the union of Echidna and Typhoeus (the
greatest monster of them all) are born the Chimaira (a three-
headed combination of lion, serpent, and goat with wings), the
nine-headed Lernaian Hydra, the two-headed dog Orthos, and
Kerberos, the fifty-headed (Hesiod) or three-headed (Apollodoros) dog of the underworld. To this list Apollodoros adds a
third Graia (Deino), the Caucasian eagle that tortures Prometheus
(2.5.11), the Crommyonian sow killed by Theseus (*Epitome* 1.1),

Ladon (2.5.11), the Nemean lion killed by Herakles (2.5.1), and the Thebian Sphinx (3.5.8). In the *Theogony,* however, the Sphinx and the Nemean lion are the offspring of the dog Orthos and either his mother Echidna or his sister Chimaira.

To this list we should add the Harpies Aello and Okypete, daughters of Thaumas and the Okeanid Elektra and sisters of Iris, the personification of the rainbow and a messenger of the gods. The Harpies appear sometimes as wind-spirits (storm winds in the *Odyssey*), and sometimes as bird-women who carry away the souls of men; in the latter form they are the disgusting persecutors of the blind prophet Phineus (Apollodoros 1.9.21).

While there is no single explanation for the hybrid form of such creatures as Echidna (serpent/woman), the Harpies (bird/woman), or the Sphinx (lion/bird/woman), it should be recognized that it is always the upper part which is human, while the lower is usually some animal with phallic associations. One might plausibly suppose that these figures represent the male child's curiosity about the usually unseen parts of the female (typically, the mother's) body, a fantasy in which the mother often appears as actually possessing the phallus, or threatening to take the phallus away from men, or both (the vindictive and castrating "phallic mother");[28] in general, children's fantasies concerning sexuality, like their fantastic theories of birth, take almost any form but the right one. There are several representations of castrating "phallic" females in the monsters of Greek myth: for example, the Gorgons, who had snakes for hair and rendered a man impotent by their look, and the Erinyes, who also were often portrayed with snaky hair and, as we have seen, were described by Aeschylus as concerned with emasculation and its symbolic equivalents, such as decapitation and blinding. It should also be noted that the name of the Harpies, usually derived from the Greek *harpazo* (to snatch away) would seem to be associated as well with *harpe,* the sickle with which Kronos castrated his father. Like Harpies, Gorgons, and Erinyes, the Echidna and Sphinx are also threatening figures of female malevolence (Apollodoros 2.1.2, 3.5.8). There are other recurrent features that seem connected with the derivation of these fantasies from the earliest mother–child relationship, in particular the prominence of orality and ambivalence. Emphasis on orality appears in the multiplication of heads (on the same or

Figure 4.2

different bodies), in the Harpies' and Erinyes' causing men to starve to death, and in the Sphinx' eating of those who fail to answer her riddle. Ambivalence, the leading characteristic of infantile emotional relationships (in a matter of seconds, it seems, a child can oscillate between love and hate, trust and fear), may be seen both in the incongruous attempts to assimilate disparate features in a single figure and also in the conflicting portrayals in myth and art of these female creatures' physical characteristics: for example, the Erinyes are often "rather beautiful,"[29] the Echidna is described by Hesiod as "gleaming-eyed" and "fair-cheeked" (*Theogony* 298), and the Gorgon Medousa herself is said to have com-

peted with Athena in beauty (Apollodoros 2.4.3) and to have attracted Poseidon as a lover (*Theogony* 277–79).

After describing the progeny of the other Titans, Hesiod comes at this point to Kronos and Rhea and their children (*Theogony* 453–506), but he interrupts his account of the conflict between Zeus and Kronos to tell the story of Iapetos' son Prometheus and the creation of Pandora, the first mortal woman (*Theogony* 507–616). He then tells how Zeus freed the Hundred-Handed from captivity, revived them with nectar and ambrosia, and with their help defeated the Titans and confined them in Tartaros after a war lasting ten years (*Theogony* 617–735).

GOLDEN RACE AND GOLDEN APPLES

As we have seen, it was during the rule of Kronos that the first
men were created by the gods. Perhaps because Kronos was associated with this blissful golden race of original mortals living in a
symbiotic paradise, a derivative myth arose in which Kronos was
released after his defeat by Zeus and ruled over the "islands of
the blessed," another paradise in which selected heroes enjoyed a
nirvana-like afterlife. For these members of the heroic age (fourth
of Hesiod's five ages: gold, silver, bronze, heroic, and iron), the
earth produced fruit and crops three times a year, a miraculous
bounty reminiscent of the self-producing fields at the time of the
golden race (*Works and Days* 167–73):

> But, giving to others a life and home apart from men,
> Kronos' son, father Zeus, settled them at the ends of the
> earth, and they dwell with carefree heart in the
> islands of the blessed by deep-whirling Okeanos;
> happy heroes, for whom the fertile earth bears
> honey-sweet fruit, ripe, three times a year;
> they are far from the immortals; Kronos is their king.

By the fifth century we find in the odes of Pindar not only the
islands of the blessed but also a kind of half-way paradise, where
the good live a life of total ease (as did the golden race):

> With nights always equal,
> having the sun in equal days, effortless is
> the life the good receive, not troubling the earth with strength
>   of hand,
> or the water of the sea
> for an empty living; but near the honors
> of the gods, those who were pleased to keep vows lead a
>   tearless
> life, while others suffer unsightly pain.
> As many as triply endured,
> waiting on the other side, to keep their soul from all wrongs
> take the road of Zeus to the tower of Kronos,
> where ocean breezes surround
> the island of the blessed with
> their breath, and flowers of gold blaze,
> some on land from glorious trees, others nourished in water;

from these they weave bracelets for hands, and crowns,
under the upright counsels of Rhadamanthys,
whom the great father has ready, seated beside him,
the husband of Rhea, whose throne is highest of all.
                                            Olympian 2.61–77

For them the sun shines brightly while it is night here.
The area before their city is shaded by balsam in rose-
red meadows and laden with golden fruits.
                                            Pindar *fragment* 114B

The essential characteristic of paradise, whether it is located at the beginning of life (the golden race) or after death (the island[s] of the blessed), is that it is a place of effortless gratification, a place where nothing can be desired because nothing is lacking. This aspect is also emphasized by Homer, whose name for paradise is the "Elysian field," here described in a prophecy of the sea-god Proteus:

for you, O Menelaos of the race of Zeus, it is not the
gods' decree that you die and meet destiny in horse-
feeding Argos, but the immortals will send you to the
Elysian field and the ends of the earth, where light-haired
Rhadamanthys lives and life is easiest for men;
there is no snow, great storm, or ever rain,
but always the breezes of Zephyros blowing clear
are sent by Okeanos to refresh men.
                                            Odyssey 4.561–68

The presence of paradise at both the beginning and end of life is, of course, not peculiar to Greek religion; many religious systems similarly locate the lifespan of humanity in the hiatus between two paradises (for example, the Judeo-Christian tradition of the Garden of Eden at the beginning and heaven at the apocalyptic end of the human race). This equivocation makes good sense in the light of individual psychology: the original paradise is the *memory* of the symbiotic situation, and the final paradise is the wish-fulfilling fantasy that answers the unconscious *desire* to return to symbiosis, a fulfillment possible only after the death of the individual.[30]

Since the desire for symbiosis appears regularly in the form of a desire for fusion with the mother, we should expect to find some representation of maternal presence or nurturance in the

fantasy of paradise. This appears by implication in the total ease
that characterizes paradise, since in the earliest state of the infant
all needs *must* be satisfied by the maternal environment. But there
are other indications as well, both general—as Motte has demonstrated in detail, gardens, meadows, and fields in Greek religious
thought bore an archaic association with female sexuality or the
maternal genitals[31]—and in specific details. The Greek word
pedion, for example (Homer's "Elysian field" is an *Elysion
pedion*), means both "plain, field" and "(sexually mature, i.e.,
maternal) female genitals." Also, the color *gold* and, especially,
golden fruit or plants seem to have a pervasive connection with the
Greek notion of paradise. The first humans were a golden race,
and the islands of the blessed, according to Pindar, were the home
of "gold flowers" and "golden fruits." The best-known location of
golden fruit in Greek myth, however, was another sort of paradise,
the garden of the Hesperides. Unlike the Elysian field and the
islands of the blessed, this garden was not the scene of the afterlife of the good; although mortals could occasionally visit it, it was
a garden of the gods, not of men. But it is described in much the
same way as the afterlife paradises, and scholars of ancient religion
have suggested that it shared with Elysion a derivation from pre-
hellenic traditions.[32] It also was located in that imaginary world
at the ends of the earth; Hesiod mentions the Hesperides (daughters of Night) three times and places their garden "beyond famous
Okeanos," "towards Night [i.e., to the west]," and "at the borders
of the earth." In one of these passages Hesiod describes the garden
as a "soft meadow with flowers of springtime" (*Theogony* 279),
and *leimon,* his word for "meadow," has like *pedion* associations
with the female genitals[33] (Hesiod uses the not uncommon word
leimon only to describe the garden of the Hesperides, and Pindar's
single use of the word occurs in the description of paradise [*fragment* 114B]). Hesiod also places the union of Zeus' brother
Poseidon with the Gorgon Medousa in the garden of the Hesperides (*Theogony* 279), and for Euripides it is the place where
"springs of ambrosia flow before the marriage-bed of Zeus" (*Hippolytos* 748–50). The fullest account of the connection between
the marriage of Zeus and Hera and the garden of the Hesperides
is found in a fragment of the early Greek mythographer Pherekydes (in the scholia to Apollonius Rhodius 4.1396): Gaia produced a tree with golden apples and gave it as a present to Zeus

and Hera on the occasion of their wedding; Hera then requested that it be planted in the garden.

The golden apples appear at two other notable moments in Greek myth, and each time the context has to do with marriage. At the wedding of Peleus and Thetis, the greatest social event of classical mythology, Eris (Strife) rolled a golden apple inscribed "To the fairest" before the assembled guests; the ensuing quarrel between Hera, Athena, and Aphrodite led to the judgment of Paris and, consequently, to the Trojan war (Hyginus, *Fabula* 92). The other occasion concerns the virgin Atalanta; the story is included in fragments of Hesiod, and is told with most detail by Apollodoros (3.9.2):

> Iasos and Klymene, the daughter of Minyas, had a daughter Atalanta. Her father wanted sons and exposed her, but a female bear came often and suckled her until hunters found her and raised her with them. When Atalanta grew up, she kept herself a virgin and was always fully armed, hunting in the wilderness. When the centaurs Rhoikos and Hylaios tried to rape her, she shot and killed them. She went with the heroes to hunt the Kalydonian boar, and she defeated Peleus in wrestling at the games in honor of Pelias. Afterwards she found her parents, but her father tried to get her to marry; she went to a place suitable for racing and fixed a three-cubit stake in the center. She sent her suitors to run from this point, and ran after them with her weapons. If the suitor were caught, he received immediate death, but if he were not caught, he could marry her. Many had already died when Melanion fell in love with her and came for the race; he brought golden apples that he had gotten from Aphrodite and threw them down as he was pursued. Atalanta picked up the thrown apples, but lost the race and so became the wife of Melanion.

Why are the golden apples regularly associated with marriage and weddings? Since they appear as wedding gifts we might suppose that they, as is the original meaning of all traditional wedding gifts and rites, are symbolic of fertility and compatibility. But we can be more specific: whether as symbols in a dream, or in medieval paintings of Madonna and Child, or in the Greek language itself, apples can symbolize a woman's breasts. One of

Freud's patients, who was having an affair with an actress, recited to Freud these lines from Goethe's *Faust* in his associations
to a dream:

> FAUST: A lovely dream once came to me,
>   And I beheld an apple-tree,
>   On which two lovely apples shone;
>   They charmed me so, I climbed thereon.
> THE LOVELY WITCH: Apples have been desired by you,
>   Since first in Paradise they grew;
>   And I am moved with joy to know
>   That such within my garden grow.
>   *Part One, Scene 21*

As Freud says, "There cannot be the faintest doubt what the apple-
tree and the apples stood for. Moreover, lovely breasts had been
among the charms which had attracted the dreamer to his actress."[34]

Specifically, then, apples symbolize breasts; more generally,
they represent the maternal and nurturant role that a woman un-
dertakes in marriage. This is why the golden apples are appropriate wedding gifts and why Atalanta loses the marriage-race to
Melanion by stopping to pick them up. After spending her life
trying to be the son her father wanted, a wish that had led him to
abandon the daughter he had instead of a son, Atalanta now re-
nounces this role in favor of marriage and maternity (which is
clearly what the apples represent, despite statements by authors
such as Hyginus [*Fabula* 185] that Atalanta was betrayed by a
women's attraction to gold). This maternal symbolism is verified
linguistically in the use of "apple" (Gk. *malon*) by the comic
playwright Aristophanes to mean "breast" (for example, *Lysistrata* 155–56: "Menelaos took a glance at naked Helen's apples,
and threw down his sword") and by the fact that the only meaning
of the Greek word *malouchos* (literally, "apple-holder") is "bras-
siere."

Herakles must win the golden apples of the Hesperides for his
eleventh labor, and it is clear that the real meaning of this task is
not to demonstrate strength and bravery (although Herakles must
defeat Ladon, the guardian serpent with one hundred heads, and
outwit the giant Titan Atlas) so much as to signify Herakles'
acquisition of immortality (in this respect the apples are a variant

of the fruit of the Tree of Life in the Garden of Eden)[35] and at the same time his fulfillment of the wish to be reunited with the nurturant mother. Herakles' journey to the symbiotic paradise is thus a repetition of an event from his infancy; Hera, tricked by Zeus, Hermes, or Athena into nursing the baby Herakles, fed him with her own milk, and it was this milk that made him immortal (Tzetzes on Lycophron 1328).

There are, of course, many reasons for the symbolic valuation of gold: its scarcity, its association with royalty, its relative incorruptibility, its seemingly infinite extensibility. But the underlying psychological significance of the golden apples and the golden age, of paradise (wherever its location in time or space), is the attraction of the nurturant mother who embodies the fulfillment of the wish to return to symbiosis. And whether paradise comes at the beginning or end of life, Kronos is its ruler.

THE SECOND REVOLT

After Kronos overthrew his father Ouranos and succeeded him as chief sky-god and king of the world, the steps he takes to protect his position clearly derive from his memory of what had happened to his father and his intent that nothing similar will befall himself. Ouranos, as we saw, foresaw a threat to himself from his sons on the basis of his own experience; since he had married his own mother, he figured that his sons would try to replace him, and so he did not allow them to emerge from their mother's body. But he had failed, and Kronos knows why better than anyone, since he had received from his mother the sickle that he used to castrate Ouranos. In order to prevent his sons from overthrowing him, Kronos now reasons, he cannot keep them in their mother's body, but must keep mother and sons separate as well as suppressing the sons themselves. The obvious answer to Kronos' problem is the one he adopts: If the mother's body will not do, he will use his own instead, and so he swallows his children as soon as they are born. The lesson Kronos has learned from the fate of Ouranos is basically misogynistic; he sees that it is the woman as much as the son who is his enemy. His children must not be allowed an independent existence and, especially, they must be kept separate from their mother, their potential accomplice.

The choice of Kronos is logically very simple. He cannot kill his children, since they are as immortal as he is. Nor can he imprison them anywhere in the world or under it, since this is equivalent to keeping them in the body of his mother Earth, the failed strategy of Ouranos. Their mother is Rhea, not Gaia, but Rhea is surely a double of Gaia and as much an earth-goddess as Kronos is a sky-god. The only method remaining, a simple but significant emendation of Ouranos' tactic, is to imprison either his children *or* his wife in the other parental body, in his own rather than Rhea's. Kronos must swallow either his children or his wife, and his choice of the former meal is presumably because the latter would not only leave his children running free but also deprive him of a sexual partner (and if he is anything like his father Ouranos and his son Zeus, unceasing sexual activity would seem to be the essential function of his role as a Greek sky-god).

The oracular warning given to Kronos by his parents is therefore superfluous. It merely reminds him of his own experience and tells him nothing new, except that he will make the wrong choice. Zeus in turn will be faced with the same situation and the same choices, but, as we shall see, he will choose correctly (that is, he will swallow his wife instead of his children). By choosing thus (which involves no great thought, since it is the only alternative left), Zeus will establish himself as the most notable exception to the underlying law of myth as well as of life that fathers are destined to be replaced by their sons, and he will exemplify the male wish that what he wanted to do to his father will not be done to him in turn.

One important and identifiable source for the myth of Kronos is the Hurrian-Hittite myth of Kumarbi, a myth that contains both castration of a sky-god and (perhaps) the swallowing of a son or stone,[36] and a second sure source is the myths and cults of Minoan Crete. The myth of Zeus' birth or infancy in Crete (Hesiod is somewhat more vague than later writers about whether Zeus was born in Crete or smuggled there as an infant) would seem to be derived from the Aegean cults that pre-existed the arrival in Greece of Indo-Europeans and their paternal sky-god. The religion of Minoan Crete may have included a cult in honor of a male fertility spirit, who was born and died each year and was represented sometimes as a bull, sometimes as a young man named Kouros, consort and son of the mother-goddess.

Later writers embellished greatly the tale of Zeus' childhood in Crete, and we may recall here Apollodoros' version (1.1.6–7):

> Angered by this [the swallowing of her children], Rhea went to Crete when she was pregnant with Zeus. The baby was born in a cave of Dikte and entrusted by his mother for nurturance to the Kouretes and the nymphs Adrasteia and Ida, daughters of Melisseus.
>
> The nymphs therefore nursed the child with the milk of Amaltheia, while the Kouretes took up arms and guarded the baby in the cave by striking their shields with their spears, so that Kronos would not hear the child's voice. Rhea meanwhile wrapped a stone in infant's clothes as though it were a newborn child and gave it to Kronos to swallow.

Although Hesiod says that Zeus was hidden in a cave on Mount Aigaion, later writers said the name of the mountain was either Dikte or Ida; Apollodoros' compromise is to name the mountain Dikte and one of the nurses Ida. There was a similar confusion concerning Amaltheia, whose milk fed the infant; some said she was a woman, while others said she was a goat. Apollodoros here seems to follow the more common version (as in Kallimachos' *Hymn to Zeus*) that Amaltheia was a goat, since he names Adrasteia and Ida as Zeus' nurses and later (Apollodoros 2.7.5) identifies the horn of Amaltheia as the "cornucopia" or "horn of plenty." But in the same passage he says that the horn Amaltheia had was a *bull's* horn and mentions Amaltheia's father Haimonios; this may be due to a tradition that regarded Amaltheia as a nymph who hung the baby's bed from a tree, so that its cries could not be heard in heaven, earth, or sea (Hyginus, *Fabula* 139). In this version the goat whose milk fed the baby is Aix, daughter of the Sun; she was so ugly that the Titans begged Gaia to hide her in the earth, and Gaia put her in a mountain cave of Crete (Hyginus, *Poetica Astronomica* 2.13). According to these same late sources, one day the baby Zeus broke off one of Aix' horns while playing and gave it to Amaltheia, promising that it would supply inexhaustible nourishment. Later, when Zeus fought against the Titans, he made the skin of Aix into a protective shield or breastplate, the *aigis*.

The Kouretes were men who, in orgiastic dancing and ceremony that may have involved the slaying and eating of a bull, summoned their god Kouros and identified themselves with him. As various items of the Aegean religion were assimilated into the beliefs of the Indo-European invaders, the cult of Kouros merged with that of Zeus (who came to be called the "great Kouros") and the armed dance of the Kouretes became a device to save the life of the infant Zeus.

From the variety of sources available to him, some of them mutually contradictory (the Cretans insisted on identifying Zeus too closely with their Kouros and would even point out to visitors the grave of Zeus on Crete), Hesiod and the Greek tradition following him fashioned a myth of striking psychological logic: this archetypal story of oedipal rivalry, marital antagonism, and maternal preference is reduced to a series of binary choices leading inevitably to the emergence of Zeus as the greatest and permanent sky-god. To recpaitulate: Ouranos, in order to prevent his sons from repeating what he had done, must restrain either his wife or his children; having decided on the children, he then must choose whether to put them within the mother (Earth) or himself (Sky); he chooses the former and is overthrown; Kronos, faced with the same choices, also tries to eliminate the children, but by putting them inside himself, and he also is overthrown. When the turn of Zeus comes, he will have to repeat the same choices or he will have to put not his children but his wife inside himself; there will be no other alternative.

THE DISPENSATION OF ZEUS

Kronos and Rhea had six children, the first Olympians (so called because their base in the war against the Titans was Mount Olympos in Thessaly): Hestia, Demeter, Hera, Hades, Poseidon, and Zeus. The position of Zeus as the youngest son is connected with his role as the successor of Kronos, just as Kronos had been the youngest of the twelve children of Ouranos. In myth it is the youngest son who typically inherits the father's position, and it is not difficult to see the psychological reason for this in the dynamics of sibling relationships. From the perspective of an older child, it is always the youngest who inherits, who displaces his predecessors in the affection and attention of his parents. The same situation occurs frequently in the Old Testament; perhaps the best-known examples are the deceitful victory of Jacob over his older twin brother Esau and the triumph of Joseph, Jacob's son, over his jealous older brothers (Genesis 25–30, 37–45).

In the Greek succession myth the conflict between the societal law of primogeniture (inheritance by the eldest) and the psychological law that the youngest child must usurp the privileged position of his older siblings is neatly solved by the imprisonment of the children as they are born in one or another parental body. When the Titans are released from the body of Gaia or when the Olympians are disgorged from the body of Kronos (a kind of second birth), the order of birth is reversed. Kronos, the youngest of the Titans, is closest to the surface of the Earth and thus the first to be (re)born, and Zeus, youngest of the children of Kronos, moves to the position of eldest by escaping being swallowed and subsequent rebirth. In this way youngest becomes oldest, and psychological reality is mythically verified.

After the defeat of the Titans by the first Olympians, the three sons of Kronos divided the world up between themselves, with Zeus as supreme authority. Hesiod speaks simply of their "honors" or "prerogatives" (*Theogony* 885). Homer, followed by Apollodoros, is more specific, as in this description by Poseidon of the division of the world between the three brothers (*Iliad* 15.187–93):

> For we are three brothers from Kronos, and Rhea bore us,
> Zeus and I, and third is Hades, who rules the dead;
> all things were divided three ways, and each has a share
> of honor; I received from the shaken lots the sea to live
> in always, Hades received the misty gloom, and
> Zeus received the wide sky in the clouds and clear air;
> but earth and high Olympos are common to us all.

Myths are never far from a child's fantasies of dealing with his world, and in particular with his parents and siblings, the most important inhabitants of that world. Zeus, Homer's "Father of gods and men," is of course the major projection of the father in Greek myth, but in the allotment of spheres of influence by Zeus, Poseidon, and Hades we may see a splitting, or decomposition, of the father into three figures with separate though overlapping characteristics. Zeus is the head of the family as seen through a child's eyes: virtually omniscient and omnipotent (though harassed by a nagging wife), a stern if sometimes capricious figure of authority, jealous of his prerogatives (especially of a sexual nature), protector and punisher. As E. R. Dodds says, "It was natural to project on to the heavenly Father those curious mixed feelings about the human one which the child dared not acknowledge even to himself."[37]

Hades, the awful lord of the underworld, represents a certain aspect of the father (or of Zeus): he is the father who punishes, who holds the power of life and death over his children (and also, like Zeus, has a powerful sexual drive, as demonstrated in the rape of Persephone). That Hades represents an aspect of Zeus is revealed by passages in Greek literature such as *Iliad* 9.456, where he is called a "subterranean Zeus," or Aeschylus' *Suppliants,* in which he is called "the all-welcoming Zeus of the dead" (157–58) and "another Zeus" (231) who passes final judgment on the dead. The emblem of Hades, which he received from the Kyklopes at the time when Zeus received the lightning and Poseidon the trident (Apollodoros 1.2.1), is a helmet or cap that has the power to render its wearer invisible (Apollodoros 2.4.2: "wearing it, he saw whom he wished but was not seen by others"). The power of the cap of Hades repeats the etymological significance of his name itself, since *Aides* (the Epic form of Hades) means "the Unseen One." While Hades' function as a judge of the dead is usually assigned in early Greek literature to the Cretan brothers Minos and Rhadamanthys (and occasionally Aiakos), both his cap and his name would seem to indicate a paternal judgmental function. Like Santa Claus, who "knows if you've been bad or good," Hades represents the child's absolute conviction that his father knows and will punish even his most secret misdeeds. Sometimes, however, the tables are turned and the cap of Hades is worn by the hero of a myth, which portrays the child's success in viewing a forbidden sight without being caught or punished; the best-known example of this is the myth of Perseus, who wears the cap of Hades to help him decapitate Medousa and to escape the pursuit of her sister Gorgons (Apollodoros 2.4.2–3).

Poseidon, god of the sea, primarily represents the procreative sexuality of the father. This may be seen in the probable etymology of his name, which could mean "husband of Earth" (a relationship suggested also by his Epic epithets "Earth-holder" and

"Earth-shaker"), a natural derivative of the Greek idea that the earth was surrounded (or embraced) by a circular ocean; in his frequent association with the symbol of a stallion (another of his epithets is *Hippios,* Horse-Poseidon); in his emblem, the trident (a phallic implement that prefigures the three-forked tail, pitchfork, and even penis of the medieval Satan); and especially in his usual connection with the sea. Whereas in many languages and mythical systems the sea is feminine, the sea in Greek mythology would seem to have a primordial masculine value. The various Greek words for sea are masculine gender (with the exception of *thalassa,* a word of non-Greek origin), and its personifications such as Okeanos, Pontos, and Nereus are male deities. Furthermore the sea would seem to represent not merely abstract masculinity but specifically male sexuality and procreativity. Thus the most prolific of the Greek gods are the sea-gods Okeanos and Nereus, and there is a hint in Homer, as we have seen, that Okeanos himself may have appeared in an ancient cosmogonic myth not as a Titan but as a primal father-figure. In this hypothetical myth the original couple may have been Okeanos and Gaia, symbols of male and female procreation (with Okeanos preceding Poseidon as "husband of Earth"), and dynastic succession in the cosmos passed from Okeanos to Ouranos, then to Kronos, and finally to Zeus.

The sexual significance of the sea is due not only to its location embracing the maternal earth; there may also be some significance in the fact that it is a salty liquid, and as such a representation in nature of the sexual meaning that innumerable folk practices and beliefs attribute to the various liquid secretions of the body (e.g., perspiration, tears, saliva, urine), all of which share with semen the qualities of salinity and liquidity.[38] The same unconscious association underlies the English saying that someone is "the spit and image of his father"; spit, as in those creation myths where a creator-god makes the first humans from the clay formed by earth and spit (female and male symbols, respectively), is a seminal symbol, and the fact that a son looks exactly like his father is a proof of the father's seminal potency.

In Mesopotamian myths, on the other hand, this symbolism is usually reversed; sweet (fresh) water is male and bitter (salt) water is female. This reversal is presumably due to the immeasurable importance of the great river-systems in Mesopotamia. For both Greece and Mesopotamia the female principle is earth, but whereas in Greece the male principle is the sky (which produces rain and lightning) and the ocean (because of its location and salinity), in Mesopotamia the male principle is the river, which fecundates the earth. This concept is not entirely lacking in Greek thought, however, since the ocean is often thought of as a freshwater stream and since river-deities are always male and invariably lecherous.

THE STRATEGY OF ZEUS

Having led the successful rebellion against the Titans, Zeus is now the new sky-god and the master of the universe. But two new tasks await him: first he must set out to populate the world with his children, the gods, demigods, and mortals whose production will consume most of Zeus' time and energy from now on; but also, before he can even begin the work of procreation, he must do what is required to ensure that his reign will be permanent, and that he will not be overthrown by his sons as his father and grandfather were.

As I said earlier, we know, even before we are told, that Zeus will have to swallow a wife. He has learned from the fates of Ouranos and Kronos that to put his children in either his wife's body or his own is no solution, and he also realizes now that the real enemy is not his children but his wife. Therefore, instead of swallowing his children, like Kronos, he has no choice but to swallow his wife. The story first appears in the *Theogony,* in the catalogue of Zeus' wives (886–929).

The seven wives of Zeus are, in order, the Okeanid nymph Metis, the Titanid Themis, another Okeanid Eurynome, Zeus' sister Demeter, another Titanid Mnemosyne, the second-generation Titanid Leto, and finally his sister Hera; the relationships of the seven to Zeus are cousin–aunt–cousin–sister–aunt–cousin–sister. Once he has secured his reign by swallowing Metis, the first wife, it seems that all other possible relationships are now open to him. There is, of course, one important exception: unlike Ouranos, who had married his mother, Gaia, and like Kronos and the Titans, who married their sisters but not their mother, Zeus stops short of mating with his mother, Rhea. Nevertheless, just as Rhea had been virtually a mother-figure to her husband Kronos, Zeus now marries two of his mother's sisters (Themis and Mnemosyne) and two earth-goddesses (Themis and Demeter). But since marrying mother-substitutes instead of the actual mother had not saved Kronos from being overthrown, Zeus must do more than merely refrain from marrying Rhea herself.

Or, to put it another way, Kronos may be said to have married his mother under the guise of Rhea, her double, just as Ouranos had married his mother, Gaia. With Zeus it seems that the scenario will be repeated again, since both maternal figures, Gaia and Rhea, contrive to save him from his father. But in Zeus' case there is an important difference: although he has a sexual relationship with two aunts and several maternal goddesses, he observes at least a rudimentary distinction between permissible and nonpermissible sexual objects. His establishment of a primitive rule of exogamy occurs in his first marriage; to avoid having the son who will overthrow him, Zeus must give up the woman who will be that son's mother.

Zeus then proceeds to atone for this act of restraint by copulating with practically every woman in Greek myth. There is, however, one other occasion on which he observes an exogamic taboo, a repetition perhaps required by the fact that he had not abstained entirely from a sexual relationship with Metis. The several versions of this story are summarized by Apollodoros (3.13.5):

> Then Peleus married Thetis, the daughter of Nereus. Zeus and Poseidon had competed with one another to marry her, but when Themis prophesied that Thetis would have a son greater than his father, they both desisted. Some say that it was Prometheus who foretold that the son of Thetis would become the ruler of the sky, when Zeus was intent on having intercourse with her. Others say that Thetis did not wish to have intercourse with Zeus since she had been raised by Hera, and that an angered Zeus decreed that she be married to a mortal.

These three variants seem to fit together in an interesting way. Clearly Zeus forced Thetis to marry a mortal not so much because he was angry for being scorned but because he was afraid of the son greater than his father; why else would he choose as Thetis' husband Peleus, a second-rate hero with the dubious distinction of having been defeated in wrestling by a woman, Atalanta? As for

the version involving Prometheus, it must involve the Titan's revealing the existence but not the name of the woman whose son
would rule the world. In this way Prometheus, sentenced by Zeus
to eternal suffering for his theft of fire, can force Zeus either to
free him and learn the secret name or to give up sex altogether
(an obvious impossibility). For sooner or later, if that woman exists somewhere in the world, Zeus will find her in his ambitious
campaign of procreation, and he will be overthrown. She might
even be (and in one version, she actually is) the current object of
his amatory attention. By releasing Prometheus, Zeus learns that
the woman is Thetis; and by observing at least a minimal restraint,
he insures his perpetual triumph.

Zeus's successful strategy does not imply, however, that his
position is free from attack; it simply means that any oedipal assault on him will be unsuccessful. We have already seen instances
of such a rebellion (with a sexual motive) in the myths of Ixion
and Tityos, punished in Tartaros for having attempted to rape one
of Zeus' wives. Other examples of unsuccessful rebellion include
Prometheus, the Giants (whom Gaia brought forth to fight against
Zeus after he had conquered the Titans and become ruler of the
world, thus repeating in regard to Zeus the same role she had
played earlier against her husband Ouranos [Apollodoros 1.6.1–2]),
or the Aloadai, giant children who piled mountain upon mountain in their effort to scale the sky and attack Zeus (Apollodoros
1.7.4).

None of these rebels, however, is actually the son of Zeus
and one of his wives. In fact, all seven wives combined produce
only two sons (but twenty-three daughters), and the two sons,
Leto's Apollo and Hera's Ares, never pose a threat to Zeus. Still
there is one god, who may or may not have been a son of Zeus
and Hera, whose mysteriously contradictory myth may conceal a
lost story in which Zeus had to face, and defeat, a real threat from
an actual son. This god is Hephaistos, the god of fire, metallurgy,
and magic.

HEPHAISTOS

According to Hesiod (*Theogony* 927–29), Hera gave birth to
Hephaistos without having had intercourse, since she was angry

with Zeus (presumably for having given birth to Athena all by himself). In the *Odyssey* Hephaistos is clearly regarded as the son of Zeus and Hera (8.312); in the *Iliad* the same parentage is assumed by most readers of 1.578 and 14.338, although the inference seems doubtful. And in most post-Homeric writings he is regarded as the parthenogenic son of Hera alone.

The *Iliad* also contains two contradictory versions of why Hephaistos fell from the sky to the earth. In *Iliad* 1.590–94, he cautions his mother Hera against continuing her quarrel with Zeus by recalling to her that once Zeus threw him out of the sky when he attempted to help her during one of her innumerable disputes with her husband; on that occasion the fight was over Hera's persecution of Herakles, and Zeus had hung Hera from the sky with anvils attached to her feet:

> At another time, when I tried to help you,
> he seized my foot and threw me from the gods' threshold.
> All day I fell, and with the setting sun
> I landed on Lemnos, and little life was still in me;
> after I fell, Sintian men rescued me.

In *Iliad* 18.395–405, however, Hephaistos contradicts his own earlier story and claims that he was thrown from the sky by Hera, who was ashamed of the lame child to whom she had given birth. Rescued by Eurynome and Thetis, he spent nine years with them:

> She [Thetis] saved me, when I suffered, falling far
> by the will of my dog-faced mother, who wanted to
> hide me since I was lame; then I would have suffered
> in spirit if Eurynome and Thetis had not received me
> to their bosom, Eurynome the daughter of back-flowing
> Okeanos. Nine years with them I worked much in bronze,
> making brooches, curved clasps, cups, and necklaces
> in the hollow cave, and Okeanos' endless stream
> flowed around, murmuring in foam; and no other
> of gods or mortal men knew,
> but Thetis and Eurynome knew, who had saved me.

Other sources say that he also made special gifts to send back to the mother who had rejected him, a golden throne which immobilized her when she sat down and a pair of adamantine sandals which somehow caused her to hang suspended in the air

(Pausanias 1.20.3; Hyginus, *Fabula* 166). Finally the gods sent Dionysos to get Hephaistos drunk and thereby persuade him to return to Olympos; he re-entered heaven riding on an ass and freed his mother from his gifts (Pausanias 1.20.3).

Sometimes portrayed as living in Olympos, sometimes in his forge under the island of Lemnos, Hephaistos is married, but the name of his wife is variable. According to Hesiod, she is Aglaia, youngest of the Charites (*Theogony* 945), but in *Iliad* 18 she is Charis (the singular form of the plural name Charites), and in the song of Demodokos in *Odyssey* 8 she is Aphrodite, whose affair with Ares is detected and punished by Hephaistos. He catches the lovers in an invisible net, which immobilizes them and exposes them (and himself) to the laughter of the assembled gods.

Perhaps because of his lack of success with Aphrodite (which seems to have been a complete lack), Hephaistos on one occasion attempted to have intercourse with Athena, when she came for weapons to his forge. Because of his lameness, however, he could not attain his goal but managed to leave some semen on Athena's leg, which the disgusted goddess wiped off with a piece of wool. She then threw the wool on the ground, and in due time the autochthonous Attic hero Erichthonios was born from the earth (Apollodoros 3.14.6).

The myth of Hephaistos thus begins with an overt contradiction, the epic variants concerning his fall from the sky, the cause of his lameness, and even the participants in his conception. This contradiction corresponds to a basic psychological ambivalence in the portrayal of Hephaistos. In the *Iliad* 1 version he appears as a rebel against Zeus, an instance of the oedipal hero who enters into conflict with the father for the sake of the mother. What lost myths may have underlain this episode we cannot say, but it seems to be derived from an older account of the succession myth in which Zeus had to defend his claim to permanent rule by overcoming a challenge brought by his own son. As Kronos had been overthrown by Zeus and Ouranos had been overcome by Kronos, we might suppose that a similar danger would be posed for Zeus himself in his turn, and that the account of Hephaistos' fall from the sky, so reminiscent of Milton's Lucifer, is a remnant of this conjectured myth.

For reasons not immediately clear this story disappeared except for the Homeric incident, perhaps because it was eclipsed by the myth of the rebellion against Zeus by Prometheus, a fire-god closely related to Hephaistos and in some instances functionally interchangeable with him. For example, there are versions in which Prometheus, like Hephaistos, is called a son of Hera (scholia to *Iliad* 5.205, 14.295) and is said to have fallen in love with Athena (scholia to Apollonius Rhodius 2.1249); both Hephaistos and Prometheus were said to have assisted at the birth of Athena from the head of Zeus (Euripides, *Ion* 455; Pindar, *Olympian* 7.35); Hephaistos created Pandora by mixing earth and water (*Theogony* 571) and Prometheus was credited with the creation of mankind by the same means (Apollodoros 1.7.1); both Hephaistos and Prometheus were honored as the bringers of culture and technical advancement to humanity (Aeschylus, *Prometheus Bound* 436–506; Homeric *Hymn to Hephaistos* 2–7); Hephaistos was called the father or grandfather of the Lemnian Kabeiroi, and Prometheus was named as one of the Theban Kabeiroi, along with his son Aitnaios (Strabo 10.3.21; Pausanias 9.25.6); in Attica the shrines and cults of Hephaistos and Prometheus were closely associated.[39]

We noted earlier other instances of rebellion against Zeus (Tityos, Ixion, Giants, Aloadai, etc.) and there are many additional parallels (Bellerophon, Salmoneus, Keyx, etc.), but the one most relevant to our purpose and most closely connected to the succession myth is the story of Typhoeus, the most horrible monster of all and the most powerful and dangerous enemy of Zeus.

Both Hesiod and Apollodoros call Typhoeus the son of Gaia and Tartaros, and their accounts are generally similar; Apollodoros includes more details and places Typhoeus after his defeat under Mount Aetna, while Hesiod has Zeus throw him into Tartaros. In two other versions, however, Typhoeus is closely linked to Hera, her enmity with Zeus, and (either directly or indirectly) with Hephaistos. In one version (scholia to *Iliad* 2.783) Gaia, angered by the death of the Giants, complained to Hera, who asked Kronos for help. He gave her two eggs smeared with his semen and told her to bury them in the ground, predicting that from them would be born an avenger who could overthrow Zeus. She buried the eggs in Kilikia and Typhoeus was born, but Hera then was reconciled with Zeus; she told him what had happened and he killed Typhoeus with a thunderbolt.

In the other version (Homeric *Hymn to Apollo* 305–56), Hera, angry because Zeus had produced Athena by himself whereas her own attempt at parthenogenesis had resulted in the crippled Hephaistos, whom she had thrown from the sky (as in *Iliad* 18), prayed to Gaia, Ouranos, and the Titans that she would bear a son greater than Zeus. A year later she gave birth to Typhoeus and entrusted him to the serpent Pytho to raise:

305 Once she [Pytho] received from gold-throned Hera and raised
terrible and cruel Typhoeus, a plague to mortals.
Hera bore him since she was angry with father Zeus,
when he, Kronos' son, bore illustrious Athena
in his head; mistress Hera grew immediately angry
310 and spoke among the assembled immortals:
"Hear from me, all gods and goddesses,
how cloud-gather Zeus begins to dishonor me
unprovoked, after he made me his true and good wife.
Now without me he bore owl-eyed Athena,
315 who is eminent among all the blessed immortals.
But my son was born the weakest of all gods,
Hephaistos with crippled feet, whom I bore by myself.
I seized him and threw him into the wide sea.
But Nereus' daughter, silver-shod Thetis,
320 rescued and cared for him with her sisters;
she could have done some other favor for the blessed gods.
Bold and clever one, what else will you now plot?
How dared you bear owl-eyed Athena alone?
Would I not have borne a child? At least I am called
325 yours, among the immortals who possess the wide sky.
Take care I do not plot some future evil for you.
Even now I will arrange to give birth to a son,
who will be eminent among the immortal gods,
without disgracing the holy bed of you and me.
330 I will not come to your embrace, but going far
from you I will be with the immortal gods."
Saying this with angry heart she left the gods.
Then cow-eyed mistress Hera prayed at once,
struck the ground with flat hand, and said:
335 "Hear me now, Gaia and vast Ouranos above
and Titan gods who live under the earth
in great Tartaros, ancestors of men and gods.
All of you now listen and give me a son apart from
Zeus and just as strong as Zeus; rather, may he be

340 stronger, as wide-seeing Zeus is stronger than Kronos."
Saying this, she struck the earth with her great hand;
and life-bearing Gaia was moved; seeing this, she felt
joy in her heart, for she thought it would come to pass.
From then on until the year's completion
345 she never came to the bed of wise Zeus
nor to the carved chair, where formerly
she sat and planned dense counsels,
but she stayed in her crowded temples
and enjoyed her offerings, cow-eyed mistress Hera.
350 But when the months and days were fulfilled
and the seasons passed through the circling year,
she bore a child unlike gods or mortals,
terrible and cruel Typhoeus, a plague to mortals.
Quickly cow-eyed mistress Hera took and gave him
355 [to Pytho], one evil thing to another; and she received
him; and he did many wrongs to the famous races of men.

We may compare this version to Hesiod's, in which Hera and
Typhoeus are unrelated, but in which Hera similarly conceives
Hephaistos on her own because Zeus had given birth to Athena.

He [Zeus] himself bore from his head owl-eyed Athena,
the awesome, fight-rousing, army-leading, unweary
mistress whose delight is din and wars and battles;
but Hera, who was angry and at odds with her husband,
without love's union bore famous Hephaistos,
excellent in arts beyond all of Ouranos' descendants.

Theogony, 924–29

Although the *Theogony* does not mention Hera's ill-treatment of
Hephaistos, and Homer in *Iliad* 18 does not mention a quarrel
between Zeus and Hera, the two accounts along with the *Hymn to
Apollo* seem to represent a common tradition in which Hera gave
birth to Hephaistos in order to avenge herself against Zeus and
in which Typhoeus and Hephaistos therefore play similar roles.

The assaults made against Zeus by the various rebels who
attempt to usurp his position are often characterized as sexual, as
in the archetypal mutilation of Ouranos by Kronos; for example,
Typhoeus, the Giants, Tityos, and Ixion all want to have a sexual
relationship with goddesses. If Hephaistos were to appear as a
credible threat to Zeus' sexual dominion, he also would have to

be equipped with the emblems of active masculinity, a condition that seems to be met by the phallic associations of his connection with both fire and metallurgy. We have already discussed the psychological meaning of the mythological and philosophical symbolism of fire; as we saw, fire seems to represent both male sexuality and also the vital principle of generation, the dynamic creativity that occurs when male and female are brought together.

The same connotations are implied in Hephaistos's role as god of the forge and of metallurgy, laboring to produce arms and artifacts for the gods and select mortals in (usually) his workshop in a cave under the island of Lemnos.

In the Athenian festivals of the Chalkeia and Hephaistia, Hephaistos was honored, along with Athena and Prometheus, as the patron of smiths and craftsmen. In Crete Hephaistos was worshipped as the discoverer of every means of working iron, bronze, gold, and silver (Diodoros 5.74.2), a description which corresponds to Aeschylus' praise of Prometheus as the first to discover bronze, iron, gold, and silver beneath the earth (*Prometheus Bound* 500–503). Whether in Crete or elsewhere in ancient Greece, the discovery of the arts of metallurgy was usually attributed not to major gods but to primitive demonic beings; nevertheless, these archaic and mysterious gods, called Daktyloi or Telchines or Kabeiroi, are regularly associated with Hephaistos.

Although these obscure demons were generally connected with specific areas in the eastern Mediterranean (the Daktyloi with Crete and Phrygia, the Telchines with Rhodes, and the Kabeiroi with Samothrace and Lemnos), they are often said to have migrated from one place to another. They are all named on different occasions as either the same as, or the ancestors of, the Cretan-Phrygian Kouretes and the Phrygian Korybantes, and they share their chief attributes in common (so much so that, as Strabo says, the Korybantes, Kabeiroi, Daktyloi, Telchines, and Kouretes were regarded by many writers as related and by others as identical [10.3.7]). Their essential nature is threefold: they are attendants of some form of the Anatolian mother-goddess (usually appearing as Kybele or Rhea); they are wizards and sorcerers; and they were the first to discover and work bronze and iron. The Kabeiroi, whose main cult centers were the islands Lemnos, Imbros, and Samothrace but were also worshipped in Greece, Egypt, and Phrygia, were said to be either the sons or grandsons of Hephaistos by the early mythographers Pherekydes and Akousilaos; according to the lexicographer Photius, the Kabeiroi were also named Hephaistoi. Of the three groups of demons the Kabeiroi are most closely related to Hephaistos by kinship and cult, but the Daktyloi and Telchines resemble the god as much or more in their activity. Thus the Telchine are called magicians and discoverers of certain arts (Diodoros 5.55) and sorcerers who were the first metallurgists (Strabo 14.2.7). The Idaean Daktyloi are also said to have been the first metalworkers and miners as well as being wizards, and to have discovered the use of fire and the "art of Hephaistos" (Pherekydes in scholia to Apollonius Rhodius 1.1129). Sometimes represented as being tiny and dwarfish in stature, these demons have an obvious affinity with the dwarfs and gnomes of the mythology and folklore of northern Europe (e.g., the Nibelungs), who work at forges in caves beneath the earth or are the guardians of secret treasures buried in the earth.

The sexual significance of these smith-gods lies in the fact that they, who are always attendants of a great mother-goddess, work within the body of the earth (Gaia) at the task of creation. Thus they are a group of personified phalloi whose labor is production from the body of the mother, and it may be for this reason that they appear often as phallic beings; Herodotus says that the ithyphallic herms of Athens (stone boundary markers with a bust of Hermes and a prominent phallus) copied a practice connected with the rites of the Kabeiroi on Samothrace (2.51).

The two great technical achievements of early man, the beginning of agriculture and the discovery of the use of fire in metallurgy, may both be regarded as sexual acts and were portrayed in this way by the Greeks. For in both accomplishments the earth is a maternal figure who conceives and gives birth as a result of man's intervention. Unlike the earlier cultural orders of hunting and food-gathering societies, when the earth produced its bounty spontaneously and, in a sense, parthenogenically, with the onset of agriculture the earth was now inseminated by farmers who were her "husbandmen." Similarly, the discovery of metallurgy meant that the earth now produced her precious metals through the cooperation of man and the application of fire.

If we may then regard Hephaistos as a phallic god in light of his opposition to Zeus, his association with fire, and his magical craft of metallurgy, there still remains a contradictory theme of impotence and sexual failure, which runs throughout his myth. We can see this, for example, in his being cuckolded by Aphrodite, in his abortive and almost ludicrous attempt to have a sexual relationship with Athena, a most unlikely recipient of his passion, and especially in his lameness.

Since Hephaistos's disability is specifically crippled feet, we might consider at this point the symbolic significance of feet in Greek myth. Psychoanalysis has made the concept of a "foot fetish" a common notion, but the idea behind this concept, of an unconscious association between foot and phallus, is confirmed in the Greek language itself. The best-known example of a phallic foot in Greek literature in the oracle given to Aigeus in Euripides' *Medea;* Aigeus tells Medea that the oracle told him "not to loosen the dangling foot [*pous*] of the wineskin," that is, not to have sexual intercourse, until he returned home. The symbolism of *pous* is immediately clear to Medea and presumably, and more importantly, to the audience as well. From the related root *ped-* comes the word *pedion,* "plain," that is, ground in or on which the foot is placed. Taking the literal meaning of *pous,* a *pedion* is ground that can be walked on, as opposed to mountain or marsh; taking the symbolic meaning, it is arable ground, suitable to be fertilized and bring forth new life (that is, a receptacle for the phallic foot). Thus *pedion* is also a metaphor for the female genitals, usually sexually mature but depilated (as a crop is harvested), as in the "beautiful *pedion*" of the Boiotian woman at Aristophanes, *Lysistrata* 89. Related to this pattern of signification is the word *leimon* (meadow), which because it is uncultivated ground, came to mean "virgin female genitals," as at Euripides, *Kyklops* 171 (the direction of the symbolism is exactly opposite from that of such English phrases as "virgin territory"). There are in fact several instances of similar symbolism in English usage; for example, the meaning of the custom of attaching old shoes to the vehicle of a newly married couple is clearly expressed in the saying which once accompanied this practice in England: "May she fit you as well as this old shoe fits my foot!"[40]

It is tempting to ascribe the contradiction in the nature of Hephaistos, who is both phallic and impotent, to a distinction between function and myth or, alternatively, to successive variations in the myth. In the first instance, Hephaistos' phallic qualities would be derivatives of his role as god of fire, a function that must inevitably bring him into conflict with Zeus, his father and also a fire god himself (in the form of the lightning). Since the role of Zeus must remain impervious to overthrow and also because of the progressive endeavor to elevate him from a god of brute force to a deity of wisdom and justice, the potential threat of Hephaistos is eliminated by making him, whenever he leaves his forge, into an impotent and even comical figure, and by shifting the orientation of mythical conflict from father–son to mother–son and wife–husband.

In the second instance, we might assume that there was indeed an early lost myth in which Zeus had to fight against not only giants and monsters but also his own son. This myth could have been brought with them by the Greeks when they first entered Greece, or it could have been acquired during the Mycenean period through contact with Near Eastern succession myths, in particular the Hurrian and Mesopotamian.[41] However, perhaps because of the tendency to exalt the position of Zeus, perhaps (and this may be more likely) because of contact with the Cretan, Phrygian, and indigenous religions centered on a maternal goddess, perhaps for unknown sociohistorical factors occurring during the isolation of the transition from the Myceanean period to the Archaic (1200–800 B.C.), or perhaps for a combination of these factors, the father–son conflict tended to be replaced by cross-sex antagonism (especially when Zeus is concerned) and, except for the brief mention in *Iliad* 1, Hephaistos is henceforth in conflict with his mother instead of his father. We can see this tendency toward cross-sex antagonism and misogyny already in Hesiod, and it accelerates throughout Greek myth. An obvious example is the story of Pandora in the *Theogony* and the *Works and Days,* and we should remember that the secret of Zeus' success is a misogynistic lesson he has learned from his predecessors.

Despite Hephaistos' conflict with his mother, it should not be overlooked that the female enemy in the succession myth is not the mother but rather the wife, who regularly takes the side of her children against her husband. The malevolent maternal figure does make her appearance in other contexts—Greek myth is largely the record of Hera's destructive hostility toward the sons of Zeus by other women—but even this is ultimately the result of her quarrel with her husband Zeus. In the case of Hephaistos also, Hera rejects him precisely because she has failed to gain adequate retribution for her husband's abandonment of her and her maternal role.

Perhaps all we can say is that the Greeks were led, by possible internal causes and by exposure to the strongly matriarchal religious systems they encountered, to admit into their own myths a female principle who could be a dangerous enemy to both her husband and her sons. This formulation, however, does no more than provide a possible answer for the intrusive importance of Hera in a myth that might have been originally concerned with sons overthrowing, or trying to overthrow, their fathers. The basic structure of the myth remains the same. Even the parthenogenic birth of Hephaistos, which would seem to remove Zeus from the story, in actuality serves to reintroduce him, since the birth of Hephaistos is Hera's response to the quasi-parthenogenic birth of Athena and since the fact of parthenogenesis would seem in this context to be the prelude to an episode of oedipal conflict between father and son: Gaia had thus produced the Giants, and Hera (in one version) Typhoeus, for the express purpose of overthrowing Zeus.

In any case, the assumption of an historical change in the superstructure of the myth does not solve the problem of Hephaistos' dual nature as both phallic and impotent, nor can this contradiction be correlated with variant orientations of the myth, as if he were phallic in one version and impotent in another. Whether it is his father or his mother who rejects him, both versions require that Hephaistos be a phallic hero, either as a fitting opponent of Zeus on his own, or as a proper example of his mother's parthenogenic ability and an instrument of her desire for revenge on her husband. Furthermore, in both versions it is appropriate that Hephaistos be portrayed as ultimately impotent; if he is to fight against Zeus (and both versions seem to have this objective in mind), he must be defeated and the example of Ouranos show the sexual nature of this sort of conflict. As for the version which attributes Hephaistos' lameness, the constant symbol of his impotence, to Hera's inability to produce a perfectly formed child, this dysfunction is a virtually predictable result of his being the fatherless son of the most powerful mother in Greek myth. His role seems determined even before his birth, since Hera produces him precisely in order to demonstrate what she can accomplish without men, and then throws him away when he does not measure up to her expectations.

Should we say then that Hephaistos, either lacking a father or vanquished by the father, is deprived of masculinity and seeks to compensate for this deprivation by fabricating symbolic phalloi at his forge, just as Athena, born without a mother, is deprived of femininity and therefore devotes herself to a career of emulating maleness (compare her weapons, her warlike activities, her male partisanship)? That the motherless female and the fatherless male should both be striving to acquire the missing phallus may possibly be traced ultimately to the fact that they are both products of a patriarchal culture; and that the major sexual adventure of each of them should be with one another (his futile attempt to rape her) is highly ironic.

But perhaps there is another solution to the problem of Hephaistos' enigmatic sexuality. While the historical conflict of different cultures may underlie the hostility between the sky-gods Ouranos and Kronos and their wives, the maternal earth-goddesses Gaia and Rhea, the essence of these conflicts is that these goddesses are principles of fertility, whereas the gods, despite their prolific sexuality, are essentially antigenerative. Although Ouranos seems to engage in a single unending act of intercourse with Gaia—thus keeping her children inside while at the same time asserting his paternal prerogative—both he and Kronos seek to undo the fact of generation by the perpetual confinement of their children in one or the other parental body. With Zeus, however, things are different; he causes those who were bound beneath the earth to be released and sets out on an ambitious program of reproductive activity. Like his forefathers, Zeus is a principle of male sexuality, another god of rain and lightning; but unlike them he is not an enemy of generation. And it is this principle of generation that the fire-god Hephaistos seems to represent.

The distinction we are making between sexuality and generation suggests that the magical power of generation is not localized in the phallus but rather in the acivity that results from the act of penetration. Although primitive magic is much concerned with potency and conception (at the beginning of pregnancy) and with birth (at the end of pregnancy), the physiological prototype of magic would seem to be that mysterious activity that takes place within the body of the pregnant female. Hephaistos does not represent the *external* power of the phallus; he is not the fertilizing rain or the phallic lightning, but rather he, like the wizard Kabeiroi, Daktyloi, and Telchines, is the power of the phallus within the body of the mother. As Demeter represents what happens to the earth after it has been fertilized by the seminal rain, Hephaistos represents what happens to the earth after it has been subjected to the power of fire. A connection is also established between Demeter and Hephaistos by the fact that both of them live for a time in isolation from the other gods and resist all attempts to persuade or force them to rejoin the divine company, Demeter when she lost Persephone and Hephaistos when he was thrown from the sky. The world cannot live when Demeter is absent, and the fact of a similar episode in the myth of Hephaistos suggests the importance of what he represents to the furtherance of life.

In the version in which Hephaistos is born crippled and then thrown from the sky by Hera, both incidents may be viewed as metaphors for the same psychological event. The first and greatest human loss is the separation of the child from his mother, at birth or, more exactly, at the time of individuation when the child first learns that he and the mother are separate beings. From this point on the child wishes to be once again united with the mother, to be once more part of her body. There are two paths of unconscious fantasy that can represent this desire as hallucinatorily fulfilled. One is the way of the oedipus complex and adult sexuality: to be a phallic hero, to gratify the mother's desire by having the phallus she wants, to find in sexual intercourse a recapitulation of the original bond between mother and child. The other is the way of regression and preoedipal fixation, retrogressive rather than progressive, a return to the past state of symbiotic union rather than an active pursuit of some substitute for it in the future. Yet the motivational impulse is the same in either case: to be reunited with the mother or her substitute in the closest possible union or, since it is only the phallus that can accomplish this in fact, to be the phallus within the body of the mother.

That Hephaistos in one version attempted to follow the path of oedipal activity is indicated both by the conflict with Zeus in *Iliad* 1 and by the parthenogenic variant, since, as we have seen, parthenogenesis is connected with the creation of oedipal rivals. But in this instance parthenogenesis seems to have another meaning as well; opposed to the triangular oedipal structure that is one aspect of the Hephaistos myth, it expresses the dominant dyadic structure, the preoedipal relationship between mother and child in which the father is excluded. Yet this relationship may be viewed as triangular also, a triad that consists not of child, mother, and father, but of child, mother, and phallus. And if the aim of the child in the oedipal triad is to replace the father's phallus with his own, the aim of the child in the preoedipal triad is to re-establish union with the mother by being the phallus she desires. In simplest terms, the distinction is between *having* and *being* the phallus: in the preoedipal project it is not the possession of the phallic organ that matters, but rather the transformation of the entire self into a phallus that resides within the mother's body.

There is a good deal of clinical evidence for this phenomenon, and two examples from folklore and religion may help to illustrate it. First, the dwarfs of mine and forge in European legend (Nibelungs, Rumpelstiltskin, Snow White's Seven Dwarfs, etc.), clearly related to Hephaistos and the wizard-smiths of Greek myth, are little men whose whole body is a phallus within the body of the earth. As Jones says, "the conception of the male organ as a mannikin is extremely widespread and . . . often becomes personified and incorporated in an independent figure,"[42] and, according to Bettelheim, "these 'little men' with their stunted bodies and their mining occupation—they skillfully penetrate into dark holes—all suggest phallic connotations and a preoedipal existence."[43] Second, in the Phrygian rites of the mother-goddess Kybele/Rhea worshippers castrated themselves and offered the severed genitals to the goddess, thereby achieving mystical union with her. The castration is a denial of masculinity and oedipal striving; the worshipper's phallus is removed so that the himself may be the phallus that is incorporated within the body of the goddess. What he becomes is reminiscent of the role of the Kabeiroi, Daktyloi, and Telchines; it is therefore not surprising that these beings are all associated with Rhea/Kybele and usually with Phrygia as well.

We might summarize briefly how this pertains to an interpretation of Hephaistos. Separated from his mother at birth, he attempts to re-establish union with her by means of both oedipal and preoedipal strategies. In the heroic oedipal project he fails, as he must, since Zeus cannot be replaced, but in the magical preoedipal project he succeeds, since in this case he is not a sexual rival of Zeus but rather takes up where Zeus leaves off, as the magic principle of generation within the mother's body.

The cosmological projection of male sexuality takes the double form of lightning and rain, both of which travel from the sky to the earth. Thus Hephaistos, after his own flight through the sky, is associated, like the Vedic god Agni, in one instance with fire and in the other with water; one variant has him land on Lemnos, where he will establish his fiery forge within the volcanic island, and the other has him land in the sea, under which he spends the next nine years in the cavern of Thetis and Eurynome. The length of time, the cavern, and the reception by the maternal goddesses all mark this episode as a representation of return to the maternal womb. And in both instances, whether in a cave beneath the land or in a cavern under the sea, Hephaistos begins his career of magical fabrication.

Two remarkable accomplishments of Hephaistos also suggest his function as principle of generation within the body of the maternal earth: his creation of Pandora from earth and water, and, after his failure with Athena, his impregnation of the earth and the subsequent birth of Erichthonios. We have already noted the resemblance between Hephaistos and Typhoeus, both of whom were said to be parthenogenic children of Hera, but the Erichthonios episode also suggests a resemblance between Hephaistos and Kronos. In one version the serpentine monster Typhoeus appears as the progeny of Gaia and Kronos, and the story is strikingly similar to the conception of the half-serpent Erichthonios; as the latter is born from the semen of Hephaistos that has fallen upon the earth, Typhoeus was born from eggs smeared with the semen of Kronos and buried in the earth.

There is, of course, another point of connection between Kronos and Hephaistos: as the latter performs his function within the earth, the metaphorical representation of the mother's body, Kronos also lived after his birth in the earth, in this case the literal body of his mother Gaia. The difference between the two gods, however, lies in the fact that Kronos emerged from his mother's body to engage immediately in sexual conflict with his father Ouranos. For Hephaistos, on the other hand, the mother's body is both a refuge and the site of his magic generative power. We might describe Hephaistos, in fact, as a Kronos who, when faced with the prospect of oedipal conflict, chose to remain within the mother.

Still there is that vestige of oedipal revolt in the myth of Hephaistos, preserved for us in the first book of the oldest surviving piece of Greek literature. In some version somewhere Hephaistos did emerge, like Kronos, to do battle with his sky-god father. And, like Kronos, he was defeated by Zeus. But, finally, he finds his place and his victory in a preoedipal union with the mother, just as Kronos ultimately will rule over the symbiotic paradise of the Islands of the Blessed.

CHAPTER FIVE

CONCLUSION

While Hesiod tended his sheep on the slopes of Mount Helicon, the Olympian Muses appeared to him in a dream, or daydream, or vision of some sort, and told him of the origin and history of the gods. Hesiod remembered this dream and wrote it down (or dictated it), no doubt with some changes, in the hexameter verse of epic poetry. His vision became the standard Greek version of the beginning of the world and its divine inhabitants, and the reasons for its success are probably the same reasons he had, and remembered, the vision in the first place.

We know next to nothing about the Greek origin myths already in existence when Hesiod composed his *Theogony,* but we know that they did exist and that Hesiod did not invent something entirely new. Functioning like day residue in a dream, previous myths provided Hesiod with the data that he arranged in a new and satisfying pattern. In this pattern the ascent of Zeus to permanent sovereignty in the world is presented with implicit but certain logic as an inevitable fact. We know that Zeus must succeed since he is, after all, the chief god of the Greek pantheon, but Hesiod shows us why and how he must succeed where his predecessors, Ouranos and Kronos, had failed.

But this is only one aspect of Hesiod's achievement. Underlying the logical inevitability of Zeus' triumph is an emotional imperative that is no less compelling. Zeus is victorious not only because there is no logical alternative, but also because he is, at least in the *Theogony,* not so much the archetypal father as the idealized son. His triumph is the equally inevitable replacement of fathers by sons, or the older generation by the younger, and in this way the ambivalence with which Zeus is often regarded in later Greek thought is voided. Instead of being a combination of "good" and "bad" father (as in the contradictory portrayals of Zeus in Aeschylus' *Suppliants* and *Prometheus*), the paternal role of Hesiod's Zeus is the wish-fulfilling result of his oedipal triumph. He wins the stuff of divine sons' dreams—virtually unlimited sexual access to goddesses and mortal women—and, thanks to the swallowing of Metis and the avoidance of Thetis, no ambitious son appears to challenge his rule and take his place. Hephaistos, whom Homer seems to regard as the son of Zeus and Hera, would be the likely candidate, but Hesiod eliminates this possibility (in what may be his most significant innovation) by making Hephaistos the son of Hera alone and by making the threat to Zeus come not from his son but from the monster Typhoeus. Various mythical references show that Typhoeus is a substitute for Hephaistos, but in the *Theogony* (and usually thereafter) he is associated not with Hephaistos but with the Titans and Giants, other gigantic children of Gaia, and Zeus' defeat of Typhoeus is a repetition of his victory over his father and the older generation.

The potential oedipal threat of Hephaistos is also transferred to his fellow fire-god Prometheus, but even in this episode the portrayal of Zeus is favorable and quite unlike Aeschylus' version of the same story. Zeus is not deceived by Prometheus' disguised sacrifices, although he pretends to be, and in fact the whole episode can be read as an example of Zeus' beneficent justice: he will free Prometheus from his torture not, as elsewhere, because Prometheus knows a sexual secret which might cause Zeus' downfall, but because he wishes to glorify his son Herakles; instead of taking fire from men a second time, he allows them to keep the precious gift and sends as substitute punishment Pandora and the race of women (who, as Hesiod says in *Works and Days* 702–3, can be the best thing for man as well as the worst). Prometheus, a second-generation Titan, is of the same generation as Zeus; his defeat by Zeus is the result of sibling, not oedipal rivalry.

Zeus, the hero of Hesiod's vision, is the all-conquering son, the oedipal success story par excellence, and also, secondarily, the good father of unlimited power and knowledge. Whatever Hesiod's own filial position and ambition may have been, his Zeus is a figure with whom all sons (that is, all men, whether or not they become fathers) can identify.

This does not mean that the only function of the origin myth is to make men feel good by gratifying unconsicous oedipal aspirations. Its primary function on a conscious level is clearly what Kirk would classify as "speculative": to describe and explain the origin of the world and the gods. But this intellectual goal is expressed in, and energized by, a structure that recalls and reanimates the deepest concerns of childhood. Sons overthrow their fathers not because this is the way things are, but because mothers favor their sons. The principal figures of maternal partisanship are Gaia and her double Rhea; Gaia marries one son and enables another to castrate his father in her womb itself, while Rhea and Gaia together rescue Zeus from his father and make it possible for him both to become and to remain the oedipal victor. Women may appear as dangerous and evil in the myth of Pandora, but this is simply an extension of the roles of Gaia and Rhea, whose maternal allegiances regularly turn them against their husbands. The good mother is necessarily a bad wife, since she must take the side of her son against her husband; even the ostensibly "good" wife, as Hesiod says, is always half good and half evil (*Theogony* 608–9).[1]

The theoretical account of the origin of the world is grounded in the gratification of childhood wishes and the overcoming of childhood anxieties. The rule of Zeus is assurance that sons need to fear neither paternal retribution nor the loss of maternal love. As Greek culture at the time of Hesiod emerges from the Dark Age and enters upon history and maturity, its future greatness, like that of its chief god, is already promised by the good childhood of mythic beginnings.

NOTES

PREFACE

1. See Pucci (1977) 88.

CHAPTER ONE

1. Burkert (1979); Burkert (1983); Kirk (1970); Kirk (1974).
2. Kirk (1974) 28–29.
3. Kirk (1970) 24.
4. Kirk (1973) 68–69.
5. Kirk (1970) 218.
6. Kirk (1970) 253–54.
7. Kirk (1970), 261.
8. Kirk (1970) 283.
9. Burkert (1979) 1, 5, 18, 23.
10. Burkert (1979) 22.
11. Burkert (1979) 23.
12. Spiro (1951) 19–46.
13. LaBarre (1980) 7.
14. LaBarre (1970) 47.
15. Burkert (1979) 50.
16. Kirk (1974) 71.
17. Kirk (1974) 71–72.
18. Kirk (1974) 286.
19. Kirk (1974) 72.
20. Kirk (1974) 75.
21. Kirk (1974) 76.

22. Kirk (1974) 87.
23. Kirk (1970) 262.
24. Honko (1984) 41–52, especially 47–48.
25. Kirk (1974) 87–88.
26. Kirk (1974) 71.
27. See LaBarre (1958) 275–328.
28. For bibliography, see LaBarre (1970), 66–67, n. 33.
29. Kirk (1970) 272. On chemical changes due to dream deprivation, see Dement (1965) 404–8 and LaBarre (1970) 67, (1980) 40.

CHAPTER TWO

1. The classic studies of symbiosis are Mahler (1968) and Mahler, Pine, and Bergman (1975).
2. Freud (1920) 36.
3. Senility seems to repeat in reverse the developmental processes of childhood. In John Barth's novel *The Floating Opera,* a senile and wealthy old man causes consternation in his heirs by constantly changing the terms of his will. A person who one day stands to inherit a fortune may find on the next day that his inheritance consists of a basement full of pickle jars containing the old man's carefully preserved feces.
4. Lévi-Strauss (1969) ch. 5, "The Principle of Reciprocity," 52–68.
5. For Jackson Knight (1935) 98, the labyrinth is "a macrocosm of the human anatomy." The first labyrinths were the caves in which paleolithic rock art has been discovered; in most of the caves, the art is far below the ground and reached only after a difficult and dangerous journey through twisting corridors. Cave art has been brilliantly described and interpreted by LaBarre (1970) ch. 13, "The Dancing Sorcerer":

> the art is placed deep under the ground and is reached only after hazardous crevasses, low seams, and slippery tunnels have been traversed. . . . Forces greater than fear must have driven the Magdalenian and other magic artists far inside the earth, where one can easily be lost in tortuous labyrinths or be killed by accidentally slipping into time-forgotten depths . . . magic art in caves is clearly a supernatural, quasi-sexual, creative act of the shaman-artist to promote the increase of animals in the womb of the earth. . . . The concern of paleolithic art with sexuality is no mere inference of a later psychiatrically sophisticated age; the data admit of no alternative interpretation" (395, 397, 398).

6. See Ch. 4, pp. 153–54.
7. See Ch. 4, pp. 132–42.
8. See Ch. 4, pp. 149–51.
9. See Ch. 4, p. 153.
10. As in contemporary advertisements promising instant masculinity to the man who has a motorcycle between his legs, Bellerophon becomes a hero astride the ancient analogue to a Harley-Davidson. Flying and horses both symbolized victorious male sexuality in Greek culture, and there are other indications of Pegasos' role as magic phallus for Bellerophon: he is called by Hesiod (*Theogony* 286) the carrier of Zeus' thunderbolt, and both Pegasos and Bellerophon are said to have Poseidon as father (*Oxyrhynchus papyrus* 421), which would make horse and rider half-brothers.
11. "Little Hans" is the subject of Freud's famous case history, "Analysis of a phobia in a five-year-old boy" (1909).
12. See Roffwarg, Muzo, and Dement (1966) 604–19; Fisher, Gross, and Zuch (1965) 29–45.
13. See Ch. 1, pp. 16–17 and n. 29; also LaBarre (1970) 55–61.
14. See Ch. 4, pp. 176–77.
15. Freud (1916–17) 179.
16. See Ch. 4, pp. 159–61.
17. At a lower level we perform the same operations of selection and combination on sounds to form words, and at a higher level on sentences to form paragraphs.
18. See Jacobson (1956) 81; Lacan (1957) 64; Lévi-Strauss (1966) 204–8.
19. Nonnos, *Dionysiaka* 9.320, describes her act with the revealing adverb "stepmotherly."
20. See Slater (1968) 308–33.
21. For other examples, see Ch. 4, pp. 165–168.
22. Freud (1910).
23. Freud (1916–17) 178.
24. Wallon (1945) 41.
25. Holland (1968) 54.

CHAPTER THREE

1. The indebtedness of Sections 1–4 of this chapter to the summary of Greek prehistory in Burkert (1985) and to the discussion of Hesiod's relationship to Near Eastern myth by both West (1966) and Kirk (1970, 1974) will be obvious.

2. Although it has been argued, on the basis of comparative letter-shapes in Semitic and Greek alphabets, that the Greeks adopted an alphabet as early as the eleventh century, no examples of alphabetic writing in Greece earlier than the eighth century have survived.
3. Kirk (1974) 255.
4. West (1966) 30.
5. Kirk (1974) 255.
6. Pritchard (1969) 501.
7. Pritchard (1969) 60–72, 501–3.
8. Pritchard (1969) 517–18.
9. Walcot (1966).
10. Pritchard (1969) 120–25.
11. Kirk (1970) 216.
12. See Walcot (1966) 12–18 and Ch. 3, p. 124.
13. Kirk (1970) 218 and Ch. 1, pp. 4–5.
14. Kirk (1970) 215–16.
15. West (1966) 30.
16. O'Flaherty (1975) 15.
17. O'Flaherty (1975) 15.
18. LaBarre (1980) 110.
19. See Ch. 4, pp. 138–139.
20. See Ch. 4, pp. 171, 184.
21. Guthrie (1950) 121.
22. LaBarre (1970) 447–48, 472 n. 58.
23. See Ch. 4, p. 137.
24. See Ch. 4, pp. 138–39.
25. See West (1966) 321.
26. West (1966) 318.
27. Kirk (1970) 228, 197.
28. See Ch. 4, pp. 169–70.
29. O'Flaherty (1975) 99.
30. O'Flaherty (1975) 36, 37.
31. West (1966) 212.
32. O'Flaherty (1980) 333, citing Adalbert Kuhn, *Mythologische Studien,* vol. 1 (Guetersloh, Germany, 1886) 15–17, 218–23.
33. O'Flaherty (1980) 330, 332.
34. Olrik's research is summarized with approval by West (1966) 314–15.
35. The translation follows the Oxford edition of West (1966). Bracketed passages are, in West's view, later interpolations.
36. The translation follows the Loeb edition of Frazer (1921).

CHAPTER FOUR

1. See Ch. 3, p. 87.
2. Lévi-Strauss (1966).
3. Leach (1972) 49.
4. Brandon (1963) 168.
5. West (1966) 193.
6. A relevant parallel occurs in Book IV of the *Argonautika* of Apollonios Rhodios: Jason and the Argonauts have almost completed their return to Greece from the ends of the earth when their ship is enveloped by "black Chaos," which blots out the moon and the stars and reduces the sailors to abject helplessness. The stars, which provide them with orientation and security, existed before the arrival of Chaos and furthermore have not ceased to exist, but the precise effect of Chaos is that the order of the stars cannot be perceived by the Argonauts.
7. See Ch. 2, pp. 22–27.
8. Mahler (1968) 9.
9. See Ch. 4, p. 158.
10. West (1966) 18–19.
11. See Ch. 2, pp. 37–41.
12. See Ch. 3, pp. 87–90.
13. The Egyptian myth of the death, dismemberment, and reconstitution of the god Osiris is almost identical, with this exception: when Osiris is restored by his sister/wife Isis, the missing member, for which an ivory or wooden substitute is provided, is not his shoulder but his penis.
14. See Abraham (1955).
15. Jones (1974) 443–44.
16. Freud (1928) 185.
17. See West (1966) 214.
18. See Freud (1937).
19. Guthrie (1957) 20.
20. West (1966) 214.
21. West (1966) 214.
22. The three Kyklopes who make the lightning bolts, which are Zeus' chief weapon and emblem, are sometimes called the "ouranian" Kyklopes for their father Ouranos. Already in the *Odyssey* there is a second group of Kyklopes, a savage race Odysseus meets either in Sicily or on the coast of Italy. The Greeks also believed that a race of Kyklopes built the fortification walls whose ruins they observed on Bronze Age sites; they were said to have helped Proitos fortify Tiryns and Perseus fortify Argos.

23. Freud (1950) 143–45.
24. Freud (1950) 144.
25. Rose (1959) 45.
26. See Ch. 3, pp. 82–83.
27. See Friedrich (1978) 9–54.
28. See Fenichel (1945) 330.
29. Rose (1959) 85.
30. The phenomena cited by Freud in *Beyond the Pleasure Principle* (1920) as evidence for the existence of a "death instinct" make much better sense if viewed as evidence for a persistent wish to return to the symbiotic state, and the passage preceding the announcement of his discovery of this instinct reads in fact like a commentary on the symbiotic state and symbiotic wishes:

> Let us suppose, then, that all the organic instincts are conservative, are acquired historically and tend towards the restoration of an earlier state of things. It follows that the phenomena of organic development must be attributed to external disturbing and diverting influences. The elementary living entity would from its very beginning have had no wish to change; if conditions remained the same, it would do no more than constantly repeat the same course of life. . . . Every modification which is thus imposed upon the course of the organism's life is accepted by the conservative organic instincts and stored up for further repetition. Those instincts are therefore bound to give a deceptive appearance of being forces tending towards change and progress, whilst in fact they are merely seeking to reach an ancient goal by paths alike old and new. Moreover it is possible to specify this final goal of all organic striving. It would be in contradiction to the conservative nature of the instincts if the goal of life were a state of things which had never yet been attained. On the contrary, it must be an *old* state of things, an initial state of things from which the living entity has at one time or another departed and to which it is striving to return by the circuitous paths along which its development leads (37–38).

31. Motte (1971) 38–146.
32. For example Nilsson (1950) 627–28.
33. Motte (1971) 50–54.
34. Freud (1965) 321.
35. Rose (1959) 216.
36. West (1966) 20, 290–91.
37. Dodds (1951) 48.
38. Jones (1974) 78–83.
39. Farnell (1909) 378.
40. The ancient Greek word for "foot" (*pous*) looks and sounds sus-

piciously like a contracted form of the word for penis in both ancient and modern Greek (*peos*).

41. West (1966) 28–30.
42. Jones (1918) 186.
43. Bettelheim (1976) 210.

CHAPTER FIVE

1. If *genethles* (*Theogony* 610) means "child" (a more common meaning) rather than "sort" (of wife), Hesiod's words could be interpreted to mean that the "good" wife will produce evil in the form of children.

BIBLIOGRAPHY

Abraham, Karl (1955). "Dreams and myths: a study in folk-psychology" in *Clinical Papers and Essays on Psycho-Analysis*. London.

Apollodoros (1921). *Library*, ed. J. G. Frazer. London.

Bettelheim, Bruno (1976). *The Uses of Enchantment*. New York.

Brandon, S. (1963). *Creation Legends of the Ancient Near East*. London.

Burkert, Walter (1979). *Homo Necans: The Anthropology of Ancient Greek Sacrificial Ritual and Myth*. Trans. P. Bing. Berkeley.

Burkert, Walter (1983). *Structure and History in Greek Mythology and Ritual*. Berkeley.

Burkert, Walter (1985). *Greek Religion*. Trans. J. Raffan. Cambridge, Mass.

Dement, William (1965). "Recent studies in the biological role of Rapid Eye Movement sleep," *American Journal of Psychiatry* 122.

Dodds, E. R. (1951). *The Greeks and the Irrational*. Berkeley.

Dundes, Alan, ed. (1984). *Sacred Narrative: Readings in the Theory of Myth*. Berkeley.

Farnell, L. R. (1909). *The Cults of the Greek States*, vol. 5. Oxford.

Fenichel, Otto (1945). *The Psychoanalytic Theory of Neurosis*. New York.

Fisher, C., Gross, J., and Zuch, J. (1965). "Cycle of penile erection synchronous with dreaming (REM) sleep," *Archives of General Psychiatry* 12.

Friedrich, P. (1978). *The Meaning of Aphrodite*. Chicago.

Freud, Sigmund (1976 [1909]). "Analysis of a phobia in a five-year-old boy," *The Complete Psychological Works: The Standard Edition*, vol. 10.

Freud, Sigmund (1976 [1910]). "The antithetical meaning of primal words," *Standard Edition*, vol. 11.

Freud, Sigmund (1976 [1916–17]). *Introductory Lectures on Psycho-Analysis, Standard Edition*, vols. 15–16.

Freud, Sigmund (1976 [1920]). *Beyond the Pleasure Principle, Standard Edition*, vol. 18.

Freud, Sigmund (1976 [1928]). "Dostoevsky and parricide," *Standard Edition*, vol. 21.

Freud, Sigmund (1976 [1937]). "Analysis terminable and interminable," *Standard Edition*, vol. 23.

Freud, Sigmund (1976 [1950]). *Totem and Taboo.* New York: *Standard Edition*, vol. 13.

Freud, Sigmund (1976 [1965]). *The Interpretation of Dreams.* New York. (*Standard Edition*, vol. 4–5).

Guthrie, W. K. (1950). *The Greeks and their Gods.* Boston.

Guthrie, W. K. (1957). *In the Beginning.* Ithaca.

Hesiod (1966). *Theogony,* ed. M. L. West. Oxford.

Hesiod (1978). *Works and Days,* ed. M. L. West. Oxford.

Holland, Norman (1968). *The Dynamics of Literary Response.* New York.

Honko, Lauri (1984). "The problem of defining myth" in Dundes (1984).

Jackson Knight, W. F. (1935). "Myth and legend at Troy," *Folk-Lore* 46.

Jakobson, Roman (1956). "Two fundamentals of language and two types of aphasia" in Jakobson and M. Halle, *The Fundamentals of Language.* The Hague.

Jones, Ernest (1918). "The theory of symbolism," *British Journal of Psychology* 9.

Jones, Ernest (1974). *Essays in Applied Psychoanalysis.* New York.

Kirk, G. S. (1970). *Myth: Its Meaning and Functions in Ancient and Other Cultures.* Berkeley.

Kirk, G. S. (1973). "On defining myth," *Phronesis* suppl., vol. 1.

Kirk, G. S. (1974). *The Nature of Greek Myths.* New York.

LaBarre, Weston (1958). "The influence of Freud on Anthropology," *American Imago* 15. Reprinted in LaBarre 1980.

LaBarre, Weston (1970). *The Ghost Dance: Origins of Religion.* New York.

LaBarre, Weston (1980). *Culture in Context: Selected Writings.* Durham, N.C.

Lacan, Jacques (1957). "L'instance de la lettre dans l'inconscient," *La Psychanalyse* 3.

Leach, Edmund (1972). "Anthropological aspects of language: animal categories and verbal abuse" in P. Miranda, ed., *Mythology: Selected Readings*. Baltimore.

Lévi-Strauss, Claude (1966). *The Savage Mind*. Trans. by Weidenfeld and Nicolson. Chicago.

Lévi-Strauss, Claude (1969). *The Elementary Structures of Kinship*. Trans. by Bell, von Sturmer, and Needham. Boston.

Mahler, Margaret (1968). *On Human Symbiosis and the Vicissitudes of Individuation*. New York.

Mahler, Margaret, Pine, F., and Bergman, A. (1975). *The Psychological Birth of the Human Infant*. New York.

Motte, André (1971). *Prairies et Jardins de la Grèce Antique*. Bruxelles.

Nilsson, Martin (1950). *Minoan-Mycenean Religion*. 2d ed. New York.

O'Flaherty, Wendy (1975). *Hindu Myths*. Baltimore.

O'Flaherty, Wendy (1980). *The Origins of Evil in Hindu Mythology*. Berkeley.

Plato (1948). *Plato's Symposium*. Trans. by B. Jowett. Indianapolis.

Pritchard, James, ed. (1969) *Ancient Near Eastern Texts Relating to the Old Testament*, with Supplement. 3d ed., Princeton.

Pucci, Pietro (1977). *Hesiod and the Language of Poetry*. Baltimore.

Roffwarg, H., Muzo, J., and Dement, W. (1966). "Ontogenetic development of the human sleep-dream cycle," *Science* 152.

Rose, H. J. (1959). *A Handbook of Greek Mythology*. New York.

Slater, Philip (1968). *The Glory of Hera: Greek Mythology and the Greek Family*. Boston.

Spiro, Melford (1951). "Culture and personality: the natural history of a false dichotomy," *Psychiatry* 14.

Walcot, P. (1966). *Hesiod and the Near East*. Cardiff, UK.

Wallon, Henri (1945). *Les Origines de la Pensée chez l'Enfant*. Paris.

INDEX